To Windward
of the Land

ALEXANDER CHARLES, 1901–1974

He dared to go to windward of the land—that area where the seas and winds are rough, the fishing is thought to be the best, and the challenge is the greatest to the fisherman in his small boat.

To Windward of the Land

THE OCCULT WORLD
OF ALEXANDER CHARLES

Jane C. Beck

INDIANA UNIVERSITY PRESS
Bloomington & London

Manufactured in the United States of America

Library of Congress Cataloging in Publication Data

Beck, Jane C   1941-
  To windward of the land.

  Bibliography: p.
  1.Charles, Alexander, 1901–1974. 2.Storytellers—St. Lucia—
Biography. 3.St Lucia—Religious life and customs. 4.Folk-lore—St.
Lucia. 5.St. Lucia—Social life and customs. I. Title.
GR121.S24C463   398.2′092′4 [B]   79–84257
ISBN 0–253–16065–0   1 2 3 4 5 83 82 81 80 79

TO DOC and NITA
Who sent me "up de road."

Contents

List of botanical terms

babara	*Diospyros ebenaster*
bamboo	Common bamboo, *Bambusa vulgaris*
bédaf	unidentified
"benjoin"	Benzoin, resin of *Styrax*
bois canon	*Cecropia peltata*
bois diable	*Licania ternatensis*
bois moudongue	*Picramnia pentandra*
cattle's tongue	*Furernea tuberosa*
chardon beni	*Eryngium foetidum*
charpentier	Carpenter's bush, *Dianthera pectoralis*
chichima	*Curcuma longa*
dasheen	variety of coco, *Colocasia esculenta*
faydo blanc	(French) feuille dos blanc, *Chaptalia nutans*
ginger lilies	*Hedychium coronarium*
grain de lain	Linsen seed, linseed, *Linum usitatissimum*
gros deetin	Wild thyme, *Labiatae Thymus vulgaris*
guava	*Psidium guajava*
"l'insens"	Incense
jampana	unidentified
jumby bead	seed of jumby bean, *Ormosia monosperma, Adenanthea pavonina,* or *Erythrina corallodendrum*
macamboo	Wild plantain, *Heliconia bihai*
maweepoui	(French) mari pourri, *Calophyllum longifolium*
la mienne	Myrrh, from *Commiphora abyssinica*
miyuk chapelle	Manioc, *Manihot esculenta*
potasse	Potassium iodide
"safétida"	Asafoetida gum
St. John bush	*Blechum brownei*
senne	Wild coffee, *Cassia occidentalis*

shasse pawelle   Sarsaparilla, *Smilax regelii*
silk cotton tree   Fromager, *Ceiba pentendra*
tannia   *Xanthosoma sagittifolium*
taway   *Bourreria succulenta*
twef   Tref, *Aristolochia trilobata*
vin chassent   unidentified
zhebe zie bourrique Horse-eye bean, *Mucuna pruriens*

Foreword

An Appreciation, Before the Fact
Roger D. Abrahams

I have always looked at these islands from the land side, for I have lived in agricultural villages in the mountains, each one looking far out to the sea. The sea, always there in the distance, is an important part of the symbolic landscape, for it stands as the boundary of farthest reach for many of those among whom I have lived—on Nevis and St. Vincent and Tobago. Their peasant world is made up of man's place of *yard* and *garden* (cultivated fields), the *road* and *town* where they go for action, and the *bush* where nature rules. The sea to them is, like the bush, a place of nature but farther away and even more loaded with uncertainty.

How strange then to come at one of the neighboring islands from the perspective of the sea, through the experiences of Jane Beck and her friend Charles. All islanders are, as Janey remarks, familiars of the sea, but familiars who often appear as "old daddies," as *duppies* or *jombies*, those existing between the realm of the living and the dead. The *fisheners*, then, from the high-ground people, share in this half-nether world. They are held to be people who flirt with death and the Devil to bring the fish to land. It is the sea which carries people away mysteriously and doesn't always bring them back. And sometimes, if they are returned, it is years later and in altered form.

Yes, the fisheners laugh at such talk, but they use it too. They love the power of their role as well, glorying in landing, bringing in the fish, the lobster, and the turtle, calling to the land-people by blowing the conch-shell trumpets (once the master's way of calling the slaves to work) announcing that there is food to buy, food which carries all of the beauties of succulence and the magic of procreation. How often have I shared a laugh with my men-friends when the fish-tea was boiling: "Mr. Rogey. You eat this, then you go make baby, nuh?"

Charles, who displays himself so artfully and so devilishly here, engages us because of his self-conscious mastery of the worlds of the horizon. His identification with the Sea Devil and the windward side again arises out of the coming together of landscape and assigned values—for on the windward coast the rocks ride high to the reef so often. On Nevis and St. Kitts, a few hundred miles to the north, the entrance to the land of the dead on the windward side is called *soul-forgot* (or *sulfur-ghaut*, depending on who you get to explain the name to you—always described as a whirlpool-like sea and a place where you go when you die. Among the same Nevisians, the man in the white suit astride the white horse, as in St. Lucia, is also associated with death and diabolic powers, and is called (after those arcane bodies of powers) "De Lawrence Company."

To understand Charles it is important to note some cultural features of West Indian insular cultures. He, like Peter Wilson's friend "Oscar" (and even M. G. Smith's more socialized preacher-healer "Norman"), is so easily characterized as insane.[1] And so he would be treated in our culture, for he speaks a language of power that is redolent of paranoia and even megalomania. And like Oscar, Charles engages us with his instant ability to hold forth grandiloquently and to frame this with severe silences and long absences. He is erratic because the power he has obtained and the place he has made for himself are predicated on unpredictability and even a calculated strangeness. But these are characters who live within communities of limited resources, communities which have long ago learned to husband these resources as carefully as possible. Thus the blind, the deformed, the tongue-tied, the stutterer, all are cast in the role of entertainer when they come into company—a practice that seems inhumane in the extreme when first encountered by Americans. But these are actively working and playing members of the community even if they are treated in this manner by their neighbors—a dignity which we certainly don't accord such people in our culture.

Charles tells us in every speech (and it is in speeches that he usually talks to us) that he is an outcast, an inbetweener, a savage, even an agent of the Devil. But again, we must not ethnocentrically regard this as a role played simply for theatrical effect to entrance an audience. Far from it, the world in which he lives insists that the powers of healing and transforming that he has learned are the energies of the other world; the *obeah man* is master of *the bush* and its products, the intermediate between man and wild nature—an intermediacy that could only be carried out by a derelict, a homeless-one who has made his pact with nature and solitude (the Devil, if you will) in open contrast to the social contract made by the stable members of the community. He lives in constant opposition to the forces of *respectability*, caring only that his powers and his reputation be maintained.

In such communities, the oppositions between such forces as good and evil, men and women, reputation and respectability, even life and death, are never played out to any sort of resolution. Rather such oppositions are seen to be the essence of life, and their enactment through dramatization can have no real conclusion, only temporary states of truce through a balancing of these contrarieties.

Jane Beck is right in her claim that it is difficult to get one who plays this role to "open up" to anyone from outside. After all, clandestineness and mystery are his stock-in-trade, more so than his bush-teas and talismans. Her triumph is that she was there at the right time and place, findind Charles in a place of reminiscence and recollection, his final way of giving summary to his powers and the paranoid agony such forces carry with them. Like most such documents, when the words are put down in black and white they lose a good deal of their thrust and suasive, transforming power. Spoken words, especially in the realm of personal rupture and healing experience, are repetitive and have the carry of mumbo jumbo to them too often. But the book is a remarkable document of such a man, such a world, if only the reader can give up, for the moment, the expectation of new revealings in each opening up of Charles's self through his story.

Turkeyfoot, Texas

April, 1979

ACKNOWLEDGMENTS

As anyone who has ever tried to write anything knows: nothing flows straight from pen to published text. In my case many people gave me much-needed help along the way, and I would like to take the opportunity here to thank them.

For painstakingly answering my letters and clarifying a number of points for me I am very grateful to George E. Simpson and Douglas Taylor. Yvonne Lange also merits a big thanks for taking time from her very busy schedule to help with some Patois translations. For struggling through the manuscript in its various stages and making numerous helpful suggestions and criticisms I would like to thank Daniel Crowley, Roger Abrahams, Leonard and Nancy Glick, Ron Nief, George Carey, and Grace Ganter. My greatest debt, however, goes to Ione Ford, who with her intimate knowledge of St. Lucia and Patois (she herself is working on a Patois dictionary) meticulously read every word of the manuscript, picking up my mistakes, setting me straight on points where I erred, and graciously encouraging me. Any mistakes that remain are my own, but without question I benefited tremendously from the aid of all the above.

I also owe special thanks to Mary Henkels, who patiently and quickly transcribed the music of the three songs, and to JoAnn Lessard and Ann Ferm, who so capably typed different versions of the manuscript.

Last but not least I add a few kind words (after many of the other sort) for my husband and my two children who played parts in much of the original recording and then relived it over and over as I struggled to give the tapes and words some kind of form. Without all this help I can safely say that *To Windward of the Land* would never have come to the printed page.

Jane C. Beck

Introduction

WE WERE TIRED—perhaps even a bit homesick—as we sought out a telephone to initiate the long-drawn-out process of an overseas call. The scent of bougainvillea hung heavily in the air as a West Indian downpour spattered off the concrete. All thoughts of collecting and recording traditional lore were momentarily brushed aside, and we braced ourselves for the long, frustrating wait before our call would go through. We had been in the field for seven months. This was to be our first contact with the outside world, and we were looking forward to it.

We found the telephone and prepared to do battle. A small dark form swathed in a number of cocoa bags lay there, stretched out on a bench. The form opened one eye as my husband, Horace, picked up the receiver. As the call was placed the eye continued to follow us from the cocoa bags, and when we stoically made ready to wait for the operator to call back, the cocoa bags moved and a head appeared. A brown hat was squashed on the top of a black face with thin features and a jack-o'-lantern-like smile, while a blue denim jacket covered a woolen jersey to help fight the cold (to us balmy) night air. As I remember he muttered something about the telephone—expressing a view that was closely akin to ours—and we began to talk. He told us that he was the night watchman and worked from six in the evening to six in the morning, while during the day he went to sea and fished. Before we knew it he had launched into a long involved story. Our ears perked up; I silently cursed myself for having left the tape recorder behind, and we forgot all about the telephone. Alexander Charles was a mine of information, and story after story spilled out. All were peppered with beliefs of the supernatural, a topic I had found always slow in coming, usually only when the conversation had been carefully and delicately channeled to elicit such beliefs in a natural and comfortable context. But there was no stopping this man—he loved to talk and discovered he had found an enraptured audience.

He spoke of his life as a fisherman and as a sailor, and suddenly we realized that he had been shipmates with one of our earlier informants, Captain Bristol, a wonderful storyteller and singer from another island farther south. "You know he?" he asked incredulously and then launched into a long involved story of Bristol's smuggling escapades and eventual downfall—a dimension of his life the good captain had neglected to reveal. And so he talked on into the night. The phone rang, and a clipped voice told us that our call could not be completed. But we had forgotten our anticipation. When we finally took our leave we knew we would return again—and not just to replace the call.

And we did return, evening after evening. The situation was ideal. Usually we could talk far into the night and, but for an occasional telephone call or the scuttling of a scavenging rat under the door of the grocery store, we had complete privacy. For us, folklorists interested in oral tradition, Alexander Charles was the perfect informant.

Above all he was a marvelous storyteller who performed with a wonderful sense of the dramatic. As his tale unwound his voice would rise and fall. One minute he would leap to his feet, acting out his deeds in pantomime, the next moment he would let forth with a great yowl to emphasize a point. He was always moving, performing the parts of his stories.

One night Charles was relating how he had built a fire to brew a particular tea. As he fanned the imaginary fire with his hat, a huge cockroach scuttled across the wall behind his head. I had no idea that Charles was even aware of it. Suddenly, *whap* went his hat, the cockroach was dead at my feet, and Charles went back to fanning his fire. I had to blink twice to make sure that the incident had taken place. The sudden, incredibly swift action performed with a total lack of emotion was a small incident at the time, but it lent credence to later tales of his quickness and deeds of violence.

In a very real sense he performed his life. He was the hero and was projecting his image of himself for us to see. Words rolled off his tongue easily. He was a natural orator, liberally indulging in parables, proverbs, and metaphors. His imagery was based in the concreteness of folk speech yet flowed in a cadence that the public speaker often yearns to attain. The ignorant fishermen were to him "like new sheep that go in a pasture. When you let them go they can't come back at the master's house;" a person who did not know how to protect himself from harmful magic was "like a man going to fight in the war without no gun." Instinctively Charles knew when to shock, when to surprise, when to be complacent. Seldom did he just narrate. Once again he was actively reliving parts and portions of his past and he portrayed them vividly. He enjoyed the role of hero and he reenacted it in what to him was a hostile world.

Although in some ways unique, Charles's life was generally representative of the great majority of lower-class West Indians. He was born exactly one month after Queen Victoria was buried—or so his grandmother told him—but as to when that was he had no idea.[1] I said that must make him around seventy-two, and he burst into a big grin, "How you know that? I knew you would know." Orphaned early in childhood, Charles soon learned to fend for himself. He lived with various relatives, but they had numerous children of their own and he was an unwelcome mouth to feed. For a time he was taken under the wing of a ship's captain; later he found warmth and love from a missionary's wife. But always he was struggling, often living from hand to mouth or crawling into a fish barrel for shelter from the rain and the night air. As he grew to be a man he traveled north to Haiti and the Dominican Republic and south to Guyana, trying his hand at numerous jobs—from cutting cane to smuggling—finding the occupations of fisherman, night watchman, and practitioner of magic to be his steadiest source of income.

Throughout his life he received little formal schooling and could not read or write; thus all he knew had come to him by word of mouth or through his own observation. He was thoroughly steeped in tradition and had little knowledge of twentieth century technology. One Christmas I brought him a small transistor radio. He looked on, beaming, as I showed him how to work it. I told him he must be sure to hear the click of the volume knob so that he wouldn't waste the battery. He was all smiles that night when I left him and he switched on the radio to while away the hours before sleep caught him. The next evening when he came down he was totally dejected. "The radio break," he told me. Apparently he had spent the morning trying to make the tuning knob click on, and when it wouldn't make the proper noise he had no idea how to make the radio work. I went through the process again and once more he was all smiles. This story is not supposed to indicate that Charles was stupid— nobody could ever call him that—he was just totally unfamiliar with machines.

Such learning held little value for Charles. Within his own society he was thought to be highly educated in a very specialized field—the realm of the supernatural. This was a knowledge that he pursued throughout his life and had acquired carefully and methodically. But more on this below.

Charles was very much a member of the folk community[2] on the island of St. Lucia.[3] As peasant-fisherman he shared the bottom rung of the social-economic scale with the bulk of St. Lucia's population. At the top of the ladder are a few exclusive white families who through birth and inheritance have maintained a small closed elite. Their numbers are so few that they do not have much influence on the whole society.[4] As in most other, former slave cultures there is an awareness of color, but it is not necessary to be of light hue to succeed: one of the most successful families of entrepreneur's on the island is black. However, in general it could be said that the color of the upper- and middle-class workers is brown while the peasant masses are black. The former group expresses contempt for the latter, claiming they are "illiterate," "dirty," and "bad workers." This gulf is further widened by distrust and hostility by both groups.[5] When an individual rises to a middle-class level from peasant origins, his peers generally believe that he succeeded due to antisocial means—often by dealing with the Devil.

The peasantry still practices subsistence agriculture, growing garden crops on small plots of land or catching fish and selling the excess at market. Living is simple, outside purchases are few, and often an exchange of goods takes place instead of monetary payment. In the slack season a man might live on mangoes and breadfruit, often known as the "twin curses" of the West Indies. They are so plentiful and freely available that when these fruits are "full" there is no need to work, and the population tends to relax. Why should one work when with no effort or expense he can eat a "bellyful" of mangoes and breadfruit?

A number of fishing boats dot the beaches that ring the island, the larger concentrations lying in the harbors of the leeward coast. Castries with its excellent deep-water harbor is the chief port of the island and contains about forty percent of the population. At its head lies Conway, the center for the fishing fleet; often thirty or more canoes can be seen pulled up on the shore. Here boats beach and unload their fish for the market nearby and here, too, many of the fishermen live just a short distance from the waterfront.

Although when we first knew Charles he lived on Monkey Hill, in a district just behind Castries known as Marchand, much of his life was spent in Conway where he lived with a variety of women, somtimes in a "frenning" relationship with his girl friend, but more often in a "keeper" relationship with his common-law spouse. There seem to be three basic relationships in St. Lucia: "frenning," which implies a sexual relationship with a woman who still maintains her own residence, "keeping," where a couple lives together in the same household, and "marriage," with all its legal connotations and prestige value. Leonard Glick describes the general situation as follows.

During the early years of sexual maturity and adulthood a girl lives with her parents and accepts a lover or perhaps lovers. During adolescence she may be rather casual about this, but as she grows older she thinks more about settling into a stable relationship. In time she may begin to cohabit with a man, perhaps the father of her child, without marrying him (the so-called "keeper" relationship). Eventually they may separate and move on to other partners, or they may marry. Finally, having lived with a man, borne children to him, and found reasonable security with him, she is likely to marry; by which time she may be 28 or older and may be the mother of three or more children.[6]

Charles told me that he had had two wives: Edith and Ann Marie. With Edith he had seven children; with Ann Marie, three. However, he also seemed to have had keeper relationships with Baby and Enid. These were apparently of much shorter duration, although with Enid he had three children. There is no stigma attached to an illegitimate child in the West Indies, and Charles was proud of all his children. Two of his favorites, Ti Son and Septima, had different mothers, but this made no difference to Charles. Still, I think it is significant to note that it was important to him that both these children were actually married. When a young man named Chairman told Charles that he loved Septima, Charles was adamant, "No ring, no love." In traditional manner the suitor took Charles to Cannouan to meet the future son-in-law's family; Charles gave his blessing, and Chairman and Septima subsequently married.

Outside children usually live with their mother or perhaps with the maternal grandmother or aunt. In Charles's own case where both his mother and father were dead, as well as his grandparents, he rotated between his father's aunt and his mother's sister. As is said in St. Lucia, "Everyone has family," but in Charles's case his own family did not pay him much mind. This is not the general rule and probably accounts for his hostility towards his relatives.

The illegitimate child will take the name of his mother. Thus Ti Son, Charles's son by Enid, took her name and calls himself officially "Anthony Felise," although he is better known by his nickname.

Generally children are valued in St. Lucia. As Charles said, "If a woman born in this world and she haven't got a child, she is no use." The usual adage is that a woman must have the number of children that are in her belly. These in turn are looked on as insurance for old age: "that boy going to give you a penny bread and that girl going to give you an ole dress."

For a man children are not regarded so much as eventual providers but as symbols of his manhood. Sexual prowess is highly prized, and a man is expected to have outside children. He is proud when his "seed" is "scattered all about." As one young man of twenty-one boasted to me, "You want to know my top score? Twenty, with four pregnant!" It seems that the further abroad one's children are procreated, the greater the prestige. Thus Charles told me proudly, "Oh, I have children all about— Santo Domingo, Antigua, Dominica, and St. Lucia."

For the West Indian, living on small islands linked only by water (and more recently by air) the sea often becomes the proving ground for his masculinity; this was certainly so for Charles, particularly in his fishing and smuggling exploits. While fishing he dared to go to windward of the land—that area where the seas and winds are rough, the fishing is thought to be the best, and the challenge is the greatest to the fisherman in his small boat.

A man's prestige is also closely linked with his worldliness. There is a profitable living to be made through interisland trading: the more enterprising and opulent merchants will build and maintain trading vessels which will go throughout the Caribbean carrying all manner of produce between the islands. One vessel may run north with a load of mangoes, sell them, and return south with a load of contraband—cigarettes, radios, whiskey, and some other high-duty commodity. The vessel will discharge her cargo in the night and take on a load of passengers for another island. Smuggling is considered both profitable and heroic. Some believe that you can double your money on each voyage; at the same time you must have courage to deal in such a hazardous occupation. Not only is there the natural threat of the elements—and often these are very real, as many of the vessels, through age and lack of care, are unsound, carry little lifesaving equipment, and may often lack both chart and compass—but there is the constant threat of being exposed to the authorities and losing everything. In native eyes the successful smuggler is a hero. By his accounts Charles was such a smuggler. He even had brushes with the law and each time eluded capture.

The concept of courage is very important to the West Indian. As a virtue it is greatly admired but seldom accorded anyone; frequently an individual will be criticized as "he coward." The West Indian must confront the power of both natural and supernatural obstacles and stand firm no matter what the consequences. As with most ideals, courage in the face of powerful odds is seldom realized, thereby making it an even more precious commodity.

Power is another concept that is very important to the West Indian. He strives to have power or control over situations and individuals, and may accomplish this goal on many levels, from a verbal battle to an attempt to control the realm of the supernatural and therefore his fellow men. This man is a boss—a master—and as such is both feared and revered; such a position is continually sought after and is eternally precarious.

This veneration of power is closely linked with the West Indian belief in obeah and the whole supernatural world. God is the Master, the grand designer of the world. "There isn't a thing that he didn't put here." At the same time many of the things he put in the world have the ability to do evil and have an individuality all their own. The Devil, the master of obeah, is a case in point.

The Devil is not as much an evil figure as he is a fearful one because he controls great power. One must have the courage to face the Devil to obtain some of this power through a pact with him. The concept of the Faustian compact with the Devil is a common one in the West Indies and extends to most supernatural relationships with familiars. Usually a man agrees to pay an amount—either in money or in blood—and if he doesn't meet the deadline (which is usually believed to be the case) he is in the power of the Devil. As a creditor the Devil proves to be insatiable in his demands and will inevitably destroy his victim.

This compact with the Devil also leads to a belief in the power objects that the Devil is believed to provide as his part of the bargain. As Charles says, "Everything has got its master." The secret is to know and to be able to use the "master." Thus a particular seed will enable you to change shape and fly through the night, another will protect you from magical harm. This knowledge—often referred to as "science" or "obeah"—is one path to becoming a big man and thereby achieving power. It was this road that Charles chose.

Obeah, a kind of sorcery practiced by those who have attained the special knowledge of the "master," is a craft whose roots go back to Africa. Scholars have suggested the Twi word "obayifo" (or perhaps its derivative "obeye") as a possible source—the root "obayi-" meaning sorcery, and the suffix "-fo" meaning man.[7] Whatever its etymology, obeah plays a substantial role within West Indian culture. Often its sensational aspects are played up, and outsiders seldom look beyond these to realize that it is an important functional pillar of West Indian society. Through the practice of sorcery tensions of aggression, jealousy, and anxiety are relieved between individuals. Using magical means one believes he can control his enemies, thereby releasing a certain measure of fear and uneasiness.

At the same time obeah also operates as a mechanism to enforce social control on the community level. For example, there is little opportunity to climb beyond the bottom rung of the socioeconomic scale in the West Indies, as the basic subsistence economy does not allow for the accumulation of wealth, and the only way to overcome such a situation is to emigrate[8] or to remain and somehow change one's position in terms that are explainable to the society as a whole. In a society where changing one's economic status appears nearly hopeless, there seems to be a greater acceptance of the supernatural. Those who, by chance, achieve material success are thought to have won through supernatural means. Therefore, it is popularly thought that the most tenable way to success is through obeah.

Such a belief explains many of the "duppy" men and women[9]

whom Charles encountered daily. Anyone who has gained wealth and power through no visible means has to be "dealing with the Devil," according to Charles's reasoning, and is held suspect. Tainted by dealings with the Devil and using this power for his own individual ends, such a person is regarded as an antisocial member of the community. Often the man or woman will also have individual peculiarities that will set him apart from his neighbors—perhaps he will have one leg or he may have committed some flagrant social act (such as Mrs. Etienne [see page 205–06] who insulted her mother in front of a crowd of people). Society distrusts this "implied" obeah man because he flaunts economic, social, and individual convention; the "traditional" obeah man, very much a part of the community, is seen in a very different light because he achieves wealth and power in the traditional manner of receiving gratuities for helping others achieve their desired ends.[10]

The traditional obeah man or gadeur, as he is often known in St. Lucia, is treated with both respect and fear—respect because he holds a knowledge that the average person does not have, and fear because his knowledge gives him power. Often the obeah man, like the duppy man, will be set apart as odd or physically different—perhaps pockmarked, scarred, or physically handicapped. A good obeah man is known to be able to kill or to cure; thus he can do both harm and good. Those obeah men who have the greatest successes will obviously be the most in demand; often, if an unnatural sickness is detected, more than one obeah man will be tried. I personally know of one man who believed that obeah had been worked on him through a cake which, after eaten, led to terrible pains in his stomach. As a result he went to a gadeur in Laborie who gave him a special oil to rub on his stomach. But this seemed to do no good, and as the pain continued he went to an obeah woman in Castries. She said she could help him and showed him two handfuls of glass she had removed from another obeah victim's stomach. She told the man that he must return on Saturday—not Friday or Sunday as she would be telling her beads—but on Saturday and that he must bring one of his undershirts soaked in his sweat. With this she would work her own obeah and cure him. Apparently this woman was not successful either, and the man went to a third person. This too was a woman who it was believed had actually succeeded in curing the patient. The cure was effected through a tea made from the root of the moudongue and two sweet-smelling charms concocted out of herbs which the man must always wear pinned inside his shirt. Obviously the sick man's faith in the ability of the woman who had apparently cured him was strong.

Just as doctors, obeah men and women will specialize. One may be known for his ability to foretell the future; another might specialize in fishing magic, yet another might concentrate on cures. I was told about a particular obeah man who was known as a specialist in getting rid of young girls' unwanted babies. Apparently a girl whom he had treated died, and he was arrested and faced serious charges.

The magic made use of in obeah is fairly straightforward and operates on two main principles. If an individual wants protection or luck he must perform a cleansing ritual. Baths, fumigations, highly scented potions, and lotions all serve this purpose. But if a person plans to harm a rival, he must achieve a kind of putrifying ritual—one that will cause decay and disagreeable odors. These are the two principles that were constantly employed in Charles's own personal methods, and I have also found them to be typical of obeah practices throughout St. Lucia and the other islands.

But if there is magic in obeah there is also much that is not left to magic. Charles made this very clear with his discussion of different poisons and bush[11] remedies. As with all obeah men, his knowledge of bush medicine was extensive and was often used to supplement magical cures. He expressed concern that doctors' medicine was making inroads on the use of bush and at times seemed almost apologetic about going to the doctor, indicating that in reality it was his own medicine that cured him. ''Bush makes better man. Old time people never went to doctor. They knew what kind of bush to pick. Today the young people don't know."

Through recent studies it has become apparent that low income and high prevalence of disease have a strong, positive correlation.[12] St. Lucia is no exception to the rule, and one research team described the situation in gloomy terms: "There is little money, and overcrowding, parasites, poor diet and poor hygiene expose the people to a host of minor and major ills."[13] With a paucity of trained medical personnel and an innate distrust of the outsider, it is no wonder that the St. Lucian will turn first to bush medicine.

It is still common for an individual, like Charles, to have his "bush" garden behind his house; when ill, he would pick the appropriate "bush" or perhaps a number of different "bush." Then, boiling the leaves together, he would prepare a tea. Leonard Glick writes that most St. Lucians "approach illness with a limited range of ideas and associated 'diagnostic' terms. Most often one hears about *fwedi* 'coldness' or 'chill' and *apwudo* [enpweda] 'imprudency,' which may refer to anything from dietary to behavioural indiscretions, while occasionally there is a more or less veiled reference to sorcery to explain a serious or unusual illness."[14]

This is not to say that St. Lucians never go to the doctor. Like Charles, when a person has an obvious physical illness, one that is natural and not sent, and home remedies have no effect, he will turn to a physician. But the folk are more comfortable with their traditional ways. The gadeur or obeah man would speak Patois, the language of the people. Although English has been the official language since 1814, when St. Lucia was ceded to the British by the French, and must be spoken in all schools, Patois, a form of French Creole, is the language that the child of the lower classes first speaks in the home. Later he learns English and naturally comes to associate it with the upper classes, the government officials, and the well educated—those people to whom he accords little trust. As a member of these ranks, the physician would be separated by both language and class from the St. Lucian peasant.

Thus it is understandable why the folk, rooted in tradition, cling to the old and the known. The strength of their belief in the gadeur's curative abilities can be expected to contribute to his success, and his success often depends on his therapeutic psychology. Illness in St. Lucia is not just a biological phenomenon but a social condition as well. As Kiev points out to us, "Illness is an impersonal event brought about by neutral, nonemotional, natural agents such as germs." But in Charles's society a sickness is much more comprehensive, relating "to the individual's life, his community and his interpersonal relationships"[15] as well. Thus the function of a gadeur is not simply to cure an obvious wound but in many cases to cope with social conflicts that have reached a critical point of stress. In this aspect he operates as a kind of folk psychiatrist, well versed in the beliefs and traditions of the society and therefore often extremely effective in his "therapy."

Charles's attitude toward illness is very representative. He did not dwell on the sickness alone, but on all the surrounding circumstances—the nurse in white, the injections, the pills, the bed pans, the food. All these are given as much emphasis as the illness itself. In Part II, when Charles's techniques as a curer are discussed more fully, I think it is evident that a corresponding emphasis is placed on the attendant paraphernalia.

As an obeah man, Charles was an unspecialized practitioner. He coped with everyday occurrences on the general level, cured minor ailments and drunkenness, administered to those who had problems in obtaining love or financial security, and helped others who felt they had been wronged and who wanted revenge. All of this coincided with his philosophy of life. As is ninety-five percent of the population, Charles was a practicing Catholic,[16] but he rationalized,

> I believe in God, but the God tell you, "Seek, you shall find. Knock, the door shall be open." Nothing in this world that we have [are] using, that God [didn't] put it there. You sit down there and pray from Monday through Saturday and see if you're going to get it. If someone tells you he going to hurt you, don't leave it to God.

In other words, "God helps those who help themselves." In help-ing himself and others, Charles saw nothing wrong with using any means available to him, be they natural or otherwise.

Certain magical means are accessible through the Church: at the folk level prayers and religious paraphernalia are often used as magical charms. Holy water has great efficacy, as do candles, incense, or other objects blessed by the priest. Often a candle will be "fixed up" and an individual's name scrawled on it before it is brought to the priest. This is believed to have special efficacy and is thought to work good or evil on that person according to how the candle has been dressed. The same principle was involved in the case where Charles made a special bullet to kill a duppy man in animal form. To give it added strength, he took it to the Church and doused it in holy water. This level of the Catholic religion is obviously very much in harmony with the general practice of obeah. Many obeah men and women consider them-selves as good Catholics, as did the woman who told the man that she would help him but not on Friday or Sunday, because she would be telling her beads.

As I have already pointed out, the Devil is the master of obeah and indeed the master of the "unseen world." His power is all encompassing both on land and sea and enables him to effect both good and evil. To windward of the land such a master is known as the Sea Devil; he takes a different form from the hand-some gentleman in a white suit often astride a huge horse. The Sea Devil has an amorphous form which can expand to alarming proportions in size. Some say he comes first as a little piece of white sheet, and then all the sea will be a big white sheet; or first as a small patch of red blood which swells and swells until the whole sea is red with blood. Others have seen him as a huge fish with no head or tail. However, all are in agreement that no mat-ter what his shape or form, when he appears he comes to take a life.[17] When a fisherman has made a contract with the Devil in order to catch fish, the Devil is relentless in forcing the individual to keep his end of the bargain. If the individual does not produce when his time is up, the Sea Devil simply takes his due in the form of a life—usually the individual himself or perhaps a son or daughter. Often he will capsize the fishing boat, taking with him the man he wants.

As the sea is thought to be more dangerous than the land, different ingredients must be used in an attempt to harness its different powers. While different strong-smelling oils (compelling oil, rose oil, etc.) are often utilized ashore for some kind of magical purpose, they are believed to be "too strong" for sea work; thus essences extracted from the oils are used in their place.

On land the Devil's hour is midnight. This is the time one trysts him at the crossroads and strikes a bargain with him. At sea, noon is the hour one would meet the Sea Devil. Although midday is known elsewhere in the Caribbean as a dangerous hour,[18] noon is the significant pivotal hour of the fisherman's day. Frequently Charles left at three o'clock or four o'clock in the morning and, if all went well, returned around noon with his catch. The earlier the successful fisherman comes in, the quicker he can dispose of his catch in the market. Another consideration is that fish tend to be quiescent at midday. Thus it makes sense that the fisherman would be more vulnerable at noon than at midnight, and it is at noon that the Sea Devil appears to take his due.

As the chief practitioner of magic the Devil is master of all "science." He can give one the power to invoke the dead, to practice black magic which allows men or women to take members of the opposite sex and have them sexually without their knowledge, or to become a duppy man or woman and fly in the night. It is also from the Devil that one who practices "science" receives a "familiar."

Although familiars differ, the concept behind most of them is quite similar. Charles speaks of both the bolum and the snake. The bolum,[19] generally known interchangeably as a baku, bok, or backru throughout the islands from Surinam to Haiti, is the size of a small child. He must be properly cared for and in turn will bring his owner whatever he desires. The problem is that the owner cannot always keep up with the bolum's demands, for he must feed him fresh meat—chicken, goat, or sheep—daily; this is a typical variation of the supernatural compact.

Apparently the bolum is received directly from the Devil, or one can create him with the aid of certain knowledge from the Devil. According to Charles, a bolum can be made magically from an unborn foetus. Through certain charms the foetus is drawn from the pregnant mother as she passes by.

The snake is also received from the Devil and acts in the fashion of a familiar—in this case a protector as well as a bringer of riches. Although Charles simply describes it as "worse" than the bolum, it is reasonable to assume that the snake must also be properly taken care of. Thus once again we note the difficulty of keeping a contract made with a supernatural creature.

Python worship in Africa is well documented and was apparently a strong cult in Dahomey and Southern Nigeria,[20] a region from whence many of the slaves were brought to the West Indies. In fact the similarity of John Roscoe's description of Baganda practice and the discourse Charles gave me on how to keep and train a snake is remarkable. Roscoe wrote,

> Pythons were held to be sacred, and in some places offerings were made regularly to them to preserve the people. A few men kept pythons in their houses, taming them and feeding them on milk with an occasional fowl or goat. It was said that these pythons did not kill children or animals in their own villages but went further afield for their prey.[21]

With such a heritage it is understandable that the snake is frequently associated with obeah and is often thought to be the familiar of the obeah man. In Trinidad, "All obiamen keep snakes. Snake is the spirit of a dead person, a dead person who was cast out. That's why it know everything."[22] Thomas Banbury, writing of Jamaica, says that, "snakes used to be 'set' by the Obeah Man,"[23] and I myself have recorded tales in Tobago and Grenada of snakes "planted" under the silk cotton tree, as Charles also recounted.

In this context the snake seems to play the same role as the "jumby" who is invoked by an obeah man to do his bidding. A jumby is usually considered to be the spirit of a dead person, although the term is sometimes more generally used to indicate any supernatural spirit. To invoke a jumby, one must go to the grave of a person who has died "badly"—one who has not died quietly of some illness and with the rites of absolution, but rather one whose life has been cut short unexpectedly, one who has met death accidentally, or perhaps one who has experienced a violent end through execution, murder, or suicide. Such a dead person cannot rest peacefully in his grave, and it is to this grave that the individual who wishes to invoke the dead will go. Through the use of highly prized and very secret Black Arts books,[24] the invoker raises the dead and charges him to do his bidding. However, the person must know how to lay the jumby as well as to raise him, and this is why so many jumbies have been "planted" like the snake under the silk cotton tree. The silk cotton tree in Africa and in the West Indies is held in great veneration and is believed to have powerful supernatural significance. If an invoked jumby becomes fractious, causing harm to its "master," the invoker can only be saved by planting the jumby under this enormous tree for, as with the Devil, the bolum, and the snake, a compact has been made and the human must keep his end of the bargain or he will lose his own life.

The concept of invocation appears to have changed over the years. Originally the dealer invoked souls, but today the Devil and the dead have become confused. Thus when I asked Charles if one raised the dead or the Devil in the dead's form, he answered me, "When you dealing with bad spirit, well, you're dealing with the Devil." Under the tutelage of Catholicism the evil dead and the Devil seem to have merged, and the belief is now that the Devil works through the evil dead; indeed these dead are one of his manifestations. Originally the invocation of the dead was probably much like it was in West Africa. The general belief was that "an evil person can summon by incantation the shadow of a deceased person and interrogate it."[25] This was based on the general African belief that a person possesses a number of souls—a distinction often being made between the breath, the shadow, and the guardian soul.[26]

This same belief is reflected in Charles's term, duppy man or woman. Duppy, another term for jumby, is common in Barbados and Jamaica, but I have never heard it used extensively in St. Lucia. When I asked Charles, and others as well, where this term came from and if it were widely used in the old days, I never received more than a perfunctory, "Yes, it was used by old time people." The significance of such a term is seen in the definition of the word "duppy": "the spirit of the dead, believed to be capable of returning to aid or (more often) harm living beings, directly or indirectly; they are also believed subject to the power of obeah and its practitioners who can 'set' or 'put' a duppy upon a victim and 'take off' their influence."[27]

Thus I would suggest that the original belief in multiple souls has become somewhat confused with the Christian concept of the Devil. As Herskovits has pointed out, the Africans' acceptance of the Christian Devil as the personification of evil in the universe has only been halfhearted. Early missionaries tried to liken Satan to the trickster God Legba or Esu (also, I might add, known as God of the Crossroads), but in African tradition nothing is entirely good or bad.[28] Thus even the Devil is capable of doing some good. His sorcery can work good as well as evil.

Whatever the dead's relationship to the Devil, with the invocation of the dead we once more see the familiar technique of the obeah man using an agent to carry out his bidding. Just as the bolum or the snake, the jumby is a supernatural instrument used to attain certain ends.

The duppy woman (and less frequently the duppy man) differs from the obeah man or dealer in that she is an antisocial being. She deals with the Devil for her own personal ends and is therefore held suspect by the rest of society. In St. Lucia a duppy woman is believed to have the power to fly at night and thus go all about working her evilness. Like the succubus,[29] she is thought to have the ability to suck the blood of her victims, thereby gaining the needed strength and vitality to fly. She also has the power to transform herself into an animal; thus the St. Lucian is extremely cautious when he meets some animal in the road at night. If a duppy woman is wounded or killed in such a guise, she must return to her natural form. Often such a person will repent of her wickedness and will want to be cleansed. This can be done by "sticking" a duppy woman and making her bleed, causing all the evilness to come out. Such a tradition perhaps harks back to the belief that a person cannot die possessing the knowledge of witchcraft, but must pass it on to somebody before her death. The Patois term for such creatures is "gagé" (French: *engagé*), and when such a creature is made to bleed and thus is "disenchanted," it is known as "degagé."

As the duppy woman, the black magic man (and less often, woman) is an antisocial creature. While the duppy woman wreaks social harm, the practitioner of black magic, known as "magie nwé" in Patois, outrages sexual mores. Although the attitude toward sexual freedom is more permissive in the West Indies than in the United States, a license for sexual aggression is not countenanced. Thus the man who presses his sexual attentions upon unwilling recipients is abhorred. The person who practices black magic also makes a compact with the Devil: in return for the ability to penetrate any lock or closed door[30] he must pay the Devil with blood.

"La jablesse" (French: *la diablesse,* she-devil), another creature who peoples the St. Lucian's supernatural world, also has sexual overtones. She is a beautiful woman who lures men (and sometimes women and children as well) into the jungle where she loses them and abandons them to their fate. She can be identified by her "cattle's foot," but this is usually covered by her long dress and therefore is seldom seen. Many of the stories told of the jablesse indicate that she usually takes men who do not conform with social propriety. As Charles says, "If you going somewhere and you meet a woman passing, say 'good night' and go on with your business."

There is no real line of demarcation in most St. Lucians' minds between the natural and the supernatural; communication between the two is achieved mainly through the bridge of dreams. Dreams are always accorded the greatest respect and will often determine an individual's course of action. Although all dreams are considered significant, those which are most important are dreams in which a dead relative or friend appears. These "dream messages,"[31] as they are called, sometimes incorporate a request from the dead, who also frequently send advice including cures and prognostications.

One of Charles's most valued possessions was a song he had learned from an old Haitian. Through this song he was able to speak to his dead mother in dreams. At times of crisis she could give him the advice he needed but was unable to attain through natural means. The value of such a song is obvious, for it was a direct pipeline to the dead and therefore to a vast store of supernatural knowledge. As Charles boasted, "I talk to my mother when I like."

For Charles, there was no distinction between the natural and supernatural areas. One merged into the other and simple enlarged Charles's view of "reality." His was a pragmatic world with little regard for the esthetic. The emphasis was on struggle and violence, and his life was a series of episodes which took place in a totally hostile environment. As a practical man, Charles used any means that suited his purpose. He looked for the solution to solve a particular problem. Whether the key were natural or supernatural was of little note as long as the approach produced the desired results.

It took a long time to make a comprehensible whole out of Charles's monologues; throughout those evenings our relationship changed and developed. There were setbacks, annoyances, apparent inconsistencies which left me frustrated. At other times there were breakthroughs and revelations that infused new life into our project. But always there was a growing warmth and rapport between us that bound us together. I did not play at being his white daughter, nor he, my black father. We fell naturally into those roles and we cherished them.

The material for this life of Charles was gathered over a three-year period and was collected on a number of trips of varying time lengths. After our initial conversations with Charles in 1971, my husband and I discussed the possibility of recording his autobiography, for little truth has been written of the West Indian.[32] Instead he has been glamorized and characterized to charm the average tourist. We wondered how such a project would sit with Charles, and with some apprehension, almost a year after our first meeting, my husband broached the subject to him. Our fears proved ill-founded, for he was enthusiastic about the project. Whether he completely understood it or not, he was obviously flattered by such attention. I had also been worried that the introduction of a tape recorder would induce an element of self-consciousness, but that anxiety also proved baseless. We explained what the machine was, asked his permission, and even played parts back to him, but I doubt he really took in the whole meaning or significance of it, for later he often said to me when speaking of a particular cure, "You must write this down so you will remember."

That second trip our time was much more limited. My husband had to return to the States, but I decided to stay down a few weeks and continue recording Charles. As we had already established a good working relationship with him, we didn't think it mattered which one of us recorded him. As it turned out we were very wrong, but chance had made a happy choice.

Almost immediately a change was evident. Charles was concerned that now, as a single woman and an outsider, I would fall prey to countless dangers within his society, dangers which I did not understand. He became my protector and, in his terms, "made me wise." Gradually he began to teach me. At first it was just to bring me different mixtures of oils and bush that would guard me against certain evils. Later he decided to teach me how to identify pitfalls in my path and how to deal with them.

During all this time I was still recording the life of Alexander Charles; here too a significant change took place, and our relationship entered a new phase. One night he had been telling a story involving a man who had been subjected to a lashing with the cat-o'-nine-tails. Something in the way he described the beating suddenly made me ask him if he had ever felt the cat. Up to that point I had never pressed Charles. I had always been careful not to ask him a question that he wouldn't be willing to answer, but almost as soon as the words were out of my mouth I felt I had gone too far. The silence seemed interminable—painful. I kicked myself for being too impatient. And then came, "Ah, child, you want the whole story of my heart." With one quick movement he pulled up his shirt and exposed the welts—a timeless testament to four lashes of the dreaded cat. And then came his story. Words rolled over words in the stillness. Even the tree toads seemed to stop their peeping as I leaned forward to catch every syllable of his husky account. For Charles it was a revelation of the past—something he had kept to himself for over fifty years. Time had long since silenced the other participants, but for the moment Charles once again relived the agony of it. "And today, look at me. I'm not creeping and no one would ever know."

From then on our conversation was freer and more familiar. It was shortly after this that Charles began to bring me different concoctions which were to protect me from any harm. He told me that he couldn't have done that before because he didn't know me well enough, but now he trusted me as his right hand. In return I would bring him things. When I cooked supper I would take Charles a bowl and a cup of coffee. One night I brought him a tin of tobacco. I was surprised to see him put it aside because he had a pipe with him but nothing to put in it. He commented on this later in the evening, and I asked him why he didn't use the tobacco I had brought. "That's tobacco?" he asked, amazed. Unable to read the label, he had thought because of its shape that it was a tin of sardines. Eagerly he filled his pipe.

We fell into an easy familiarity. One night on my way to see him, some sport fishermen had come in with more fish than they knew what to do with. One man gave me a barracuda, and I walked down to Charles carrying it. "Who that for?" he asked me and smacked his lips with relish as I presented it to him. He then requested some salt and a knife. With the knife he gutted the fish and washed it clean. Next he made a couple of slits down each side and motioned me to pour the salt in those. When that was done to his satisfaction, he went and found some string and some brown paper and made a careful package of the fish, which he hung from a beam in the storeroom so the rats wouldn't get it. As he was doing this he began to sing in Patois. "See, you never know what Daddy will do," he turned to me and beamed. In fifteen minutes the barracuda was disposed of, and we returned to our usual places in front of the telephone. Sometimes if he was lucky fishing he would bring me a bonita, and I would cook it. He was amused at my different way of preparing fish. I'm not sure he always liked it, but he invariably ate it—sometimes one or two nights later. I can remember one evening being nauseated by the smell of some lamb chops I had brought him previously. But he sat there smacking his lips over them and gnawing the bones.

One night I came down to find him very glum. He shook his head when I asked him what was the matter. Two teeth were troubling him, and he grabbed my hand to let me feel how they wobbled. But even a toothache could not repress Charles's eagerness to perform his tales, and once launched he seemed to forget his pain. A few days later he finally lost the troublesome teeth and that night appeared with the air of the successful general wearing his new medals. Throwing back his head he bared his gums so that I could witness the newest gaps.

But toothaches were not all we had to contend with. There were other interruptions and one or two unpleasant confrontations that were much more disconcerting. One night there was a meeting in the office adjacent to where we sat. Charles was so concerned he would be overheard that I could barely make out what he was saying. But this only happened once. Our most continual source of irritation came from a Grenadian youth known as Julien. Horace and I learned from Julien's employers that Julien was "putting it about" that we were making money off of Charles. After hearing that, I decided it was time to have another chat with the watchman about what we were doing. I wasn't sure that everything my husband had said to him about the autobiography had actually sunk in. I stressed the fact that we weren't making money off of Charles, that the tapes were to go to the University, and that there was no book about the real West Indian and for this reason we wanted to portray his life. All of this seemed to please and reassure him, although he emphatically denied having been worried about my motives. He said it was Julien who was stirring up trouble and he had been warned about him by a friend of his son's. Whether his indignation at Julien was for my benefit or not, his voice began to rise as he told of sharing his food with the Grenadian and giving him clothes. "And he go and say things like that," Charles spat in rage. "Grenadians are no fucking good. They never have been." I said calmly that I didn't care what the man said as long as Charles didn't think we were ripping him off. Charles looked at me for a long moment, and I wanted to believe him as he told me he trusted me or he never would have told me about his back. He reiterated that he had never spoken of that to anyone else. I nodded my head and, feeling somewhat better, went off to cook supper.

But we were not rid of Julien yet, and those following nights proved to be frustrating ones. Every evening Julien would turn up. He seemed oblivious to any taunts Charles might make to him—and there were many. One night he slouched up as we were talking and sprawled down in Charles's chair as he was enacting some scene. Julien was wearing a wool cap, and Charles took one look at him and snapped, "What's the matter? Is your head sick?" Charles's voice, pitched to an irate shrill, made it clear to Julien that even the most profane language would only elevate him. Through the sheer volume and volley of his words a lesser individual would have been felled. But not Julien. He smiled serenely and sat there, apparently unconcerned, until another youth, Randolph, appeared and lured him away. Randolph had come to sit at Charles's feet to learn, but as Charles said, he didn't want to teach him too much, too fast, because he was young and wanted too many things.

The next evening Julien was back again, and the next and the next, interjecting comments, monopolizing conversations, and generally acting as an inhibiting force. Finally Charles told me he was going to put an end to him and that he would blink the lights to let me know when the coast was clear. True to his word, the lights flickered off and on around nine o'clock, and I heard a shout. I went in to find Charles fuming about Julien. Apparently he had tried to beg some more food from Charles, but Charles would have none of it. At any rate our menace was gone and we had the evening to ourselves.

Another night two boys hung around, waiting to hear what would be said. But that night Charles didn't want to talk at all, so I gave him some coffee, chatted for a few minutes, and then took my leave. The next evening we were once again free from intruders. And so it went.

I returned home; the next trip down my husband was with me, and we resumed our old habit of seeing Charles together. We continued to obtain rich material concerning Charles's past, but there was no more talk of bush or magical medicine until one night when Horace was called away. Immediately Charles asked me if I needed any more "messages," and for the rest of the night our talk was along those lines. From then on Horace and I decided it was best for him to come sporadically. And in those hours when Charles and I were alone he began to instruct me in earnest.

But mostly I was concerned with his autobiography. My plan was simply to elicit as much information concerning Charles's life as possible. In the earlier sessions I let him drift along at his own rate, figuring that the most important events of his life would come first. Only very slowly did I come to have a grasp of his whole life. To make any chronological order of events was initially baffling. It was only later, after a few major experiences could be dated, that any kind of order was realized. This was of no concern to Charles. It was the experience itself; whether it came before this or after that had no significance for him whatsoever.

Our sessions together were in blocks of two or three weeks,

and during the periods in between, when I was at home in the States, I went over the tapes, transcribing them in general form, attempting to gain an overview. When I was unclear about something I marked it down to ask Charles at a later date. I found there were many gaps in his story and I slowly tried to fill these in to make a comprehensive whole. When he died I still had many questions, but these were mainly for greater clarity; the bones of Charles's story were all there. It only remained for me to put them in some skeletal order and flesh them out as best I could from the existing sixty hours of tape.

My biggest problem was in verbally understanding the man. This difficulty was greatest at first, but as our association continued—as we talked night after night, and as I listened to the tapes over and over—the problem disappeared. I found that earlier narratives that had confused me now were clear, or at least clearer. There were always those words that were unintelligible, for often his actions in depicting a scene interfered with the clarity of recording. Sometimes if there were people present his voice would drop so low that the microphone could not distinguish it from other background noise. But by and large, the tapes are of good quality and have all been transcribed to the best of my ability.

Charles generally spoke to me in English although I knew he used Patois exclusively with his family. In teaching me bush remedies and cures he usually was careful to teach me both the English and Patois names, having me repeat the latter until I pronounced it as nearly right as possible. He was comfortable in both languages and could break from one to the other with no apparent break in continuity.[33] He also spoke Spanish fluently from his five years in Santo Domingo, and I found that whenever he was telling a story in which Patois- or Haitian-speaking[34] people were involved, he would break into passages of Patois or Spanish and then translate them for me. This was another touch which led me to believe that Charles was once again performing, or perhaps recreating, the past.

There were times when I heard the same story so often that I thought I had plumbed the depths of Charles, but another night a new series of narratives would prove me totally wrong. Because I was constantly looking for new or more extensive information, I inwardly bemoaned the constant repetition of certain incidents. Later, when I had a chance to compare them, I realized how helpful these repetitions were. I was intrigued by the fact that many of these narratives were often duplicated word for word, which said something to me about their veracity as far as Charles was concerned. As he said pointedly on a number of occasions, "A man who lies cannot remember his own words."

The retelling of these incidents also served to underscore the most traumatic events of his life. Among these were his sicknesses, particularly those of unnatural origins, a trip to Carib country to be cured, his activities in Santo Domingo, and his smuggling escapades. However, one sickness dominated all others in Charles's mind: he was convinced that this illness had been "put" on him by a fellow worker who coveted his job. For three months Charles lay helpless on the bed, until at last he remembered the song of the Haitian. As he began to sing it, he fell asleep, and his dead mother came to him, explaining the cause of his sickness and how to cure it. Charles followed her instructions to the letter and the next morning he rose from his bed, cured. Over the three-year period he told this same story to me at least six times and referred to it many others. Almost always his words were the same, the narratives only differing in details that he thought to add from time to time. For Charles this symbolized the greatest trauma of his life, but through his knowledge he was able to save himself and triumph over his enemy.

Many times I asked Charles how he came by his knowledge. His answers varied, indicating a large number of sources. "I spent my time with old people[35] when I was a young boy." Or on other occasions he told me, "And I paid for that knowledge." Most often he prefaced his remarks with "What you plant is what you reap," and explained that a charm or cure was given to him in return for a favor. This was certainly the case with Anton, the old Haitian who apparently was Charles's single greatest teacher.

During those five years that Charles was in Santo Domingo he met Anton, who had "a big head of hair on his face." When Anton complained that he had no one to cut his hair, Charles offered his services. In return for this favor Anton, who was a king of "wangawanga,"[36] tutored Charles for a month and a half.

The Carib Indians of Dominica also instructed Charles. For seven years as he came and went trading out of Dominica, he had a close association with these people. "The Carib people are very good people—nice people. Carib strongest obeah people in this world." It was from the Caribs that he learned much of his bush and magical medicine. These aboriginals have long been known for their extensive plant lore and particularly for their medicinal and magical cures.[37] As Hodge and Taylor point out, "The rarer the plant the more marvelous are its properties as a charm among the Island Caribs."[38]

But not all his knowledge was learned from such foreign sources. "My uncle learned me too and after he learn me he tell me, 'I learning you this because you haven't got no mother or no father.'" Thus Charles's knowledge was a compendium learned from many sources—from the Haitians, the Caribs, from his own people. He picked up information from a Guadeloupe man, from an East Indian. Anyone who could contribute to his knowledge he listened to. This is significant because it is not unique with Charles. In the West Indies it is usually the case.

Much has been made of the pluralistic nature of West Indian society,[39] with the many different groups of people living there, but the differences seem to merge when one examines the supernatural realm. In regard to the supernatural world the structure is one of belief integration.[40] From Guyana to Haiti, different cultures share a common belief in the supernatural, and it is interesting to note that the two extremes of the culture area are known to be the most potent sources of supernatural knowledge. Proximity to one of the poles seems to dictate a preference for that source of the magical arts—Grenadians swear by the dealers in Guyana, while St. Lucians seem to prefer Haiti. It is no accident that Charles learned from a Haitian.

Just how extensive Charles's knowledge was, no one will ever know, for he believed that one must never reveal more than half his learning.[41] I was aware that I had only scratched his surface. His competence in such matters seemed implicitly accepted, and he was continually sought out with questions. It was noised around that if anyone wanted to "know anything" he should see Charles, and young men like Randolph saw fit to sit at his feet and learn.

As time goes on and one talks to an individual night after night, it is very difficult not to become emotionally involved. There is no question that that happened to me. I became very fond of Charles, and a warm relationship grew up between the two of us. The gulf between foreigner and native, black and white, diminished, and we were two human beings enjoying each other's company. As a folklorist I tried to keep my perspective and wondered how much I influenced the way Charles portrayed himself.

Was it because I was white that he lingered on his debt to the white man, telling me that it was the white people who had "let me come big, not the black" or that "A man can say what the hell he likes about black people, but I tell you, black killing me. Give me white people." This sounds very reminiscent of the Haitian proverb, "Kill a hundred Haitians to save one white man." I suspect that both concepts had been deeply ingrained into the system and were an automatic response when the right button was pressed by a white skin. This response was also tempered by the fact that as far as Charles was concerned, white skin was synonymous with money. Therefore his policy was simply, "You don't bite the hand that feeds you." He was successful in his interactions with whites, but he was equally so in his relations with blacks and Caribs.

Throughout our conversations it was clear to me that Charles was very conscious of a person's color, but he was also very tolerant. He told me indignantly about a brown-skinned girl who had publicly insulted her mother in front of a crowd of people, claiming, "I don't know why my father took somebody black like you." As he explained to me in a backhanded manner, "Love is very funny—even [if] you black, I could love you." He had been forced to learn the standard gradations of color and the stereotyped attitudes attached to each, but when it came to the clinch it was the man who was important to Charles. Perhaps white people required more money to live, as his white boss tried to explain to him. He knew they didn't eat the same kind of food. He told me English people didn't like West Indian fruits. Such strange tastes were hard for Charles to understand, but he seemed to accept that whites were somehow different, with their own peculiarities—that they couldn't live on salt fish or a penny macamboo. He could go along with their different life-style, but he couldn't swallow the fact that a white man would be paid more for the same job than a black man simply because of the color of his skin. He made frequent use of the proverb, "The same thing that bite the white dog, bite the black,"[42] and often he would put his arm next to mine to accentuate the differences in our skin and then he would point to the heart and say, "The two are we so" (bringing his fingers together). Thus in dealing with whites as a group Charles was expedient, but in his individual relations he was a true democrat.

As our relationship grew Charles was anxious for me to come and meet his family and to have them meet mine, so we planned to go to his house one Sunday. Although he always walked to work he insisted that he get a car to drive us—the sun would be too hot, the walk too long. That morning he came for us a little after eleven, dressed in his Sunday best—panama hat with a brown band, a light shirt with a turquoise collar, cocoa brown pants, and brown shoes. He ushered us into the car with great dignity, and we drove to Marchand. Up the road we went, winding higher and higher. Charles gave us a running commentary, pointing to visible evidence of stories he had told me to indicate their truth. There was where he had once lived, that was the breadfruit tree he had refused to climb, that was Mrs. Branch's house, and so on. Finally the car stopped and Charles motioned us to follow him up a winding track. It was a narrow, steep path with water rushing down it from the latest shower. Charles marched up, surefooted as a goat, stopping only to show us the house of a duppy woman, Mrs. Alcindor, who had plagued Charles. Abandoned and decaying it stood with her death bed remaining as a final testament to her fearful nature—otherwise someone long ago would have "tiefed" (stolen) it.

Another fifty yards or so and we reached Charles's house. A little wood building about eight by fifteen feet, carefully patched, it stood by itself on the hillside, surrounded by mango, breadfruit, and papaya trees. Outside the smell of chicken arose from a coal pot bubbling over an open fire, while his wife washed the breakfast dishes in a big pan. Charles's three youngest children, Simon, Zander, and Angela, were all there waiting expectantly. The boys were neatly dressed, while Angela, the youngest, ran around *au naturelle*. Upon our appearance this was quickly remedied and she soon appeared in her best Sunday dress. "Come in, come in," Charles urged, as he stepped on the flat rock that served as the doorstop and climbed across the threshold.

We followed into a small, well-scrubbed room. A cool breeze blew through the open window which looked north out across Castries Harbor to the French island of Martinique. Two tables, a shelf of the best crockery, a large Victorian mirror with a frame of mahogany veneer, and a number of chairs overwhelmed the space. A fresh white tablecloth covered one of the tables and close by stood a chair with a red satin pillow which Charles plumped up and motioned me to sit on. As I did so I tried to absorb my surroundings. They were much like those of other houses I had been in throughout the islands, with one difference. There were few extras—everything was functional. There were no little china ornaments or knickknacks, no plastic fruit in bowls which so often adorn a West Indian home. The only decoration was to be found on the walls—a number of cheesecake pinups, with a glassy-eyed picture of Christ staring out from their midst. Near the door hung the sole photograph that Charles possessed—one of Ouioui, a grown son in Demerara.

We had brought Charles a bottle of rum for the occasion, and he placed it on the second table next to the door along with three glasses and a pitcher of water. He sent Simon to a nearby shop for some ice and, in traditional West Indian fashion, poured us each a shot of rum to be followed afterward by some ice water.

The children lurked around waiting to see what the strangers would do. Angela sat wide-eyed and staring in her own chair, looking dwarfed under the huge mirror, while Zander, who was about four, hopped from spot to spot, a perpetual grin on his face. Meanwhile Simon, the oldest, ran errands for his father. Charles wanted to make sure we saw everything—particularly those things which held the most importance for him.

He beckoned Zander to crawl under the bed that literally filled the second room and to bring out his "grip," a well-battered, black suitcase, while Simon fetched the key from its hiding place among the cups. With great care and pride he unlocked the bag and gingerly unpacked it. On top was a heavy overcoat, obviously the product of a colder climate, but it was the clothes underneath that he wanted us to see. These were what he was to be buried in—all clean and pressed, in anticipation of this final solemn occasion. My husband audibly gasped at such grim forethought, but Charles roared with laughter, regaling us with the need to prepare ahead of time and proudly displaying the white shirt and the black worsted suit that were to be his final garments.

Next he sent Simon scurrying after his own confirmation clothes. Simon had been confirmed a few months before and Charles had outfitted him with a new three-piece brown suit and matching shoes. "It cost forty dollars," he told me beaming. Simon appeared with the suit—carefully protected by a plastic bag—and Charles pulled it up for us to see, making sure we inspected all three pieces. These two suits were more than clothing for Charles. They were a measure of his and his son's distinction and respectability. Nobody could fault them on their appearance. Often in Charles's narrative he is careful in his description of how people are dressed. This concern is typical throughout the West Indies, for appearance is thought to be indicative of status. Frequently an individual will refuse to be photographed in old clothes. Instead he will vanish for a period of time, only to reappear dressed to the nines and will then strike a serious pose and await the click of the camera. This is how he wants the world to see him—formal and serious—a truly respectable personality.

While Charles was showing us his worldly goods, his wife continued to cook outside. She seemed shy and uneasy and did not come in until he called her. She spoke no English, but smiled and politely told us good day in Patois, then once again retreated outside where she took the coal pot off the fire, tapped a live coal into her pipe, and stood there smoking, gazing off down the hill.

I had brought my camera, as Charles was eager to have me photograph his children, and as I went outside to do this I noted other houses further up the hill. It seemed as though all the occupants were outside staring openly at the strangers. Everything was observed. There was no way to escape their watchful eyes. In that moment I could understand why Charles constantly expressed the desire to have no one know his business: very little appeared to be private.

After a couple of hours had passed, Simon came to tell his father that the car had come back, so we said our good-byes and once again Charles escorted us down the track. As we left, Ann Marie gave him a tongue-lashing in Patois concerning his drinking. Charles waved unconcernedly, "She'll beat me when I get back." As we stumbled downwards over roots and loose rocks, I asked him how he made it up the path when he was intoxicated. He chortled at me, "I don't come home when I'm drunk." He seemed delighted that we had come. "Now you see everything. Now you know what I tell you is true. Now you know where to find me if you come back and I not 'watchie' at Mrs. Ganter's."

What follows is Charles's book. It is a spoken book, one that was meant to be listened to rather than read. In the first part Charles recounts his life in a straightforward manner. As I have already suggested, this is not how he presented it; the chronological order is mine. I found a framework to be necessary in gaining some kind of perspective on his life. Erecting this framework was perhaps my most difficult task and I am sure that I have erred in places. I believe the general structure to be correct, although in one area I have changed it somewhat. For example, Charles fished on and off throughout his life. However, I have put all his fishing anecdotes together in one section for the purpose of consolidation. This in no way harms the narrative but rather makes it easier to follow. In no instances do I put words into the mouth of Charles. I have simply edited the tapes so there would be a flow to the narrative. In a few cases where his words were garbled I have attempted to make his point clearer. I have maintained his use of the tenses. Generally he used the present, but he was inconsistent in speaking and sometimes changed tense in mid-sentence. This perhaps makes it more difficult for the reader, but after a great deal of thought I decided it was important to uphold the authenticity. Although this may prove disconcerting to the reader at first, as he adjusts to the flow, a kind of speech rhythm results. It is this that I have hoped to preserve.

The second part of this book is one of conversations and therefore, in a sense, is much more personal. It was during these conversations that Charles imparted much of his own knowledge to me, and therefore it contains much to expand the reader's understanding of his philosophy and belief structure. This is perhaps the heart of the book.

The last section contains my own comments and observations on the text. Although I expect the text will speak for itself, these concluding comments hopefully will add one more dimension, shedding further light on the book and on the West Indian as a whole.

Part One:
Autobiography

The Early Years

I SAVAGE. I grow up like that because I lost my mother and my father when I was just a little boy going to school. Before my mother die, she always talked to me and tell me, "Keep off from strangers. Keep off from strangers." My father too. When he was small his father tell him to keep no friends. If he mix with friends my grandfather whipped his backside. But he still got friends. My father was a bourgeois[1] from Dominica and he was a big captain with a vessel. When you're traveling you have plenty girls, and he come to St Lucia with cargo and see my mother and love her.

I lost my father together with my mother. My father had a kind of boat they call a "cobble,"[2] and she went out from Guadeloupe carrying cargo and making message. In coming back a heavy squall meet her in Dominica Channel just by Devil Table Ground,[3] and the boat and everybody gone. That's the place I lost my mother and my father, and each time I reach there, I shake my head.

I was born one month from the day Queen Victoria was buried in my father's land—Roseau [Dominica]. My father belong to Portsmouth, but my uncle stay in Roseau because he was chief of police. I have a brother and a sister, and another sister too, but I ain't studying her.[4] My brother, George, he died a big man. That day was a hell of a day. It was because of the same bloody "friend." He going to dance and all about and he get into some kind of fight causing an injury inside—an abscess from some

3

blows he got. I can remember that good. He stand a nice, good-looking black man and he come thin, thin, thin—his face was paling. We all asking, "What's wrong with you?" and he answering, "Nothing." He was a man leaving the house. He don't tell nobody nothing. When he come back from work he dress up and went all about drinking rum, visiting girls—he doesn't obey Mama. That day he died he said he wanted to eat cucumber salad. Before he say "cucumber" my mother had it on the table. And after he eat it the abscess must have burst, for he puked blood and was dead—not on the bed but still sitting by the table.

My sister, she was the one taking care of me. Anywhere she went I was there with her, helping her work, helping her carry cane. But she kill she ownself—not to say, commit suicide. She ironing, and she took two ripe banana and put them by the fire to roast. My mother warned her, saying, "Nenen, that fig you roasting there will kill you. If you put it in the fire, you would properly roast it and you could eat it, and it wouldn't hurt you, but when you put it by the fire it will only half roast, and inside will be cold and will cut your stomach." Nenen did not listen, and when night come she fall sick and start to shake, shake, shake. By the time it was eight o'clock next morning she dead. That banana catch her because it was too cold and she was ironing.[5] She dead a young girl.

Misery, you think I don't see misery. I pass a lot of misery until I come big. When you're small, if you have your mother alive you is a king, but if you haven't got a mother, then you is a hustler, and don't believe you going to have it easy. I stay in Dominica with my father's people, but they don't give a blast about me. It was there I learn to make coal [charcoal]—to cut the wood, put it in a heap, catch it fire, cover it over and after your wood burn, drag it out bit by bit. Then so long as I have a tin to carry it, I know I could eat tonight. Sometimes I fill two carrying tins.

There's a kind of green tree in Dominica—its leaves are thick—and the root of the same tree is food [probably taway]. People used to dig it, boil it, and eat it. And God help me to know that tree and I use it when I hungry. I go off in the jungle and I go and find one of these trees. Then I come back, light my wood, and put my root to cook. Sometimes I help a fisherman pull his boat, and he give me two flying fish. I help him and he give me fish, and I go back and make my broth and eat.

One day a Carriacou man called Captain Broco was in Portsmouth taking cargo—ripe bananas—and everything to go up to Antigua. He have a big, four-masted schooner, and I stopped there watching him. Each time he go aboard he ask me, "What's wrong? Would you like to go aboard and sit?" I say, "Yes, Captain." He tell me he can't take me, because he would have to go and see my mother. "But Captain, I have no mother or no father." He say, "Where do you live?"

"With my aunt, Choco."[6]

"Will you go?"

"Yes."

He tell me to go and get my clothes, but I tell him I don't have any clothes. "The only clothes I have are the ones I got on my skin. They don't give me any clothes. They take no care with me. When they finish eating, they call me and give me a piece of food. If I go and do something for someone—working in their garden or picking coconuts—when I come back they give me food, or if Christmas is coming they might feel to give me a pair of pants or a shirt because I cannot work for myself yet."

The captain look at me and said, "All right. If I take you, where are you going to stay?"

"I will stay on board."

You know what they used to call me? Captain Broco's monkey. I start to wash pots for the cook and do everything. When Captain Broco was eating he would tell me to hold the wheel. He showed me how. At that time there was no wheel—it was a jackass tail [tiller]—and there was a block and tackle, and you pulled and you slacked, 'cause there was no wheel.

When it came time to be paid, Captain Broco told me, "Boy, I don't give you your money, you know. I'm going to give you something in your hand. I'm going to buy clothes for you." He watch out for me good. One day a man want to have me.[7] He was stowing cargo. At that time we carrying cement by the barrel. When he tell me to push, he catch the barrel on my leg. Captain Broco see it and tell him good, "You son of a bitch. You want to hurt the poor boy. You are no bloody good." And when we reach in Roseau, he put him ashore.

But Captain Broco went back to Carriacou, and I find another captain who says he going to St. Lucia and Barbados and I ask for a passage. When we reach St. Lucia Captain Becker want me to go up to Barbados with him. I said, "Hmmm." And I stop at the wharf and disappear with my little parcel in my hand. I left about seven o'clock in the night and go to my auntie's, my mother's sister. I tell her I had come to stay, but she say no, she have no room for me. The son of a bitch, I bury her.[8] And she was not poor. She was picking cocoa and selling it. But she say, "I got nowhere for you. I got nowhere for you." And she there cooking breadfruit and tripe. I see the food, and my belly hurting me, I so hungry. But the woman chase me away and don't give me any food. My mother's own sister.[9] I say to myself one day I am going to come big.

I remember there was a big riot in St. Lucia when I was a young boy.[10] I forget nothing. The riot started on Tuesday afternoon—people shooting, and policemen shooting people like birds. It start up to Roseau in the cane fields. There was fire and wagons to mash up the cane. It was a strike for more money. The next day cane burning, and they killing people like sand. If you running they shoot you. They burst open the shop, throw all the goods outside, and take what they want. They go out to the manager's place and use his woman and his daughter. For a month that went on. They kill the cattle and hit the manager with salt fish. Finally the jail couldn't hold all the people, so they send some to Grenada. At that time I was on top of Plum, suffering by myself. Suppose you tell me to go in the country with you, I go and help you bring down a load, and you give me something for it. At night if I can't make it up, I throw myself down by the wharf, and God help make a man of me. Sometimes I sleep in a salt fish barrel—a cask used in the dry season to wet the street.

They fill it with water and drag it behind a horse to wet the street and keep down the dust that go in people's faces. I shove myself inside and I very glad to sleep there until the next morning. I get up, nobody know where I sleeping. Yes, I have family, but they'd like me to die before I come big.

When I come from the bush I go and wash my clothes in the sea water. I have soap, but I can't get it to lather. A woman come and say to me, "Oh, little boy, don't you know sea water doesn't take no soap?"

"Mama, I don't know." And she tell me to go in the bathroom and wash my clothes.

One night I go by the market and I see Mr. Jim Stray. He used to call in Dominica and he say, "Hello. What are you doing here?"

"I came here looking for something to do."

"Well, what kind of work do you think you could do?"

"Any kind of work you ask."

"Could you bring a horse? Could you groom?"

I say, "Yes sir." And I start to groom. I take care of the horses and I begin to feel myself a man now. I drive the buggy, and Mr. Stray show me how to drive the trap. That was no buggy. It only have two wheels. I learn, I learn, and I come perfect.

Later I worked for a white woman called Avonise DuBoulay for eight shillings a month. Now, she tell me she feeding me, but you know what she do? When she finish taking her tea, she throw some hot water in the pot—she washing the pot and she sweeten that water for my tea. Or after she eat, she mix up a plate for me—you could see where she pull the flesh from the bone and leave me the bone for my breakfast. If I wait for what she give me I would suffer too much. Sometimes I tief some bread-fruit and put it to boil, and I get a piece of salt fish and eat my belly full. But that only in breadfruit season.

One day she called me, "Charles."

"Yes, Madame."

"Do you know Mrs. Minwell?"

I said, "No."

"Well, pass by the Governor's house and go to the building below there. Go inside and take that nice bouquet to the lady for me."

Little did she know that she had gone and make a whip for sheself. I go and I tell Mrs. Minwell, "Good morning, Madame."

"What a nice little boy. Where do you work?"

I say, "At Mrs. DuBoulay's."

"And how much does she pay you?"

"Eight shillings, Madame."

"WHAT! What kind of clothes do you have?"

"I don't have much clothes."

She tell me, "Come here. See this room."

"Yes, Madame."

"See, it is a nice room—all fixed up for you. Come and take work today, son."

"But Madame, they would bring me up in court because I didn't give a month's notice."

"I don't care. Indeed, if they bring you up, I will pay the money, Charles. Come down and meet me."

I go back to Mrs. DuBoulay's and I clean out a piece of the stable good. When I finished a week I ask her to lend me four shillings. "Huh, I can't give you four shillings."

"All right." I get vexed.

I hear, "Call down and tell the boy to fix up the trap to take me up in town."

I say, "Who are you talking to? Me?"

"Yes!"

"Donald will bring it," I say, "but not me."

"Come here!"

"Donald will bring it, but not me!" I just turn on my heel and down I go to Mrs. Minwell's. When I reach, I sit down in the kitchen, and before long Madame call, "Charles, come and I will give you food now." You should see the kind of food I get, and the bed she give me with a blanket. Before, I have two books for a pillow and a piece of bag on the ground to lie down on. When Mrs. Minwell see the bag she tell me, "You won't need that any more." Since that I have a sheet and a bed and a mother to love me up. Food don't bother me anymore, because I have that at my mother's house.

In a week's time I see a policeman come to order me to go to court for leaving work without notice. When I got to court the magistrate rise up and say, "Alexander Charles."

"Yes, sir."

"You have a charge against you. You working at Mrs. Avonise DuBoulay and you leave this work without notice, and you had a good salary too."

I say, "I am guilty, sir. Self-defense."

"Let me hear you."

I tell him "Mrs. DuBoulay give me eight shillings a month, and I get more than eight shillings a week at Mrs. Minwell's. You would have left, too."

"All right. I will charge you fourteen shillings. How will you pay it?"

"I will pay it right now."

I hear Mrs. DuBoulay say, "What. . . ." And Mrs. Minwell turn to me, "Let's go, Charles."

Do you know why she started to love me more? She used to buy coal by the barrel, but the property have big trees and all kinds of fruit, breadfruit, plantain, and wild yam. (She never eat that because English people don't like those kind of things.) So I say, "Madame, buy an ax and a cutlass for me."

"Charles, what are you going to do with that?"

"Make a surprise for you."

"All right. John, give him a rein and send him to buy them."

I go and buy an ax and a cutlass and I start to cut down some small trees. Well, I cut wood, I cut wood, I cut wood, and when I finish I took the hoe and the pickax, and I dig a big hole and pack all the wood in carefully. I cut grass and I cover the wood over nicely with grass and then with dirt. I make my hole and when I start the fire, I call them to come.

"What are you doing?"

"That's a coal pit," I tell them.

"You're not making coal?"

"Sure," I say. "The same coal you buy every day by the bag."

"Hmmm, I will see."

The next morning when I come, I found the pit flat. "O.K.," I say, "Burn steady." After it burn for about four days, I take the hoe and I start to pull coal. "Madame, Madame," I call.

"Yes."

"Bring a big bucket of water for me. Come quick!"

"What's wrong with you?"

I say, "Come now."

"All right." She and her daughter, Miss Flora, come down and each of them have a bucket.

"Look out for the fire, Miss. Stay back. Give me the bucket." And I start wetting the coal. My master come to see then.

"Indeed, Charles, that is coal?"

I say, "Yes, Master."

"Really?"

"Yes, Master. Wait awhile and you will see." I cover it, and at night I come again and wet all the coal with water. The next morning I have to pick up the coal. I don't call anybody, and when I have a big heap I asked Madame Minwell to get John to go to town to get five bags of sugar and then empty the sugar to put it up, bring the bags, and a little water. When she come she say, "Oooh, it's coal."

I say, "Yes, that is the way we do it." And you know what she do. She cook dumplings. She tell me she going to have a proper nice breakfast for me.

From then on I make all the coal. When people come and say, "Good morning, Madame, do you want any coal?" she answer, "No, no, I don't need any coal." The house was full of coal.

Reverend Minwell was a parson, and every Sunday morning I hear *ding, ding, ding.* I know the bell and I hurry to put on a suit—nice clothes and a rake hat. Courtly I is. We would climb into the buggy, a four-wheeler, the parson behind, and I in front there and go to the Wesleyan Church. I make my time there until they went to Hong Kong. Then Reverend Minwell transferred me to Governor Moore. They was the same kind of people, and that's why he turn me over to him.[11] Reverend Minwell tell him I a good boy of nice behavior and have a nice character. The first thing I used to do there was clean shoes—have them clean and nice for the evening. Governor Moore try me with big money in my hand to see if I would run away with it. He was a good man, and if he there still, I would be there, but he go to Hong Kong too. When I leave Governor Moore's I could stand the gigging. I big then and I know I could understand my ownself.[12]

Do you know what they call a "stow'way?" Well, four of us, Amady, Crefoot, Masel, and me went aboard a vessel coming to land coal.[13] One boy bring two coconuts, and that's all we have to drink. The fireman come down and find us. He ask us what we doing. I tell him that St. Lucia have nothing and that we trying to get a living. He say, "Here's ten cents money. Go and get a bottle of rum and bring it secretly on board." I buy the rum and come back and meet him. Then he put us all in a dark place in the hold—behind a piece of board. We hide there in the day, and at night we help him parcel the coal and trim. But we get hungry. He tell us he would fix things up. "When I tell you to go up, go up. Go two by two. It's all right. It's all right." As we reach there was a big man in a chair, his pipe right there beside him. Our friend knock. "What do you want?"

"Stowaway here, sir."

"Stowaway, aboard my ship? How many of them?"

"I don't know, sir."

"Well, bring that one."

I have no hat, nothing at all. "Good morning, Captain."

"What are you doing aboard my ship?"

"I don't come to do anything bad, Captain. If I speak to you, I hope a man like you could have sympathy."

He tell me, "You speak, and I will hear what you say."

I ask him, "Do you have any son?"

"Sure. I have a big family and a lot of sons."

"Well, I lost my mother when I was small and I don't want to follow bad company. I try to look after myself."

"That's good," he say. "Give him a couple of old pants and give him a good bath. Anybody besides you?"

I say, "There remain three more."

"Jesus Christ! Brown, take them and put them in the hold. Give them something to eat and bring them to me when you have cleaned them up. Put one on deck and another below to pass coal and help the trimmer. You go in the galley and be a mess boy. How will that do you?"

We were going to New Orleans, and when we reached we go ashore. My shoes were too long and I block them up with paper, and anyone could see the pants were not mine, but I make them fit. We go ashore and we feel ourselves comfortable. Then a big American ship come alongside, and two men come and call us. We have a bag of old clothes and a couple of dollars in hand, and they take us in charge and carry us away. We don't know it to wait for a boat going back to St. Lucia. We think we going to have a time where we going. That's how I come back to St. Lucia and I live here till I come big. I pass trouble here but I never a stow'way again—not me! That was just before the war.

During the first World War—the Kaiser War—I tiefed a pants and a shirt and I went up to the Canadians'[14] barracks, and Sergeant Gibson tell me to go back and wash my mother's pots. I cry, I cry, I cry. He tell me, "When we want you, you can come all right, but now you are too small." But I get a job with them. At the time, I working in town carrying meat, beef, and everything for the soldiers. There were two kinds, black and white, and the Jamaicans didn't like the Canadians. All the Jamaicans come down with tamarind whips in their hands, and anywhere they see a Canadian, they beat him. The Canadians said they would come down on Saturday to take their revenge. Now the Canadians' chief cook named Harry, and he involved with the daughter of a big merchant. I see him come out from the girl's house and go to take the shore boat to Vigie. I call him and warn him about the Jamaicans and tell him if he go with me he'd be all right. I take him up to my aunt's house. Sunday morning Harry told me to go with him and he give me a job. I go up with the

Canadians and I get the wash. I thought I'd kill myself during the war. I up on top there by the women's quarters washing pots, cooking, and I riding a bicycle. I don't want harm. And there I grow. I grow big and when I come out I have shoes, I had boots, plenty of Canadian pants, Canadian hat. All my friends Canadians and the discipline I have was Canadian. It not black people's discipline. If it was for the black people, I wouldn't be here today. When I was working, when my pants were dirty and I had no shirt, nothing at all, Mrs. Minwell ask me if I want to stay with her. And today I come big. Who let me come big? It's the white people.

Prison and
Santo Domingo

W HEN I COME a right ageable man, then I say, "Well, settle down in St. Lucia." And I settled down. I married up with my concubine[1] and continued going up in the country, until I got four stroke of the cat-o'-nine-tails. I was keeping a man at my house. One night I didn't go home to my wife and as I was going down, he see me passing. He tell me, "You're playing great."

I say, "What the hell does that have to do with you?" He reach up his hand and he give me one cuff.

My wife say, "You shouldn't continue to do things like that." And he grabbed me wife's breast. Then I went. I run. I couldn't fight the man, because he was too big for me. I went at my home and I take my razor, and I come back and I give him one lash. I take him from the back to the guts. I go for his neck, but I miss him and I take him on his back.

When we come to court I say, "I'm guilty. Self-defense." I tell the judge the same way it happened. They give him my conduct in writing, and when they tell the judge what kind of man I am, he say, "It's a pity to send you to prison, Charles. I got to go with the law, but I will be easy on you. I will give you nine months' hard labor and four strokes of the nine-tails. I said, "You son of a bitch—is that the way you're easy!" Four strokes of the cat-o'-nine-tails. When you get one, you get nine. When you get two that's twice nine on your back. When you get four it's four, nine. Check it up. Both your hands are up above your head, and a man

14

behind you with the whip—nine strands, a mixture of twine and wire.

When I come out from this my back was on fire and bleeding. But I did not bawl once and I fought that whip in my back. They touch me, like that, and I pull the muscles to make my flesh come hard so they could not inspect my heart. When I have three, I strut up for the last one. They come and unbuckled my hands, ready to carry me back to my cell. I walk straight. When night come I had to lie down, but I could not lie on the cuts. It was just like they had burst—like I had no back at all. The next morning they send you to bathe. They have a kind of white medicine— embrocation [liniment]—that they rub on my back. This thing burning, you know. They put on a piece of cloth and they finish with you. You got three days to come back. Now this thing going to soak and it going to dry. When they come to take it off, the skin come too because it is all wet. Then they give it to you again. They don't touch you—just one big drop of embrocation and they put on the next cloth. Your friends got to spread you with cocoa grease. I help you, you help me. That going so every day. I suffered for one month.

Judge Plunkett, it's he that give me the cat-o'-nine-tails and send me to jail, but he was a good man. He give you what coming to you. That's all. How you make your bed is how you lie down. If you don't make the bed too tough, you won't be sorry. You'll be happy. If you shake it, he will deal with you properly.

The judge have a little boy who always ride a white horse. One day he riding the horse and he fell in a gully near where I working.[2] I run and pick up the boy. I don't know him and I don't know who the father or the mother is. I take him and put him down, and I go back and do my work. One day I get myself in trouble,[3] and the boy see me come in the yard and he ask me what I doing there. I tell him what I done and he run off, saying, "I'm going to tell Daddy about you." When I come the boy say, "That's the man who helped me and took me up from the horse." Then Judge Plunkett tell me what to say tomorrow morning and give me a form to make application to see the chief of police and the governor and the keeper of the prison. Two weeks go by and there was nothing on the slate. Plunkett ask me again. "Did you do what I said?"

"Yes."

He tell me to make out an application by tomorrow morning. I do that, and Major Tanner, the chief of police call me. "Alexander!" [feigning an English accent].

"Yes, sir."

"What do you want to see me for?"

I say, "I have a long time in prison and I wish you would review my paper."

"Oh, yes, indeed. Plunkett, there's the paper."

"I've seen it already. We have got to give him satisfaction, because he is a man worth doing for."

Major Tanner say, "Well, I am going to put you in the bakery with Brother Paul. From the bakery you will go in the kitchen and help Bangi. That will do you?"[4]

I say, "Thank you."

"But don't be beating people anymore. I tell you, the next time anybody troubles you, come over to headquarters, and we will give you a free trial. But don't lift up your left hand or next time you will be hanged. A small man like you—the Lord put you so because if you were big, you would hang well, sir."

I came out and saw Mr. Braffett, keeper of the prison. "Turn him over to Brother Paul in the bakery and from the bakery put him in the galley. Guard, come take Alexander in charge." Braffett vexed. He want me to go in the bush and work. He was a bad man. He cause two men, Blast and Jet, to run away from prison. They hide in the jungle, but when they see they can't stand it no more they go back and report themselves. In the morning when the porter come he ask Blast and Jet why they come back after they run away. Blast said, "I got to run because Braffett beating me too much."

The porter say all right and go to call Major Tanner and Captain Sharp. When they reach, they bring them to court and they call Braffett. Major Tanner tell Braffett, "Everyday is fishing day and catching fish, but one day you will be counted. These men don't run away from jail. They run away from blows. If they run away from jail, they wouldn't come here in the middle of the night. You should be ashamed of yourself. Well, Braffett, I won't discharge you for the first time. I will charge you fourteen pounds[5] each man for the time they were suffering under the bush for the sake of you. You will work seven months' salary for those prisoners."

Braffett, he don't care, because the money he suppose to pay he could take it off the cat-o'-nine-tails and the tamerind rod— the cat's a pound and the tamerind rod, six shillings. [In other words Braffett was paid for each beating.] If there ten men for the cat-o'-nine-tails, that's ten pounds, so he still taking out his money, and when you see he going to beat you, he so happy you believe he a man going to be married. Braffett rejoicing to catch an animal, but one day it cost him. The cat-o'-nine-tails soaking in water and when you take the towel away it stand up, so. He drink whiskey—(that not allowed)—and as he lash them all those people scream and use their bowels. He amused when they show their backs in blood and he lock them in the cellar.

Now there was a devil of a man called Gobi. And he warn Braffett, "Braffett, although you are friends with my daughter, you treat me like that. When I come out I'll have you dead. Chow." Gobi knew about a kind of grass—it was water grass and guinea grass—and he make something for Braffett with it.[6] His six months were up at five o'clock.

"Gobi."

"Yes, sir."

"Come down and get your clothes and get a bath. Go and trim your hair, because you are leaving today."

When it was noon on Saturday all the prisoners come inside. It was a half day of work, and nobody going out again. Everybody wash off and clean up. Braffett come in. "Gobi."

"Aah, Braffett. I am going out today, Saturday, Braffett. Saturday to Saturday is eight days and I know that Saturday week, at this time you will be happy, but when it is eight o'clock you will be in Dormitory House upstairs crying." *Bang,* Gobi put it on him and Braffett never knew.[7] He there laughing. Another fellow, Chapman, watching and he tell Braffett, "Your old man speak to you. He do you something. You laugh, but you laugh on your ownself."

"I laugh on my ownself?"

"Yes. Your old man give you the word and you cannot catch it. You laugh on your ownself."

The next Saturday I was in the bakery. Braffett locked me upstairs because we come at eight o'clock to set the yeast for one o'clock. A man come up. "Paul, Charles," he called the next three men. "You know what's happened? Just now you're going to hear a cry. Braffett take the chief of police's car and go and mash it up in Hospital Road."

I say, "What!"

"Wait, they're coming with the keys now to lock him up. He's crying."

Paul, the baker, call, "Who's crying?"

A new prisoner say, "It's Braffett crying. They bring him and lock him up because he mash up the chief of police's car."

Paul say, "Gobi tell him that two things would happen. Grass and water grass. Now look at the water grass." Braffett sleep there that night. Sunday they lock him up. Monday at ten o'clock they bring him down.

I come from the bakery when Major Tanner arrive. He was a big, big white man. "Bring Brother Braffett down." When you working for the police and you don't like the man, you send for him. Everyone was laughing because nobody like Braffett.

Tanner say, "Braffett, I don't want to hear nothing from you. My car was in the pound yard, locked up, and the gate was locked. You take my car and go and mash it up. Don't fool ashore with a brown-skinned vampire [another woman]. Who do you think you are? Are you a bigger boss in prison just because you're catting people like criminals? Now your time has come. That's the end of you. You won't cat anybody again. From now on you wipe with the mop. You have lost your job and from next year you'll be chief water man. And you've lost your whole month's salary as well. Get out from that gate now. Take off your shirt and jacket and pants, Braffett, get out!"

"*Booo hooo.*" He walk down the road. He have a wife and four children and he go behind that brown-skinned vampire and play with fire in the night—taking the chief of police's car. He have to suffer for it. You know where he and his wife are now? You see them sitting down in the poorhouse, like this. He hardly has a penny bread to put in his mouth. He come old and he cannot do nothing for himself. And his hands that he was catting people with—giving them pain and wounds—his hands are dead. They're all bent over like he's still holding the cat.

When I come out from prison at twelve o'clock on the day my time was up, I was more bad than before I went. If you don't scald in hot water, you wouldn't be frightened in cold. When I come out my people start to call me and talk to me. They tell me, "Well, you see what happened to you. You get yourself messed up for cutting your own friend." I sat in a chair, a crowd of people around me. They tell me they wouldn't treat me as a friend, that I don't belong there. They hope I would change.

I say, "Yeah. I will leave now. I come to say good-bye. I believe now I am no criminal like before, because I have nothing to be scared of. From now on I will keep off from friends. I want nobody to come at my house or sit down like before. If I die the government will send someone to pick me up. I want no mercy upon my chair. I come up to bid you good-day. I'm leaving the country." And *bam*, I was bound for Santo Domingo. We had a contract to go down there to work. Now we were carried down, but we didn't want to go back because we were working for plenty money. Some run away from immigration.[8] Plenty people remained. I passed five years in Santo Domingo and I have been all about.

I was in a place they call Samana. All those people in Samana have a face full of prickles[9]—their nose, their ears, all prickles. I had never seen that before and I found it strange. Since I was born I had never seen any prickles like that. Now I don't know what to do. It was Sunday, and everyone who I want to speak to have those prickles. I finally say to a man, "Come here."

"Yes."

"Is here named Samana?"

He tell me, "Yes."

"I find prickles on everybody, and you have it too."

"Sure."

"Is that a mark the government stamp you with?"

He say, "No. All Samana is like that. It's the kind of way we is." I spend the whole day in Samana, but I don't drink a drop of water ashore, even when I go in the rum shop and want a drink. I was frightened and I wonder, if I drink the water, whether I could come like the Samana people.

When I reach a place they call Barahona in Santo Domingo, I find all Haitians there. They were so black I almost believe I white. I am black, yes, but a different color from them. I believed it was tar they dealing with. When they see a stranger coming, they won't even tell you "Good-night," they watch you. When they see you pass straight by, they laugh and make jokes. They keep away from strangers because they frightened of them. It was months before he become close to you.

When I come and join the Haitians, I become friends with the Haitians. And I thanks Haitians seven times more that I thanks any St. Lucian, for Haitians taught me how to save my life. That was Anton.[10] He taught me many things, but Haitians don't like white people. A Haitian would wait until he come home from work in the afternoon. When you stoop down to fire the stones and put the pot there, he catch you and cut your neck right off, and then he go clear away in the cane field. And why he do that? For cane. If you cutting cane and he cutting cane, he call you to give him a hand to load his cart. You give him a hand, but when you go to load yours, you won't see him again. You could call him and call him, but he won't come. The man know you going to tell him, "Come give me a hand because I give you a hand," but he tell you he's got to cut cane more far—that's why he can't come help you. If you cook one night, another night he cook. He call you and give you back the same food you give him last night. The next day he won't cook. You have to cook because he won't cook you no more food.

I like Haiti. Haiti was a good place to learn. I spend two months there—a happy time—but then I come off from there. But you must never take Haiti for your country. Haiti is easy. Just pass a leaf over your husband, like this, and he would turn a kind of cow. One day a man might see you and he would say, "Eh, eh, your flesh is soft." Next morning he would eat you with peas. "Coma gente," that's Spanish. "Coma gente"—it means a man who eats people. Haitians could turn you into a cow. The Haitians good at that.[11]

In Santo Domingo I learn how to fight with a knife. I had to go and pay five dollars every fortnight to go and fight with a parasito.[12] Every afternoon I go, take my shirt off, leave my shoes on, and go to fight Haitian. You pay your money and you learn to fight. If you going to come and fight, you salute—lift up your hands. He be so quick. He shove the knife and get you already. The kind of knife they use, it called a "cinco clava." It have a brass around the collar and a point. If you talking with a man and you see him shove his hand in his shirt, keep off because he will stick you. I got it right here in my breast. I run at him with my head and give him a kick. Then I throw my hand in my bosom and pull my cinco clava and shove it right in his guts—"You son of a bitch, endure this, Campadre"—and he dead. In Santo Domingo they have no jail. The man that is dead first is wrong.

I walk down to the doctor. You can see where he pass the needle, and the whole time I don't do nothing, I don't say, "*Uhh.*" He tell me that I looked like a bloody hog, and I a lucky man. And after he finished sewing me he put on a plaster. If I wasn't a hero I don't believe you would see me today.

It's there I learn if two people fighting, it's not me and I not going to see. I know better. I see a gang of men and women going up a side road in Santo Domingo. A man was cooking some food—rice and smoked herring. The girl passing calls, "Ah, how are you, Papasito?"

He answers, "Hi, Mamasita." The police man come up, said, "Come on." He had no right to talk to a prisoner. That woman was so smart and wanted to get even. She calling, "Papasito." They lock him up. The rice stop there for no one to eat. Fined and confined. He had to take seven days in jail. Seven dollars he pay. When you see a flock of people going up the sidewalk— prisoners, everybody—I just stay away. They watching them passing. I'm not even cursing them. When you hear a fight, you're going to see a bottle fire—too late. Why didn't you stay at your home?

One time there was a woman and she got a man. But she find out he living with another woman.[13] She call the woman and say, "Let's fight for the man. If you win you get the man. If you lose, I get him." They went at it—big brassiere, no dress, just bare panties—and each of them had a cinco clava. Somebody go and tell the man, Manuel, and he ran down with a bull pistol, chopped at the girls, and told them to go back at home. And still Cornelia—that was the girl's name—come next door and kill the other girl while she was dancing the same Saturday night. Just one knife in the back. Cornelia was a fast cutter.

I make five years in Santo Domingo and I tell you I see dead people. I see dead, I see dead, I see dead. One kill another. In a dancing house, Easter Saturday night, you saw people dead like ants. No law for that at all.

When you get paid, the country people are going to ask you what you have, and then they take it away. They stab you and take your money, or cut behind your neck with a machete. You have no chance. Nobody would do nothing.

There was a man there they call Mr. Charles. He have a cook shop, and a man eat there for a whole fortnight, and when it come time for him to pay, Mr. Charles can't see that man. His wife went at the man's house looking for the money. A message come down for Mr. Charles. "Your wife is dead."

"What happened?"

"The man kill your wife. He shoot your wife."

Mr. Charles say, "Ah, my wife."

"Yes."

He go and take his gun and he lock the shop and up the road he went. When the man see that Mr. Charles coming he fire two shots, and Mr. Charles fall down on the ground. He believe he caught Mr. Charles, but Mr. Charles don't get shot, he waiting for his chance. He give him his own and he catch him. Now the man lying there like a bull. He fall on the ground, and every person there kill heself laughing. Now a policeman come. Mr. Charles kick the man on the ground there and he took his gun.

The policeman ask, "Mr. Charles, what is the trouble here?"

The other man speak up, "He shoot at me."

Mr. Charles tell the policeman, "If you come and tell me you're on the side of that man, I will kill you, I will kill your mother, and I will kill your father." He come up to him and he have a cinco clava. He roll it, like that, in his hand. "Look, we need no constable."

"O.K., Mr. Charles."

That night Mr. Charles meet the man at a dance with his girl friend. As he make a round Mr. Charles just do that with a kind of dagger he had and just split his belly in two. The man never feel it. Oh, they have everything in Santo Domingo.

I work cutting cane, I work in the carretera,[14] but the best man I work for in Santo Domingo was Mr. Wally. If I had not been a St. Lucian and immigration hadn't got me, I would be there still. It happen so funny.

I come from the cane field. And you know "tasso"? A kind of big bull cow they're killing. They put it in a press and in a barrel to soak. It swells and that's what they call tasso. Well, I had a piece of tasso and a kind of tannia, long, and you cut it and inside there it is red. Well, I cooking it in a tin. I there blowing the fire and I hear *backala, backala.* When I look up I see a horse coming with its foot caught in the bridle. The bridle humbugging him and he stop. Well, I go. It was a big, big horse, and I take the bridle and I hook the horse by my home. I go and take off the tannia and shove the stick in it. I see it cooked, and I put it in my room and lock the door. There was no key—just a piece of wire they give you to pass over it—you hook it. Then I put the horse behind my back. I don't ride it. If you ride it, that would mean you took the horse. I go. I walk, I walk, I walk, I get fed up. I bust [come to] Pintado, I bust Barahona, I went to a place called La Noria Campina. I say, "Shit, I will leave the last corner. If I don't see nobody, I give up." Well, I never see Blanco. As I go around the corner I see one big buckaroo. He had a big, broad, nice sombrero hat and a big belt with two guns. When he see me, he do so [put up his gun].

I say, "Naw, don't shoot."

"Why?"

"You cannot shoot like that, sir. Listen, I meet the horse going down. Somebody unhook the horse. Where you put the horse?" He say, he put the horse in the orange tree. I say, "Well, you have no sense. You have a roll of rope. You should take off the bridle from the horse's neck and put the rope tight upon the orange tree. But somebody unhook the horse from where you hang it and chase it away. That mean you would have to walk down, and who ever do it would get you."

"I believe so. I believe so. Those Haitian beasts never liked my people. What is your name?"

"My name is Charles."

"Where did you meet the horse?"

"Pintado." When I tell him that he jumped, because Pintado is close to Guaymate.

"Jesus Christ! And you walking the horse. Why didn't you ride?"

"Naw, if I ride, I is the one that take it."

"Where you from?"

"Dominica."

"Dominican or Dominica?"

I say, "Dominica. I am a Dominican from St. Lucia."

"Oh, I see. My name is Mr. Wally. Are you working in Pintado?"

"Yes, I am cutting cane."

"A man like you should not be cutting cane. Would you like to work for me? I'm from La Noria where they have the Haitians, but I only speak English. Do you speak Spanish?"

"Yes, I speaking French and Haitian."

"Really? You speak Haitian? Well, that's the kind of work you do. When can you come down and meet me?"

"I got some cane in the ground."

"Well, pick up your cane. What about Saturday morning?"

"Which batey[15] do you live?"

"La Noria. Look, ask any car you meet and tell him to take you to Mr. Wally in La Noria. Then you will come at my house. Now I will give you some money to pay for the car and I'll give you something for your trouble. Twenty bucks for the car and twenty bucks for your trouble. You saved my life. If I walked into town somebody would like to stab me in the back. I am quite sure of that."

I ask, "How is that?"

"You haven't heard about Mr. Wally, the chief immigration master?"

"Yes."

"Well, that's me."

"Oh, I see."

"O.K., Charles. Be good. Keep your word."

"You can bet on that."

I go back by Guaymate, and I go and buy a bottle of wine and I sit down there and eat. I shake my head. I ain't going to cut cane anymore and I got money. I go and pick up the cane that I have in the ground, and I go and give the next man the first cane. When he done he come and help me. I put the cane in a corner and I bide my time. Saturday they pay me a few cents. I throw away my old cocoa-bag hammock. I throw away the skillet and an old shirt. I put on two pants and two shirts and go without no grip so that everybody think I going to cut cane. I go down quietly. Now the bagon[16] in the cane field. There were steps to take you up, and there I was, high in the air. When you get in there no one can see you, and I on top of the cane. The cane was sweet, and I ate my belly full. I lie down in it comfortably. Six o'clock, seven o'clock, nine o'clock, eleven o'clock. I hear *Woo-hoo, woo-hoo, woo-hoo.* Aha, it coming. *Ahoc, ahoc.* It hooking. The hook made and Engine Number 11 coming for the cane. When the train start nobody on the wagon and it made *con-ton, con-ton, con-ton* until it reach Higueral. It stop there to take on water, and I come down and go into the office. "Bueno nochas," I say to the man there. The way I say it, he think I was a Haitian because I speak Spanish. I knew Haitians are the worst of all people and that they don't like English men. If I speak English, I would be dropped right there. Well, not so. As long as I was in Spanish country, English could go to hell with me because I saving my own life. He ask me if I want some rum. I say no and go by the pipe to wash my face. Then I go. I see the same road Mr. Wally tell me to go down. He said, "Follow it. At the end of it is my building." I walk, I walk, I walk. I got my brother on me, and if anybody going to harm me, I would shove my cinco clava in their guts. I have no family. Me one alone, walking. When you have shoes you don't feel too tired, you know, because your feet not hurting you.

I reach in a shop. You know this kind of nation they call Chinee [Chinese], well, a Chinee owned the shop. He watch me and he laugh. I tell him I don't want no flesh, I want only rice and peas. Do you know why? Chinee like to cook dog too much. Chinee stuff you with dog. "Bowwowwow sweet." They have a kind of savage dog and they have a kind of syrup. They just squeeze the syrup upon the dog and as he licks it, he falls. Then they pick up the dog.

The Chinee give me some food, and I go on. I know I almost reach now and I meet a black boy with a bucket on his head. I say, "Come here." He run. I say, "What you run for? You come here. What are you frightened of? A nice human like you. You're black and I'm black." He watch me.

"What do you want?"

"Is that Mr. Wally's building?"

"Yes, do you want him?"

"Run now at Mr. Wally's and tell him that Mr. Charles has arrived." I watch the boy. *Bang, bang,* I see Mr. Wally shove his head there and he tell the boy to bring me up. He said, "Oh, Charles. My wife is coming." He call his wife. "That's Charles. Look, Charles has arrived. That is the man who saved my life in Pintado."

Madame tell me, "Thank you very much, Charles. You saved my husband, and I will never let you down. I will take care of you as my son. Are you hungry?"

I ain't shame. I say, "Yes."

"Come, man, and take a cup of tea and a piece of bread. I eat and drink, and then Mr. Wally show me all the mules and the horses and all the things I do to carry on that work. He blow a whistle, and all the Haitians come. "That's the man you have now," he tell them. "He is the captain." They watch me. He tell the whole gang that they working with me now. I black and they black. For a whole week I sweep. Mr. Wally never tell me he'd give me a dollar, he never tell me he'd give me six shillings, but I do it. He give me a horse, a saddle and a parasito—a kind of thin canas, longer than a cutlass. You got it by your side in your saco. You have a purse, you have your bull pistol—a kind of whip with a clout on the end and wire inside—you have a coil of rope, and you have your brother, your gun. But the fastest is the parasito.

When a couple of weeks went by, fire. I hear, *Woo, woo, woo, woo, woo.* Mr. Wally just say, "Charles, fire." I blow the whistle. All the Haitians got a tin to out the fire. You got to keep that tin in your hand, because when you reach by the river you pick up water to throw on the fire. We go to work. Fire, fire, fire, fire, fire. It's dry season and the leaf is brown. The ground flat, no hill atall, and you hear *pucka, pucka, pucka.* Fire in the night. I working and I see Mr. Wally in his nice panama hat. I see him cut the corner and I watch him. Now a Haitian was so anxious to kill Mr. Wally that he rush Mr. Wally as he bust the corner. But he miss him and take Mr. Wally's horse with the knife instead. The horse fall on Mr. Wally's leg. But the Haitian don't know I is in the corner, coming. I passing and I don't know nothing. As I cut the corner I see it all, and the Haitian running right at me. I sweep him up like a lizard. The same way you cutting a lizard, the same way I make his head come off from his body, because he would have killed me, too. I have a kind of long canas, long and thin, but it cutting bone mostly. I was on my horse when I do this. I see my boss on the ground and the Haitian coming by. I could not do anything else. He was a fucking pig!

Then I go and help Mr. Wally. I call some men to help raise the horse and take out Mr. Wally. I got under the horse, so, and pulled Mr. Wally's leg. His leg was not broken, but it was flat. I put him on my horse, he in front, I walking behind to his yard. When we reach two men take him and carry him up. "You will see me later," I tell him. "Take care of yourself." As I go, I say to myself, "Ah. . . ." and I just turn from man to beast. I pull out a piece of this kind of flat tobacco and *uh,* I bite it and I swallow the juice. Man to beast! I take no chance with the Haitians. When I tell them, "Go in the fire," I mean *go.* I ask nothing. If they could do Mr. Wally the meanest thing, it could be me next. Sometimes I beat, sometimes I carry water. We cut cane, but still the fire passed. The green leaf lighting more than the dry leaf. Fire go in people's shop. They have to run and let the shop go. You take sausage, you take bread. The owner don't worry about that. Fire everywhere. When you come out from there you're black. The only thing that could help you is rain. The whole night you work and you're begging God to make the rain come to out it for you—begging God to wake up. And in the morning you know what happen? Rain! A hell of a big shower, and the fire was out. It bound to be out. The rain was heavy.

In the afternoon I rush up to see the boss. His wife tie his leg all up and hear what he tell me. "St. Lucia finished for you from now on. It's a very good time I meet you, Charles, because today you saved my life. You have saved my life twice, but you really saved it today. If you hadn't come, that Haitian would have killed me for sure. Look, that is the end of it."

It is very funny in Santo Domingo. First come, first served.

There is no court. They pick you up and put you in a box. If you fall in head or tail, that's the way you lie. They dig a hole and they done with you. The Haitian was buried just like a pig—I won't say a dog, because you would have a dog before a pig.[17] He was a criminal. He was a man who would kill you in the night when you passing—cut your hand and take your grip, shove the knife in and take the money in your pockets and kill you.

Mr. Wally suffer a whole month with the pain in his knee— right there in the bone. I work for him for about three years. I would never have left, but immigration caught me. I was a happy man in Santo Domingo. I have a nice white lady with blue eyes. I got child in Santo Domingo—a girl. But that thing came so very easy. I stand up in the forenoon and I see the lady coming. One beautiful girl—tall—and she have a kind of hat with a flower around it. "Buenos dias, Mamasita."

"Buenos dias, Papasito."

I say, "A good-looking girl like you, where is your husband?"

She tell me, "No, no, no, I don't have husband, and the hell with that because you're a beautiful man."

"Yes."

"What's your name?"

I say, "Charlie."

She say, "Call me Lita." She take a cigar and she smoke it a good while and then give it to me. I take it, and she smoke a next one.

I ask her, "Where is your sweet boy or your husband?" She say she haven't got any. I tell her she telling me lies. She ask me if I had any. I say, "No, nothing."

"Come, because we're going right away on the tram to Guaymate. We're going to spend money in San Pedro de Macoris, the capital." We go. She sit down there and put her arm around my neck, and I say nothing. When we reach, she take out her wallet and MONEY! Then I pull out my money and she say, "No, no. Take me to a hotel." They ain't got no rum, but brandy, beer, and good food—roasted pig—and women—even more pretty. I

greet one. Lita said, "No, no, no, you're with me." She tell me
they come to make money, "but we don't come to make money.
You come with me." She ask me if I want anything—all that I
want she will give me. We go all about. We drink, we don't even
dance. At half-past four I go and sit down inside the van—the
cabre de familia—a long, beautiful car. At seven o'clock I was
degorara with Lita. She tell me she want to see where I live.
"O.K., I carry you to my place." We go to my room. Me one
living there. If I have a girl on Saturday that I like, I take her
there. If you know you can get a girl, don't take her with a wife.
In my room I got my hammock, I got my bed, my table, and two
chairs. She stop the night with me and the next morning she tell
me she spending three days—the Sunday and Monday, and
going Tuesday—that she don't have nobody. Every time that I
working she take my clothes and go to the la plune and wash all.
I got lots of girl friends in Santo Domingo.

I believed I was safe. I didn't think anyone would find me. It
was just as if I came from there. I go into town. I don't have
nobody watching me and I don't know that anyone looking for
me. If I not a St. Lucian I would be in La Noria today. I didn't
leave Mr. Wally. It was the immigration master. I coming from
my work up to my home at twelve o'clock to eat. I meet the son of
a bitch right by Mr. Wally's. He right there speaking to Mr.
Wally. He tell me, "Ah, here you is, Mr. Charles." He knew me
because he was the St. Lucian immigration master who carried us
to Santo Domingo and he searching for me. I had done gone, and
he couldn't find me. His job was to search to find St. Lucians to
send them back to their country. He know Mr. Wally taking
immigrants to cut cane for him. Mr. Wally suppose to see if there
were any St. Lucians there—that was his job.

I tell him that I want to stay in Santo Domingo and I don't want
to go back to St. Lucia. "You know what happen in St. Lucia
already."

"No! No! No! You've got to go because you've been here too
long already. You have given people plenty trouble. I am going to
take you."

Let me tell you. If they're searching for you, don't you believe, if you allow them to catch you anywhere, that they are going to give you any chance to get away. They say if they let you go you are going to disappear. They're taking no chances. They put rope on your hand and throw you upon the horse. You cannot go back to your home. You could tell them that you have pants, you could tell them you have a grip, but they won't let you go. The bastard tell me, "You are not going anywhere. We have caught you and you are going to St. Lucia with what you have on your skin." It was quite the next week that I was leaving. But my intention was to be back to Santo Domingo because there was all kinds of immigration every year. But after one bloody man go and cut another man—the man's guts drop out on a stick—and he tie him on the chimney, like that. Fire in his backside. After that they stop immigration. No more Santo Domingo for St. Lucians.

We was out one night, and the next night before we reach St. Lucia, the captain say, "Son, we have a fire!" The more we go, the more we see. The more we go, the more we see. When we reach in the harbor, fire in Castries.[18] We can't anchor because we don't know which way the wind was going to go.

When I land, I land with a straw hat, brown shoes, gabardine pants, and a silk shirt. I stay there with a jetty girl for a couple of days, then back home. I going to sea. I'm fishing sometimes and I'm sailing.

Employment with Mr. Barnard

F OR A TIME I worked for Mr. Heben. We take logwood[1] and carry it to St. Pierre. One night I watching this same logwood in Castries, and my sister, Enwille, come and tell me, "Do you have nothing to give me? I need six shillings and some whiskey." She did not have the same father. She was from nasty hand people.[2]

I say, "Well, I don't have any now. I will give you what I am going to get Saturday next." Saturday she come down and I give it to her. Monday I meet a man who tell me, "Hello, today you have got plenty money. I bought your sister's property. Did she give you something?"

"No."

He say, "Yes, I just give her a lot of money now. She is going to the bank." I just went *feeeeeww* — I go down. I said, "Heyyeyyey." She was drunk. I say, "I don't want nothing. Give me my six shillings. You don't tell me today that Mr. Doxine bought the property.[3] I am not asking you for that, I come for my six shillings." You know what happened? She was the girl friend of a policeman called Jeffers. He take all the money. When the money gone, he gone. She tell me she could sell her house if she could live with me. I say, "No, I don't like you." From then on I never put me foot in her house. Septime, her son, tell her, "The same thing you do to my uncle, the same thing happen to you now. Don't speak about it. Don't tell me anything." That same Septime left Anse la Raye and come and stay with me in my

house. He tell me, "I have nothing to do with my mother." When
I working he cooking. He go to school, and when he come back I
would give him a piece of bread. The boy come big where he
was. Today he working for a man called Mr. Francis, who has a
rum shop by the market. He has a car, is well dressed. His wife
sells black pudding and souse,[4] and why doesn't he help his
mother? If you don't take care of me when I am small, I won't
take care of you when I come big. You who was my sister was a
fool. Now when I meet her in town begging alms, I don't give
her a cent.

When I leave Heben there was no work again so I fish. Then I
join another vessel, Captain Maymay's, carrying logwood to St.
Pierre. Logwood for making dye and all kind of stuff. That time
money was next to nothing. We working by the trip and we make
two trips a week. When you come back you would settle up because it was not by the month. You paid in shares—four
shares—two sailors, the captain, and the boat.[5] That's the way
we get paid and sometimes the captain shove his hand deep in
the money.

One day Mr. Barnard[6] call me and ask me, "Charles, where are
you going now?" I say that I going to St. Pierre. He tell me, "I
understand they will have a strike on me. Can you stay?"

"No, I cannot stay, because I done load the boat already to go
to St. Pierre. I got to carry it."

"All right, but if you hear there is a strike in St. Lucia what are
you going to do?"

"Nothing. I'm going to reach here before the strike. There may
be a strike, but when I come everything is over."

"Are you sure of that?"

"Yes." Before I leave I hear that when the collier come we going
to have a strike. I go to St. Pierre and make two days there landing logwood. We have to carry it ashore in the shore boat. When
we finish this it was eight o'clock Sunday night. Tomorrow morning at daybreak we gone. When I reach in St. Lucia the strike
going on hard, boy.[7] Nobody ain't working. At this time we have
soldiers here—recruits up on the Morne. They take the recruits
to the ship to carry coal. When I come I find the troops there, but

they were too slow with it. Mr. Barnard ask me, "What are you going to do, Charles?" And he tell me, "If you break this strike you will work here for the balance of your life."

I say, "You say that now, but when the strike is over you will keep me for a month and that's it."

"I would never do that."

"All right." I go up in Marchand—Monkey Hill—and I go to a man they call Daddy.

"Daddy."

"Yes."

"I want you to bring the tambou[8] down. Put it in the collier and start to sing and beat the tambou."   -

"How much money would I get?"

"If you will do that you will get five dollars apiece."

"Good. I will come."

When the man bring the drum, Mr. Barnard watching him, like this. There is four of them, two men and two women. One man stand up on the deck of the ship, the drum between his legs. The other in the hold. And Jesus Christ—the two men and the two women beating and singing in Patois:

	(*English translation*)
Calaloo . . . Calaloo	Calaloo . . . Calaloo
Nous kai soupe	We have supper
Calaloo	Calaloo
Nous kai soupe	We have supper
Calaloo	Calaloo
My farine thin	My farine thin
Chou ma maou	Your mother's ass
Ça pas en rien	That is nothing
Ça pas en rien	That is nothing
Ça pas en rien	That is nothing

My farine there
Chou bo chou
Ça pas en rien
Fuck you

My farine there
Ass by ass
That is nothing
Fuck you

Calaloo
Every Sunday
Calaloo
Lundi, mardi
Calaloo
Kai ma Lulu
Pas ni rien qui doux comme ça
(Beat, beat, beat of drum)

Calaloo
Every Sunday
Calaloo
Monday, Tuesday
Calaloo
My Lulu's house
There is nothing sweet as that
(Beat, beat, beat of drum)

Kai ma Lulu
Pas ni rien qui doux comme ça
Nous ka vini la kai ma Lulu
Nous ka quitte jusqu'a jour ouvert
Calaloo . . . Calaloo

My Lulu's house
There is nothing sweet as that
We have come to Lulu's house
We do not leave until daybreak
Calaloo . . . Calaloo

Calaloo . . . Calaloo
Lundi, mardi
Calaloo
Every Sunday
Calaloo

Calaloo . . . Calaloo
Monday, Tuesday
Calaloo
Every Sunday
Calaloo

Calaloo . . . Calaloo
Every Sunday
Calaloo
Calaloo . . . Calaloo
Every Sunday
Calaloo
Every Sunday
Calaloo

In a minute's time there were no baskets by the wharf. The drum was hot, and everybody singing and carrying coal. They have a barrel full of rum by the wharf, and anybody could take a drink. I don't have enough baskets to give.[9] The music was hot, and a collier got four holds.

They fire the man who set the strike—he was a one-hand man—and give me the job. There were two colliers in the harbor, and for the whole week those people were down aboard the ship carrying the coal and singing the songs.

Before I become foreman I put up the staging in order to walk and to go carry coal. You put the stage down and the more you're taking coal, the higher you come up and the more staging you need. One time a man reach on a beam across, like this, and he just give it a turn, but he don't tie it. He tell me, "Go up on the beam and loose that rope."

I say, "Fuck you. Do it yourself." The rope was loose, and I would have fallen down inside the ship and broken in three. I tell him, "Look, I don't want that to happen to me." He watch me and laugh. He try to set me up, but before the week done he catch it himself. We were picking up a stage in the winch. You pass the wire under the stage and heist it to bring it in board. When he say "heist up" his hand was in the winch. His finger catch in the wire and he hanging in the air. He go, "*Goo-goo-goo-goo*." He stay in the air hanging by his finger until the wire cut it off. He fall on the concrete and was dead on the spot.

I put in charge of the baskets at Barnard. At that time the man who cause me to go to prison in charge of baskets at Chastenet. I had never paid my debt to him for the badge he left in my back. I call him to come after we get paid. He start to drink and he tell me, "Ah, don't believe that I have forgotten you, because the last time you cut me." Now we don't want to leave this time without consequences. The word don't have time to come out of his mouth—*badam*—right in the pit of the stomach. That put him down. I cover him. I shove his tooth in, and his tongue come out long. If people hadn't of pulled me off I would have choked him to death. Next morning I meet him and I say, "We don't finish the fight yet, boy." I had some black electric wire in my pocket and I say, "With that I will fight you." I touch him the same time he touch me with the left. I go around him and choke him. I never touch him upon his back. I say, "Ah, you meet your master today. You didn't know Mr. Charles was looking for you."

"You motherfucker, you!"

"You want to fight again?"

"No, I respecting you now." He don't know that he would get his death from the kind of lash he got in the eye. He start to go blind, and they carry him in hospital. He say he get a lash in the face, but the doctor fuck him up. The injection the doctor give him cause him to be blind. He go into the hospital to tend his eyes and he never come out. Fuck him. I give him tea, breadfruit and money. And he going after my wife.

Don't you believe this job of foreman don't have trouble in it. The first one hear a mice in a bucket of water. His wife tell him, "Get up and go and take the mice out of the bucket because it is making noise." The moment he go out from his bedroom into the hall, somebody lift him up and throw him 'round and cut his tongue right off. People do that for the sake of the same job he have. His name was Mr. George. Teddy was in the same job. They throw a stage on him and break his back. He was so sick he couldn't sit down and he could hardly drink some water. It was after Teddy that I take the job. You think that when they have coal down by the wharf that this is playing. It foreman against foreman.

One day we finish working a collier, and three men and a woman tell me as I get paid, "Carlo, you got all this money. Save some for sickness, because you can always spend plenty money." I say, "I always save something for sickness." It was Monday, and I was going up to the racecourse to see the sport when I just feel myself go up in the air. My toe lift up in my shoe. I bawl and I fall right there in the street. They have to carry me up to my house. When I reach there, they break some eggs for me and make a kind of medicine and give it to me to drink. The pain was so heavy I just swallow the bowl so I could go back into my bed. For three months I lay there on the bed suffering. I can't move and I can't speak. If you want to pee, somebody has to help you. If you want to use your bowels, somebody has to hold you there. That's the time when I come to know bedpan. At that time I was living with an outside woman—Baby. She was hustling aboard the boat carrying coal to get something to give me to eat. There was a lady by me called Mistress Taylor—a big, big woman—

and I got to call her and tell her I have to pass water. I had been a good man to her, and she came and nurse me like a baby. I was no use to anybody any more. Behind my head it just like a dispensary—so many bottles. They rub me. They give me drinks to drink and every day that same man come from the next room and spoil the medicine, turn the medicine.[10] Every morning he come, "Haha, how you do, Charlie?" Baby would tell him I had a bad night, that I suffering. "Put him in the almshouse because he will never be the same again. He is no use to anybody." He saying that to get my job. "Send him to the poorhouse. He won't live."

"I won't put Charles in the poorhouse, because when I friends with Charles I take him well. And today he sick. I got to bury him."

He say to Baby, "I tell you be friends with me, or I won't give you no baskets when the boat comes." So say, so done. He do it, too. A boat come with one hundred forty tons and he don't give the girl a basket.

Finally when I see I was going to get no better, I call to the Haitian man, Anton. I say to my heart, "Anton, you told me, any time I was sick or something wrong happen, to sing the song you taught me, to sing that song in my heart, the tear would come from my eyes, and I would drop asleep and see my family which had died, return to me." I put my two hands across my breast and I begin to sing. When you are singing that song in your heart, you're bound to sleep, and the dead are bound to come up in your eyes. I see my mother come with a white bowl, and she give it to me to drink. She ask me if I speak to three men and a woman. I say, "Yes." And she tell me they were the people who done this. She take the balance of the bowl and washed me from head to foot and rubbed me down. She tell me that I got to get up, take the main street, and go down straight to the burying ground. When I reach the spot of the burying ground I'm to turn my back and pick up three stones. I'm to take these up and make a cup of tea.

Now when I get up from the sleep I open my eyes and stretch. Then I put my legs down, and both legs answer. I stand. I turn my whole self. I turn back. My legs so weak I was trembling. I sit down. I can't go yet. I lie down on the bed again. When you're on the bed, you're sure, but when you get up, you're weak. I shove my feet in my pants and I do the same thing with my shirt. The bed helping me. I put on my cloak and I go in the yard. I going to carry on the job now. When I reach at Calgary[11]—going to climb the hill—I feel I can do it. I go up and I go in the cemetery. Then my legs start to shake, but still I go. I bend down and I pick up three stones, just like a monkey shoves his hand in a trap and he hold three tight. I hold them with my right hand. I won't put them in my pocket because I don't trust it. From there I go straight down the road and home. I got my fire going and the pan begin to boil. I take a grain of salt just how my mother tell me and put in the stones. When I see the salt on the stones I feel my body come hot, hot, hot. I drink a teacup full and keep the balance for the morning. When I finish my medicine I make some coffee and drink it. Do you know that those three people taking care of me were in the house sleeping—all this happened inside the house—and they cannot wake. My mother give them a strong sleep so they not know what was going on.

Mr. Barnard come in the morning. He blow the horn for Baby and ask her if he could come in. "All right." He open the front door, come inside and sit down by me. "How are you feeling?"

I ask him, "How much more time before the collier comes?"

"About two weeks now."

"I will work the collier."

"You! Charles, you have a good mind but you, never."

"How is Miss Mildred [Mr. Barnard's daughter]?"

"Miss Mildred is good. You will see. She will come and see you again."

"I want to meet Miss Mildred this morning. Before you go in the office, go home and take Miss Mildred down for me. Tell her to come and see me."

"What, are you dying? Are you going to die?"

"No, I won't die, I want to show you something when you come back with Miss Mildred."

I call the three who tended to me. I say, "Well, I will thanks you all for the kind of way you treated me when I was sick. And God going to help me. I will pay you all that." All three of them start crying. And you would have been crying too, the kind of way I was speaking from my bed, lying there on my back. That would hurt your feelings, for a man who speaks so is going to die. When they start to scream, I say, "Shut up. What are you crying for?" They cry more. "Naaw, shhh. I am cured."

"You're cured, Charles?"

"Yes." And I swing my legs over the edge of the bed. I get down and I walk. All three grab me. "Charlie, Charlie!" And those three people dead today—yeah, Baby dead, Pagina dead, and Marie dead—and I still here.

"Are you satisfied I get better?" They say yes. "Well, don't tell nobody. If somebody come and see me, tell him I can't be saved."

When Miss Mildred come she tell me she bring me something nice that I was going to like. "What's happened to you now, Charles?" I get up and show Miss Mildred. My mother told me, "When you get up you got to make a service for the dead and give the church a shilling." Everybody go to that service—Mr. Barnard and Miss Mildred sit down and enjoy it. When we come back, we drink.

Now that man come. He ask Baby how Charles passed last night. She say, "He's worse. I don't think Charles will see twelve o'clock because of the kind of way he spent last night."

"I told you to send him in the almshouse. If you don't send him in the almshouse I won't give you a basket next week to make your bread when the collier comes."

Baby say, "I'd rather go and serve the next man's donkey than before I friends with you for giving me basket."

He say, "All right. Next week Thursday the collier come." That's to break my heart more because he was going to be in charge. Now his people happy. They going to have things the way they want. He go and scatter it all about that he would be the one in charge of the back store giving baskets. Now people used to come and see me before. But the kind of way they find me, they pull off because I was not working in the back store anymore. My mother tell me, "When you get up from your bed, then you will know who is your friend. When you was foreman you have plenty friends, but now that you are not foreman you will see." I call my mother back in my sleep and ask her what I got to do, and she tell me. She tell me about a medicine I was to buy in the drugstore and she tell me to go work the collier—that I would go back in my same job.

Early Thursday morning a parcel come to me—a two-color brown shoe, cocoa-brown pants, a silk shirt, and a cocoa-brown felt hat—that's my suit to go in the back store. Baby sponge me down with cold water, and I dress. Mr. Barnard come in a car, and I get in. He tell me, "Charles, this man would kill you, but I don't believe you will take him to work for you anymore." I say, "Don't worry, boss. Leave it to me." I sat in the car, so [twiddling his thumbs], studying. You know what I was studying, I was thanking my mother.

When we reach by the store I go up in the office. I step right in with my gum shoe and my cocoa suit. And I take off my jacket and I come out in my white shirt. He didn't see me. "Yankee Charles" was looking at that crowd of people like Lord Kitchener, because he was the one that was going to give everybody baskets to go and carry coal.

I say, "There you are, Mister. Take off your penknife from the key and give over my key. You're fired. You are not coming in this back store again. Go by the wharf and get a job. I is my boss."

"You can't tell me that!"

"Go by the wharf on the first stage. I don't want you in my back store. Now that I've come back from my sickness, your mother and your brother and your uncle will have to climb the hill seven times higher before you kill me. I am sure I will take my revenge."

I go down and I hit the door—*bamb*. I kick the padlock. I say, "All right, I am going to open you now," and I go and throw that padlock away in the sea, and I put a new padlock on it and locked it up. I go inside and I cut father, son, and holy ghost baskets.[12] I cut every rope because they was against me. They were glad when I was crippled, because they believed Yankee Charles would be in charge of it. What they couldn't do with me, they would do it with him. I got my gang, but I wouldn't give baskets to his gang. All my gang—my people—come to see me when I sick, but his gang don't come so I know who is his gang. My people's baskets there to the side. This row is his, that one is mine. Well, I cut off this row—cut off the rope—and I start upstairs and throw down the baskets in the ground. People were fighting for them. If you don't fight, you don't get a basket because those country people are big, strapping men. When they see the baskets fall down they throw you down and unload the basket from your hand and take it. You can't be stronger than country people.

When I finish throwing all his baskets and my baskets inside, I went by the wharf to the first stage. Those country people have the baskets, and his people come and beg me for baskets. I say, "No, go ask Yankee Charles. Don't ask me." Everybody go by the boat. The boss ask me if I want any more baskets. I say, "Hold on. I know what I am doing." I have my people now. "Come up and take your baskets." This one took his here, this one took his here, this one here, and the balance I scatter out. That was four holds working. I was drinking stout like water. I stand up on board the ship with Mr. Barnard by the rail, watching. People come with full baskets and back up. I tell them, "Fill it for me and I will give you something." Twelve o'clock my breakfast come from right on top of Barnard Hill. Miss Mildred send the servant to bring my breakfast. I take time to eat.

When I finish the collier I go back, and I call my mother in the night and I speak to her just how I speak to you. And she tell me what to do—and I do just what she tell me. Yankee Charles could not sleep in his house for six months. My mother was responsible for that. His house was hot like fire. It's nothing when you have been with the dead people. My mother say, "Son, leave it to me." All that time he have to go under that tree from six or seven until six in the morning. Every night. That was his punishment.

When he get up from that he was thin, thin, thin. Just like a feather man. You think he suffer, I suffer! I never do him nothing. Me and him were good pals. We go and drink together. If I have twelve shillings, I give him four. And he try to kill me for my own job. He was my second. I have four hundred baskets. I do two hundred and give him two hundred. He want all the four hundred for his own so he put me cripple. He's dead now, though. Because why? The cold was not good for him. The fucker.

I pass fourteen years with Mr. Barnard. I got my own boat while I was there—a canoe—and I used to go out towing [trolling].

It all happened so funny. I was sitting down so in a chair at Barnard and I see a woman passing. I watch her and I say, "Jesus Christ, what a nice black woman"—a big woman. She have an arm just like that. I get up as she turned in at her house.

"Madame, chez la?"

"Oui. Come in." I laugh, and she bring a chair for me. I sit down and we talk.

I say, "A nice lady like you—you have a sweetheart?"

"I don't have nothing. My husband is a lazy man. He don't want to look for work."

We take some more, and I tell her next Saturday to come on the boat and ask the captain if I send any message for she. I get a box full of presents for her. The next week a basket come up full of cashew—russ cashew—and bread. Enid and I are courting now. I carry the basket to Mr. Barnard. He open it and say, "That is good. That girl love you. Do you love her?"

I say, "Yes, boss."

Mr. Barnard say, "I'm giving you five pounds. Send it down and tell her to buy things and bring it up."

"O.K." He take the pan of cashews and carry it for his son and wife in the store. "Look, Charles's girl send this. She's a big girl. I like her."

A lady's man always pays for it and a raven [craven] man going to pay for it, too. If you don't give your wife nothing, if you don't kiss she—a nice looking girl—it won't help. I send the girl a big box full of fried jack fish and onion on the top of it. Sugar, rice, coffee, thread, those kind of flat sweet biscuits, and cheese. The husband stoop down on his backside and open the box. He not studying what was behind that—that Charles love the girl—he eating the biscuits and cheese. He never asking her why she getting these things. But she tell him, "What you enjoy, your backside is going to pay for." And she was right, too. He never ask no questions. He just say, "Charles is a good friend of yours" and all the time he's calling Charles to come in. He was stupid. She have no connections with him. No sir—he not ride her anymore! He can't get that again.

One day the lady come up and give me a joke by the table where we were eating. I laugh, and the woman tell me, "Charles, now I feel I've got a husband." She was dead for me. "You are the onliest man I know, the kind of way you is."

"What do you mean?"

"I come here and you speak to me nicely, upon the chair. You don't ask me nothing—if I have a man or if I don't."

"It's not that I wouldn't love to know what you is. If my mind is to be friend with you in house, you won't come again because you will say I am too anxious. I'll have enough time to meet you. I want you to know that I friend with you."

"That's what I'm saying. You don't want to know anything about me."

"I don't tell you that I don't want to know anything about you. I tell you the day I have a meeting with you, you is mine. Then I could rest my head on your shoulder."

She bust a laugh and say, "Well, I will take a drink on that." We have wine and we drink a big glass. Then she say, "All right. I will come up to meet you. But the house you have there is too small. Get a bigger one and I will come up in two weeks' time. I won't be frightened for me because I have a husband in my house, and I won't be frightened for you neither because I trusting you."

I got a big house—a big room. At that time a house was cheap, and for four dollars you could get a big one. I move my things and I put them at the house. The next week she send her boy, Francis, to tell me that she was coming up the next week. When the boy come he was thin, thin, thin. He dressed in an old flour bag with all the markings on it. He come and sit down on a chair in the office, and when he do that I see the old flour bag. I run quick and buy him silk shirt and pants and I take off the flour bag and throw it in the garbage box. I tell him, "Put these on and when they ask you where you got that you tell them I is your father." I put him to school and I dress him, and the boy come one big boy. Now he is bo'sun on board the boat going to Antigua and Barbados. When I go on board to see him, he lifts me up, and I am a feather for the boy.

When the lady come up—trunk, bed, chair—and two girl and two boy. The first night she sleep there, *pow*, child stopping in her belly. That was Ouioui, the biggest boy. Later we make Ti Son.

I had one row with the other man. It was about six o'clock in the afternoon a little while after Enid had come up. All the child were inside the house there. They were merry because they not suffering. I hear him say, "Good night. I come to meet you."

His wife say, "What you coming here for? This is Charles's house."

"I didn't know Charles was your man." He start to curse. I hear a big charge come out.

I come like a buffalo. "You can't come in my house and talk like it's your own. Listen, Mister, here is mine. Now you get your ass out. You get out."

He say to Enid, "You left me to take Charles?"

She tell him, "You like too much sweetness and you're too lazy. You don't want to work. That is why I left you. And look what I have on me. Do you think you could give me that? You can't give me that. You can only let a man drown." And she sit down in the chair. Now the little boy make to join the fun.

"I got Papa, but now I got a father."

When he hear that he don't want to sit down again. "Shut up!"

he tell the boy, and he go now at Enid's uncle. He start to complain. He say the lady was a nasty girl who go and take a beast for a frat [living companion]. Mr. Andess tell him, "Hey, let me tell you. If you say that man she take up with is a beast, then I is a beast too, because me and that same man you're cursing lived together. We sleep on flour bag together. That man has got more power than you. Before your wife leave you she complain how you were doing she, and I see all that Charles do for her— all the biscuits and food you was eating. You knew something was behind that. Now she's gone to stay up there, and you've got to pay for what you've done. And let me tell you. You're going to sleep in the kitchen for a month, but before the month finish, you've got to find a place to stay because I ain't keeping you. And when I'm working, I'm working for a penny to make my shirt, so don't you come and sit down and think I'm going to feed you."

You should see the girl he pick up. He find a room and he put the girl there. When the girl had made a week she say, "How do you expect me to go and make a bone to feed you when you just sit there? Well, I can't stay with you. I'm going, and that's why your wife left you. If you don't take that to heart you will be dead." And even though he were dying, his wife would never bring him food there.

Now St. Lucian fisherman have a kind of way: if they give you fish, you see they're selling fish, but if they give you fish, they pass their hand around your neck and touch your backside and feel your breast before they will give you the fish. Well, they don't know Enid is a hog. She ask a man for six pence and he come and touch she. "I don't come to beg you for fish, I come to buy fish from you. You don't touch me. I don't come to have you touch me, because I have a man to do that." He get vex and just send the fish for the woman.

I come in the afternoon time, and she have a cup of tea there for me. "Listen," she say, "from today I ain't going by the wharf to buy fish again. You will have to get a boat for you to get your fish. Frankie tell me he come and touch me back me shoulder, and I give him a full stop. I tell him I not come here for that. I have my man and he sells me fish."

Now Mr. Barnard want a boat to fish, but he don't want to do it heself. I go up by the wharf and I find a man, Sico, who tell me he have a boat for eight pounds. "If you want it, I sell it for you."

"Where is your boat?"

"Right down by the harbor master's office. Come and see it tomorrow." When I go there he tell me that if I take it he would give me the boat hook, sail, and everything. I go up and tell Mr. Barnard that Sico have a boat there for him and I want it. He say, "Good, tell him to come tomorrow morning or afternoon for the money. Here is the money there. I want the boat paid for."

The next morning Sico come down. "Good morning."

"Good morning. Charles tells me you've got a boat to sell for him. There is the money in an envelope for you."

Sico look in the envelope. "La!" He get the money, and I don't tell him I'd done nothing.

In the afternoon I go and wash the boat. I give it a coat of paint and I change the name. I put the name *Sundown* on her. Everybody was watching the canoe. I take the box of line and I put it inside. The sail was in the air. When everything was ready I take a bottle of rum. I hit it a lash on the boat and break it— everybody stand up there, and then we take a drink.

Frankie, the same man who want to touch Enid, was selling flying fish. I shove me hand and take two and send the money into the boat for him. He ain't say one word. I take the fish, put it on a wire, and kept it there for my bait. He don't know, he thought it was for cooking. The next day was Sunday, and the boat going out. I come back at one o'clock in the night, and it could not take one pin again. I loaded from forward to aft with flying fish. When day break in the morning, my lady sit down at the boat, watching. I sit down with her, and we drink coffee, watching the fish. When everybody come, *"Wohye, wohye!"* Flying fish—shining. We don't let them bleed, we send water on them. I left to go to work, and my wife selling flying fish. When I come back I find the money and share it with the men.

From then on when I come home from sea, she would watch to see me come, and she so big she just pick me up from the boat like that. That woman love money. I'd go home and take off my clothes. The boat full of flying fish, and she there selling. I could go and wash up myself. When I finished I'd sit down, so, eat my belly full, and go to work.

After I was in charge of baskets I worked inside the back store, packing coconuts to send to Montreal. I was there about two o'clock in the afternoon when we hear, *OOOOOH*. There's a volcano going up to Micoud Estate, and two hills joined together there.[13] Plenty people die. They sweep up people, sweep up people, animals, cow, cattle, everything. What a pity. People that have nowhere to sleep, they take them up on the Morne. All the people which they find they bury in a cemetery there. They say that them people over there was cruel and God make an end of them. Everybody was cursed. Two hills become one, and each one blowing and coming. I was sitting up in Barnard's store— right by the door. They tell me to come. I say, "Who, me?" I don't want to go in the bush. What the use of going up there? At that time they were carrying down dead people to the hospital. Then the rain come. I ain't inquisitive. If two people are fighting, I'm not going to see.

I was at Mr. Barnard's when the Germans torpedoed the *Lady Nelson* and the *Umtata*.[14] It was a Sunday night, and I was shipping coconuts. That time cooley,[15] black, white, all kind of people die. There was a white woman living right up there in a building by the market. She was a spy. The enemy submarine was outside and she send and say what time *Lady Nelson* and *Umtata* coming out in the afternoon. But they do not come out because the enemy was outside, so the submarine come straight in the harbor and blow up the two ships. The steamer—the *Umtata*—come clear on the wharf. It kill a crowd of Indians and pitch them ashore. The *Lady Nelson* take two shot and canted over on the next side. It kill all the passengers that was in her. All little child, young girls, old, everybody. It was loaded with passengers going to Barbados and cargo. Everything land in St.

Lucia: pig tails, ice cream, all kinds of clothes and the market in Conway—you can't pass, there were so much things on the ground. It all blocked up with food—flour, rice, butter. It was on the ground, stinking. You can take what you liked and go with it. So many barrels of pork, corn beef, oil. You can take shoes, hat. Don't talk about ice cream, cheese, butter, milk. You don't want all that. You block up your house.

There was a woman who was going on the *Lady Nelson* who forgot something at home—a parcel she have of beef and peas. When she come up to her house by the market, she hear, *Budu, budu!* The only thing that saved her life was that parcel, because if she had been inside that boat she would have been deaded.

I don't have much to do with German people. I see with my two eyes what they do. The Germans make French people run away from Martinique and start to shoot and kill in the ocean during the war. St. Lucia block up with French people saving their lives. The Germans had dealings with you and after, they'd shoot you. They went into a house and they meet two daughters, a mother, a father, and a little boy. They kill the mother and they kill the father, but the little boy had a chance to get away. He shove himself in the grass and hide there. The one thing he have a chance to take was a small radio. After they kill the mother and father, the Germans use the two daughters. One they kill, the other they leave. What the Germans don't know is the boy had sent an SOS for his older brother who was in the war. They stand inside the house laughing and enjoying themselves as the plane was coming. The plane arrived as the first one was coming out, fixing up his pants—*pow!* When the second one coming out, laughing and fixing up his clothes—*pow!* And the last one come out—*pow!* The brother kill the whole three of them. But when he reach, he find one sister dead and the other there suffering because she was a maiden girl. You know the pain the girl would have with three men. He pick up the girl and take her to the hospital, but when she reach there, she was dead. The younger boy say, "I am going to take my mother's, my father's, and my sisters' revenge." And anywhere he go and see a German, he was dead. There was a truck full of Germans—he was on top and them below. He run a wire of dynamite up ahead and blow up the whole truck. And he say he only start to kill Germans.

During the war while I working at Barnard's I hustling on the side too, you know. I was dragging liquor from Dennery. Now we bringing liquor in casks and we have a little punch. You punch a little hole and you blow, and you could take off about four buckets of this kind of thing in a beaker. When you come down, you got to take that to make some money, because the money that they're giving you is very small. A woman get jealous and set the police on me. I give her some, you know, but she still sent the police. When I see the person coming I take him for somebody else. But when he come, he come calling me, "Charles, what you got there?"

I say, "Rum." What you think happen? They still bring me down. I said, "You're a fool to arrest me for this." Remember I going to pass a big bridge just before you take headquarters. When I reach I just throw everything in the river.

The man angry. "Go, go, go. You put me in trouble. Go, go, go."

I get a cold in my belly while I work at Barnard's. Mr. Barnard tell me, "Charles, I will send you to the hospital."

I say, "Which one?"

"The one here in Castries."

"No!"

He ask me why not. I say, "Listen, let me tell you. Mr. Augier was working at George William's and he get a hernia. He leave and go to the hospital to make an operation. He go in but he not come back. You know why? He was a big man. He have a store and property. They fucked him up.[16] And remember when you have a tooth out you went all the way to Barbados to the hospital? Well," I say, "I'm not going nowhere here in hospital. If you want to send me, send me down to St. Thomas." And he sent me. Got my papers and sent me to St. Thomas.

On the way me belly start to call me. It catch me again, and they carry me in Dominica. I stop there. When I reach in St. Kitts

I stop four days in hospital. Each time it catch me I have to use my bowels—it was a cold. That's why the doctor tell me I better walk bare foot, don't use crepe soles.

When I reach in St. Thomas they take me from the boat and carry me to the hospital. There I see people, people, white people, black people. They put me in bed. For four days they give me only milk and two pills. I see the people bringing the trays of food like macaroni, beef stew. My mouth was dry. A man tell me, "You're watching it. You will soon get yours but not now." I there and I go hungry, but the pain was on me too. The next morning they put me on a stretcher, cover me, and one hold me there. They don't do me nothing, only *tick*—that's all—just like a little pin. When they finish with me I was burning up. All me belly was burning up, and I so upon my bed. I sleep. I stop another four days and this time I only had two pains a day—one in the morning and one at night. If I feel hungry I drink water, and after a few days more they bring me milk—but I wasn't feeling hungry. A white nurse come, "How are you feeling, Alexander?"

"I am feeling much better, nurse."

"I can see that. Your face is cooler."

The next morning they bring me a big cup of pap and tell me to drink it. Saturday morning I see the nurse bringing food and I watching her. She tell me, "Macaroni and pap." I eat up. Twelve o'clock they give me food. In two weeks I start to get heavy food and I begin to pick up myself now—to feel strong. I start to walk up and down. When I come back to St. Lucia, Mr. Barnard tell me, "Oh, you've come fat, Charles. Where is the paper? Are you sure you're from St. Thomas?"

I say, "There's your paper." He read the paper. I don't know what it say, but I told the doctor I was not going back in the office because it was too cold.

"Charles, it says that you are not to work here again with us, you know."

"How you mean?"

"The doctor says that your health is too poor, and that's true."

"Yes, that's true."

"Then would you like to work at home with the roller and the bucket for when the cars pass?"

I say, "Not me." I was going to go to sea. As he leave, I go down in town to take my boat and go to sea. When I come back I bring a hell of a piece of kingfish for him. "Where have you been today?"

"I've been to sea."

"Why weren't you here?"

I say, "The job you gave me is done. Well, I give you this."

The next week I disappear. I go. When Mr. Barnard asked for me, my wife tell him I was not in St. Lucia.

"Where did he go to?" She say she don't know. When I come back he ask me where I was from. I say, "St Thomas."

"With what?"

"A sloop with a load of wire."

"Why did you leave the work?"

I say, "I don't like the work, boss." I knew he was a spiteful fellow so I moved from there. He want me to come home, "Stay home. What are you going to sea for? You nearly getting your death."

I say, "Now let me tell you. I cannot roll that big thing—me one. A big roller like that."

"Well, we have a small one, there."

"Hum." I sell the house in Conway and I get the hell away from the land before he tempt me—because I know he would try to tempt me if I don't want to work with him. He would ask that I give notice before I leave the spot, but before I give notice, I leave the spot and I go to Dominica and I come back. I don't like that roller. I too smart.

The Dominica
Years and Smuggling

W HEN I REACH Dominica I find something wrong with
me. I have no taste for life. One night I go at my Auntie's [Choco], but she don't do much for me. My heart no good,
my head no good. I ask for a plate of food. "Yes, I will give you
something." That because she was my aunt. "You want a drink?"
That was all. I go by the market in Portsmouth and sit on a bench
watching the sea. My belly in my back. And who come to help
me? A Carib girl. The Caribs are not black people.[1] Before my
mother die, I used to be friends with those people. I was a nice,
good-looking boy when I was a child, and every Saturday them
girls would come down to sell their goods and go and drink in
my father's rum shop. They would call, "Charlie, Charlie, Charlie, Charlie," and I make friends.

The Caribs are good people and dangerous people because
they know plenty obeah. They are short and they always wear
the flour-bag dress. You will see them in Portsmouth every
Saturday. They come down from the country by boat—and their
boat is so funny. They just take a piece of wood and dig a hole in
it, and they load the boat with food and come down the river to
Portsmouth. They sell their food and go in a rum shop and drink,
but don't you believe they spend all their money. They drink
because they are going to have to carry the boat up, and that is a
devil of a job. When three o'clock comes you don't see any more
in town. They all go up.

That time I sit down watching the sea, I was doped—like a

kind of lunatic.[2] My mother left two properties, and my own sister betray me to get that property. That was Enwille. Remember she sold one property without telling me. "Come and I give you thing to eat." You don't know that she has put something in your food. That's how I come to get doped. That's what she done. Then I stop like a dummy. Each time I remember my father I cry. When I see things going worse and worse I pick up myself and go down by my family, but I could not stay there, and my aunt never ask me how I was. All I want to do is kill myself. I was crying every day for my mother, and each time they tell me my mother was dead the fever take me. I come thin, thin, thin. And my mind was on my mother. I used to sleep in an old dress she had. Each time I kneel down to pray I would say, "Good night, Mama," and you couldn't pitch powder before I was asleep. My mother died in the afternoon time, and every afternoon at four o'clock the fever come to me. A whole three months I was like that. One day my mother come and talked to me—in a dream, you know. She tell me to stop it. "Do you want to come and meet me?"

"Yes," I say.

"Well," she tell me, "if you jump my coffin, you cannot come to me, but if you do not jump it and you fall in the hole, it is time for you to come." The coffin was there in the hole, just as she was buried. Well, I jump it, and my mother tell me I don't have no right to come and meet her. "Look, you jump the gutter." I watch Mama. She come over and kiss me and tell me, "Go and do your work." The next morning I get up and I eat breadfruit and [avocado] pear, and I go down by the jetty and I sit there watching the sea. All my mind tell me to throw myself in the water, when a Carib girl come up and ask me, "What happened to you?" I watch her and I don't say nothing.

"What happened to you? What happened?"

I say, "I'm not feeling good."

"No smoke?"

I say, "No."

"All right. Me come back." The kind of English she spoke I

couldn't understand it. She go and bring a little dirt pipe and a big drop of tobacco and offered it to smoke. "You are feeling no good. Me fix you up. Daddy fix you up." I followed her back to her yard. At the barrier of the yard they have a lot of little sticks, and her father sat there, smoking. "Tomorrow you are going up in the country with us. We get you better, right away," he say. "Up there you going home. You stop there. You take medicine. When you come back, you come back alive. You come back a man. Who are your family?"

I say, "Choco."

"Oh, you Choco boy? All right, tomorrow we will go. Understand? You hungry?"

I say, "Yes."

"Eat."

I ate crayfish and a kind of cassava you don't peel, but just push the skin back like a yam, and just as you put it in your mouth, it melts.

The next morning I get up and I walk, I walk, I walk. I say, "Jesus Christ!" One foot lead one foot up.

The girl tell me, "You will soon reach. Look where you are going. You see that mountain there."

"JESUS CHRIST!"

"Come. You frightened?"

When I reached I found all those thrash houses—thrash houses and little sticks and dirt. They call that "tawa."[3] They take the stick and clap it on a kind of red mud which they pung with cow dung. It's like cement and the house is very warm, for the wind cannot get in. It was there I slept. Now the mattress was made from the leaf of macamboo.[4] They roll it and splice it with two twines. I have used it since. It was night, and the girl went down by the river. There were two fish pots—a kind of wheel thing and it have a handle, like that. She lift it up and it was full of crayfish and flat crabs. She tell me to take off my clothes, to throw the things away, and she rub me down and make me bathe. Then she tell me, "Drink." Now they have a long thing that they called "gouge."[5] When it is young you peel it with the back of your knife and you take off all the seeds. Then you chop it fine, beat it, and steam it. When you see it comes soft, you put in all your messages [ingredients] and throw it in the meat, and it makes you come strong. You could do it with green papaya too—not ripe ones—peel it, boil it until it becomes soft, beat it, and throw it in your flesh [meat]. And that's what she give me to drink.

"It good?"

"Yes, it good." I take a small piece of paper and I put the seed in the paper and I put my knife on top. She never know I done that, but that's how I learn about it.

Now when I drink that medicine in the gouge, I drink good and I feel like I want to sleep. The old man had a light and a calabash full of oil, and he start to talk a language I never could understand. And he say, "Look, do you know this woman?"

"Yes, it is my sister."

"Your sister?"

I say, "Yes." Then he stop the language, and his daughter and wife come in. I didn't know that it was my sister doing that to me. I thought it was somebody else.

Tomorrow morning when I get up I drink again and go to bathe in the balance of what they give me. And I know what they give me. At twelve o'clock I drink again and from that time I was a different man. I forget my mother, I forget my father, and I begin to come straight. I become natural, just like I was before. I understand what I have to do.

It was when I come back that my aunt had missed me for a week and asked me where I had gone. Then I explained to her where I was from. She say, "Charles, if you did tell me so I know what to do for you." The old Carib know she was a doctor,[6] he knew what she could do, and still he tend to me.

I say, "Well, Auntie, I am going back to St. Lucia to avenge me." I left Friday afternoon aboard a boat they call *Pansy*. My passage was free because the Captain needed another man. He have two Montserrat men beating a St. Lucian, and he know he couldn't manage until the boat reached St. Lucia. I say yes, I would go.

I reach St. Lucia Sunday morning and I stay in town the night. Monday morning I go straight from town on the Morne, and when I reach I find those people[7] there on my mother's property. They asked me what I come for.

"I just come here for this property. I give you notice to leave that house and get somewhere to stay."

"What are you talking about?"

I say, "I told you something now."

"Oh, God!" they say. Henri, my sister's father, tell me, "A boy like you—I did like you so much and now that you have come big you act like you don't even know that you used to come at my wife's."

"Well, I will tell you. You did love me, yes, when my mother was alive. When she dead you wanted me to go and meet my mother, but you will not get the chance."

I didn't stay there. I went back in town to see Mr. George William.[8] I told him, "I'm selling my mother's property. Will you buy it?"

"Yes." The paper was signed with the lawyer, and Mr. William give me my money. I spend the week in St. Lucia and fix up my business. Saturday night at eight o'clock I leave in a shower of rain in the sloop *Enterprise* for Dominica. The captain's name was O'Farrell Hughes from Anguilla and he had come here to sell salt. At the time I didn't know he was family. I begged him for a passage to Dominica to go and see my aunt. "Who is your aunt?"

I say, "Choco." And then he come to make me know that my aunt was his aunt.[9] So I go down to Dominica with O'Farrell Hughes and then I start to sail. I sail, I sail, I sail.

I sail with O'Farrell Hughes again and we went all about—to Antigua, St. Thomas, St. Martins, St. Kitts—all about. We had a contract with Mr. Chesterfield to smuggle. He was a man who had run from a Guadeloupe jail. His wife bring him a pan of bread which have a hacksaw blade in it. During the night he take the blade and he wet the iron bars and he cut two. He have a long roll of good wire inside a bottle they bring for him, and he take that same wire, threw it between the bars, made it fast and climbed down. Behind the jail is the sea and he have a shore boat waiting there for him. After he get away he go back to smuggling again.

We left St. Lucia and went to St. Thomas with a load of wire and four men. When we reach Statia [St. Eustatius] I shake my head. Sloop *Enterprise* going without no sail. Everything was low. We reach Anguilla and we stop there for twenty-four hours. Then we *slack bam* go to St. Thomas. We meet the fishing ground where people were setting their fish traps. I lift one up, and we get two buckets of fish. We cook dolphin and couscous.[10] When we finished eating good we see the land come black—rain and wind. There was a fellow called Michel. He fall down. He cry. He tell me, "Charles, I ready to lose my life. I cannot take no more of this trip." He say he can do no more. He was too tired.

I say, "Go in the hold." But he tell me he cannot. It was too blocked up with the electric wire we were carrying. I say, "All right, Michel." My cousin, Hughes, he have the main sheet in his hand. His hand come stiff and raw—pull and slack, pull and slack. When it was twelve o'clock we pass by the bell and get inside the bay at St. Thomas. We drop anchor. Everywhere was wet. Where were we going to sleep? On top of the wire? I just throw the sail on top of the deck, crawl inside, and I sleep more than if I had a cotton bed. In the morning the harbor master come aboard—call us and wake us up. "Under this weather, where have you all come from?"

Captain Hughes answered, "St. Lucia."

"Give me all your papers. Give me your names and give me your book. When are you leaving?" We tell him we leaving any time the wind cut. We shelter there a whole week—we inside the gate, and the wind blowing outside. We unload the cargo and we have a happy time. We take on a load of Chesterfield and Lucky Strike and dry gin. We have a load of onions and salt too, for a fake. This was going to Guadeloupe for Chesterfield. He was the man dealing in contraband.

When we leave St. Thomas we meet the same kind of weather again—same wind, same bad weather. We reach in St. Martins at

Christmas time and we only have one little pig's foot for four men. We stayed there a couple of months[11] before we could go to Guadeloupe. One day a man come by the boat and talked to me. I watch the man—the kind of way he was.

"Got some fish?" I give the man some fish and a cup of tea. He take it and tell me he don't want to go fishing. The man say, "Well, Mister, what's your name?"

"My name is Charles."

"Where you from?"

"St. Lucia."

"Well, come ashore and we will have a good time, a spree."

I say, "Listen, I can't go ashore without money, without anything. How could I do anything? I am a stranger. A man can't go anywhere without a cent."

"Well, put on your clothes and come with me. Hurry up!" And I put on the clothes that I have and I follow the man. My foot want to go back more than to go in front. He take me in a shop and give me a rum. I sit there in a big chair while he say he would go get dressed. When he come out—silk shirt, thick-cut soles, and pants. "What do you say now, Carlo?" He sit down and he ring the bell, *ding-dong.*

"Yes, Master."

"Bring some whiskey here."

I say, "Nice place."

He ask me, "Who do you think is the boss of this?"

"I don't know."

"That's my brother." Then I could sit down proud because I know how I stand. We drink, and he say, "Well, I will tell you. The kind of way you treat me there I see you was a good man and that you were good and happy in your heart. If I was hungry, the same way you would have warmed my stomach. So I will take you as my friend, and you will have a good time today."

I say, "Yes. I don't tell you no, I won't have a good time, but I can't have a good time because I have no money."

"You can have all mine. Come on, I'll give you money." He put some down on the table and when I pick it up I see twenty dollars, twenty dollars, twenty dollars. He say, "That's good." We went outside, and I saw a car.

"Who's is that car?"

"Get inside. We are going up to Dutch country."[12] When I reach there I had a wool cap on my head. He tell me, "Throw away that. While we're here I'll get a hat to fit you." It was one nice panama hat. When it was twelve o'clock we leave Dutch country and come down in town. We eat until I don't have no belly to put food in—ham, pudding, everything. I don't go on board for three days, and when I go down he put a box full of stores in the car. When we reach, everyone was watching me come down. I was wearing different clothes and I was carrying the box. I put it down so, "Where is the captain?"

When he come, he say, "Charles, since you went ashore I haven't seen you yet."

I don't tell him nothing. I just say, "I got twenty dollars on me. Here is a box of stores."

We don't stay there. All the onions start to get big. Chesterfield come on board, and we hide him under the shore boat in the day, and he come out at night. We got a couple of sugar bags, and he just lay on top of them. Then we leave port and start to work down. We pass to windward of St. Kitts and when we reach Montserrat, Chesterfield tell us we must go low, low down and drift for the night. We do just that and when it was seven o'clock we go back to sail again and cut in under the land [Guadeloupe]. You see Chesterfield's house on top of the hill and then you proceed under the hill. There were three stones right in the same passage, and Chesterfield himself went out to push the stones aside. Then we take the cargo ashore in the shore boat. A gang of people come and carry it on the road. We do that very fast because it was dangerous, and the moment we reach the boat we heist the shore boat on board and we start to heist sail. I see a light, a little bit dim. We try to hurry but the anchor was humbugging us. The light came brighter until you could pick up a pin on deck. Misery is good to talk, but not nice to see. Just as we get the boat under way we hear, "Boat ahoy. Halt. Where are you from?"

"St. Kitts."

"What's your cargo?"

"Salt." All that was left aboard was salt.

"Why do you pass so close under the land?"

O'Farrell say, "We are going to Dominica and we don't want to reach so early, so we hang on here to reach at daybreak in Portsmouth Harbor."

"Hahahahaha. Get me the rod. Don't put that trick on me, because I believe I know better than that." And that was right. He come aboard with the rod. He was covered from head to foot with a shield. You can't hit him anywhere. You can't see him. You can only hear his voice, and his voice was very terrible. He say, "Let me tell you now. I know you are loaded with salt but you have something after the salt." We laugh. He say, "What did you discharge before?" He tell us that we land Lucky Strike and Chesterfield and he suppose we land liquor too. You see he have two buttons, here, and when he squeezed one a thing came out like an elephant's beak. It was long. He put the rod into the salt and drew out what was inside there and he smell it. The smell remain in the boat and when he press the button he say, "Hmmm. Fine, Captain. You're smart, eh. Salt in front and something else behind the salt." The salt was right after the mast and all the Lucky Strikes and dry gin had been right in front. When we took out this cargo the front was bound to be empty. He want to know why it was empty. He say, "You move number one cargo, and number two cargo remain and that's the one you say you have." We had not the chance to throw the empty cartons overboard. A few cartons we let go but they did not sink. They were just floating and we knew that would give the man the proof that we had those articles on board. When you're in trouble your heart is beating out your side. We thought we were dead. The man watch me. He say, "What do you think you are?" I say, "Well, Captain, I think I am a human being just like yourself. After a man in a boat, he got to work the orders. If he don't obey orders it's jail or be shot. Well, after the captain speak, I got to obey." He say, "That's right. Bring a carton of cigarettes and bring a bottle of whiskey. I will give you a chance. When I leave my home this afternoon my wife tell me not to kill. 'George, don't kill for the sake of the young kids.' He tell O'Farrell to drink first. O'Farrell don't want to drink because he thought as he drink the man would cut his throat. "I can't drink."

"Drink, God blast you. You drink. You are the captain." He drink. The man give me a cigarette, and I light it. "O.K., I won't kill you, but after today put 'WOD' on your sail and on the chock, and anytime I see that mark I will know it's you. And the next time I catch you, I will give it to you anywhere I meet you, and I will give you twice as much for the one time." He take all of our names and he go, "All right, good-bye."

I say, "Good-bye, Cap." O'Farrell sit down there, so. I say, "Mister, before we move, wire money—share it, the contraband money—share it."

"Here are the keys. Go down below and get it in the trunk and bring it up." I go and get it. "Put it there. Good. There is five of us. The boat make five."

I say, "All right, that's yours, that's mine, that's the boat's. If I dead, I dead with my money in my pocket."

All that time Chesterfield was in the shore boat covered with tins and bags and everything. If Chesterfield had only coughed we would have been done for. That man would have been glad to catch him, because he had run away from jail. If he had held Chesterfield that would have been bound to make trouble, because he had two guns on him.

Frightenness can kill you. O'Farrell Hughes had to go to his bed to lay down. When he got up I got to throw water on his pants—clean him up like a baby. He use his bowels he was so frightened. I got to take a rope and tow the pants—tow it by the boat—and let it wash up. When we reach inside of Portsmouth we throw the shore boat over the side and call O'Farrell to get up. He can't get up. We have to pick him up and take him at his house in a car. He make three months straight on his bed.

After that he tell Chesterfield, "This kind of business, after today, you get a next boat to do it for you. I will never do it again. What I could do is drop the cocoa for you, but the St. Thomas affair—not me. I am not going."

"Who will go? Charles?"

"Who will go, Cap? Huh! Not Charles!" One day Chesterfield say he have four thousand coconuts in bulk to carry to St. Thomas. I tell him, "You can go yourself, but you won't find me there." He ask why. I say, "Don't you remember what happened last time? Well, I ain't going to take nothing. If you want, take a next crew and go, go ahead."

In Portsmouth in Dominica when they hold you, they lock you up in a cell by the bay in a little house, and the next morning they take you in a boat and carry you in Roseau and put you in jail. I won't say I wouldn't take jail, but not for contraband. In Guadeloupe, for contraband they sink your boat, break your neck, or shoot you. Chesterfield, I think he was a moron. It's been a long time since I meet with him again, but I certain sure he still alive. If he were not alive you wouldn't see that house on top of the hill.[13]

We still had some liquor on board, covered with ropes and some other contraband. I try my best to help O'Farrell because he could not work. I get four cocoa bags and I fill them with butter. Then I go inside a rum shop in Portsmouth. A nice, good-looking girl was there, and I call her and asked her if she want anything. "Yes, Charlie. How many you got?" I said, "A couple of bags of butter."

"All what you have, bring it."

"What time?"

"Anytime you're ready."

"All right." I go to the boat and I get the contraband and I take it in the shop. Now people were carrying cargo. I have some rum on deck. I don't put it ashore, I just leave it in the shore boat. Miss Harris is there already waiting. She know what I was carrying. I tell her, "I have some things I got there in Antigua." I was sitting on the boxes, rowing. She tell me, "The man isn't coming, Mr. Charles. Come now, because I want to go aboard the boat." I row her out, and she give me the money. Then we come back ashore, and I pull the boat up. As we go down the street, the man come and take his rum.

When O'Farrell was sick, I was captain now and it was then I come to find out what he was doing. He used to drag cocoa and coffee to Antigua to sell for that same Chesterfield, and each trip he made was worth twenty pounds. He never gave us a cent of the twenty pounds. He gave you a share of the cargo he brought from Dominica to Antigua, but the money for the contraband, he kept it all.

When you go to Antigua there are two things you like to get: coffee and tobacco. People from Tortola brought tobacco and sold it there for nine shillings a pound. A bag of coffee was ten shillings. There were people in the steamer working—unloading cargo—and they came by the boat and they used to call me, "Charles, do you want a bag?" I'd buy it, but if you get caught by the customs, you got locked up. I don't sell the coffee in Portsmouth. I brought it for a woman, and Sunday, if I want to sleep there, aah—see that one better than the coffee. I getting in it.

One time there was a man who was in the war, Captain Pantobe from France. He took the plane from France and was dropped in Vieux Fort. A car brought him up in Castries, and when he reached there he inquired if he could get a boat to take him to Guadeloupe. I met him on the wharf, and he asked, "Where is this sloop going?"

"It going to Dominica."

"Well, I would like you to take me straight to Guadeloupe. After you reach Guadeloupe you could return to Dominica. What is your cargo?"

I say, "Coca-Cola." That's for true. That's what I carrying.

"All right. You will take me?"

I watch the man. "Yes. I will take you. How much money will you pay me to go to Guadeloupe straight?"

"I'll give you one hundred dollars to pass straight there."

"All right." I call my cousin—the same O'Farrell Hughes. I tell him I find a trip which was going to Guadeloupe straight. He say that he not going in Guadeloupe.

"Well, I am going."

"If you're going, you're going alone on the water. But I won't interfere."

I say, "I don't give a blast what you say, but I know I'm going in Guadeloupe."

The gentleman call me aside. "Tell me, what is your name?"

"Charles."

"Charles, do you have some money?"

"Yes, boss, I got a few pieces." He tell me to go buy a pack of cigars and four pounds of ice for him. I go and do so. Then he tell me to go down at that rum shop there and I would see five grips, three small ones and two big ones. I say, "Yes."

O'Farrell vexed. He could see that the gentleman was nice. He was big and tall. The man's shoes, you could put them on top of your head to carry. His hand was big like that and his neck, thick. About six o'clock we leaving to go to Guadeloupe and bad weather strike—thunder and lightning. I make ready to cook. Captain Pantobe ask me, "What kind of man is he?"

"I don't know. They say he is family."

"Well, he's nothing more than a pig. I will treat him according to how he behaves. Now don't you tell him anything."

When we reach outside I take a ballahoo [fishbait] and I put it upon the hook and I slack it. It have time to run about five chains, and *bam, feeee.* I bring in a dolphin. He tell me the dolphin come alongside, and he bend his hand like that and grab hold of the dolphin right there, so. "Well, what do you think!" He pull his dagger and he clean the fish better than me. He take up the fish, put it in a pan, wash it, put in lime and everything. Then he say, "Dinner?"

I say, "Sure. What you want? The head or a piece behind the neck?"

He tell me, "The head. It is sweet because it have grease in it." I cut a chunk and a big slice again and I say, "Tip the water on the fish. We're going to eat the head and we need more water."

"I know. I know."

"O.K." I give every man his share and we sit down and eat. Captain Pantobe get up and go and get a bottle of champagne. He bust the wire, pour it, and drink. I drink and put the bottle there. We drink the whole bottle and then throw it over the side.

O.K. Day break. We were in Guadeloupe Channel going down *slack-bam*. He tell me, "Charles, let the next boy come and take the wheel. You go and get the bucket, put a rope on it and collect some sea water to wash my back with." I do so. I throw the bucket on top of his head. He take a sponge and make me sponge all his back, all his head, and he was rubbing all his face. Then he tell me to take a cup from the water cask and throw it in the bucket. "I want to rinse myself."

We see a man passing in a shore boat. Captain Pantobe tell him to come. The fellow say he not come because the boat was going down to Guadeloupe and if he come on board they would lock him up. "Ah, yes, what he says is true." Then he call to the man, "Go down to the harbor master straight quick and tell him that Captain Pantobe will soon arrive—get ready." The man pull the boat, hard. I just see him do so—he don't even tie the rope—and he ran to the harbor master's office.

Captain Pantobe shove his trunk down and went below after it. He say, "Charles, give Captain Jab that." He called O'Farrell "Captain Jab." "Ask him if he knows that man." The man was on horseback with a big hat with a feather and he got a uniform with all the regiment hangings—going to fight the Kaiser War. O'Farrell say he don't know this man. Captain Pantobe say, "Very well. Tell him it is me." O'Farrell don't say anything. "Look the next one. That's the German War." He show him. "That's me. I win the two wars." He show me a stick. It was the first time I ever see white gold. Do you know those baskets made of coconut tree leaf? Well, he have one of those all in gold. That's what he was carrying for his niece. When he lay down on the bed he scratched his back with a gold comb. That was another present he was bringing. Then he start to dress. When he come up, I couldn't say a word. My belly cut me. I just watch, my mouth wide open. He say, "Don't be frightened." He come out with one gun here, one there, and round shot in the waistband. And he have spurs on both feet. From there, so, his medals, and on his head a hat with a big feather. "Well, Captain Jab, here is Guadeloupe."

We come through the mark and we hear, *rrrrrr,* the launch come with all its flags to take Captain Pantobe. Before he leave he take my measurements and a good while after I see a boy come with a parcel. He tell me that Captain Pantobe tell me to dress myself and a car would come and take me and the rest of the crew. So I clean myself and I dress up myself in the nice shoes and the nice shirt he sent. We go ashore. Captain Pantobe meet us and show us all his buildings. When I tell you buildings—that man got a theater, he got a whole place where he had bananas, he got a store, he got a café, and he got a place full of women. When you go in you stand over there. The house full of people, cooking, and there was an old white French woman there. She opened the big door and it was just like a hospital. You know when you go to the hospital you see patients [gales of laughter], well, it was just like that—a bed there, a bed there, a bed there, and all had young girl there! He take us into one huge building where his mother and sister and brother live. He tell all the people he meet, "Bonjour," because he had just come from France and had come to cheer the people. You see, he was making money off of them. He take us in his home and tell us to sit down. I was just like a sprat in the chair—it was big and all carved. He tell his mother, "Take care of this man anytime he comes here in this country. I don't believe he will forget this place, for I will keep him here. This is the man that take me from St. Lucia in the little sloop. And the captain refuse to take me—I hear all that he say, because they don't know I can speak English. The kind of way Charles treat me in the little sloop, I am going to treat him the same way." Then he say to O'Farrell, "Captain Jabber, you refuse to take me. Well, I won't do you any harm, but I will give you a small little punishment. You got to remain here three months[14] before you leave, and when I tell you to go, then you're going to go. If you make up your mind to leave here before I give my permission, then the boat will remain here. I am Captain Pantobe in Guadeloupe!" O'Ferrell don't say yes and he don't say no, but he know in his heart that he have to stay. "Now, my brother will take you to the next place to go and drink with your friends, but Charles will remain here with us." We take dinner—all kind of meat and everything. When we finish he gave me twenty dollars in American money and he say, "Put that in your pocket and let us go and show my people what kind of a man I have found."

The next morning he send to carry us to see his estate. He show us all that he have—fig, orange, pineapple, grapefruit, all kinds of fruit, coffee, and cocoa. I get twelve bags of cocoa for myself and six bags of coffee. How much do you think he give O'Farrell and the crew? One bag apiece. Don't talk about grapefruit and oranges. When you bite the orange you could eat the skin too.

We go in town and he change the one hundred dollars of American money into English money. And he share the money—the boat's own, the captain's own, and the three sailors'. But the American money was worth more than the English money, and what was left over he give to me, as well as my share. "That's yours, too, Charles."

I could have stayed with Captain Pantobe. But if I had stayed I wouldn't have suffered. If you suffer, you're a better man, and look where I is now. I am stronger. If I had a next man with me like a friend, I could have stayed. But me, one English man, alone, no. I don't have no second. The man I call, I say, "Sandy, why don't we stay in Guadeloupe?"

"Me? Frenchmen killing people too quick. Me no stay, Carlo. You don't know what you say. In Guadeloupe!" And really Guadeloupe is a dangerous island. Guadeloupe people are hard people.

I work with a Guadeloupe man in Santo Domingo in the carretera. We finish the carretera and we sent to put in the rear line. The man tell me, "Next week we be going home."

"How are you going home next week? You tell me you don't have no money."

"I'll get the money."

"Are you going to take it?"

"No."

Now, down there when you're working and you have an accident and get mashed up, you will get a lot of money. You know what that brute do? There is a man there and a heap of iron here. You know the train rear line—it's heavy rear line. He let go of the iron, and the iron drag him and cut off his fingers. The brute bawl. A Guadeloupe man, not one finger, all four gone— willfully. For what? He haven't got no money in Santo Domingo. He was broke. Now after he get wounded he go to the hospital. He get more than two thousand dollars. And the brute do it because he say he going next month. I don't want four hundred dollars or five hundred dollars to lose a finger. But Guadeloupe people—the man got heart, I tell you. His hand burn up. When he finish they send him in Guadeloupe with all the American money—four hundred dollars, four thousand dollars, something like that.

After three days we go down to Dominica, and O'Farrell, he start to talk shit. When he reach in Dominica he don't want to come out because he have money. I say, "O.K." When he was at his girl friend, the *Pansy* was passing up from Dominica and I go with her. I sold my cocoa in Dominica and I carry the coffee to Castries. O'Farrell don't even know where one bag go. When he finally come to St. Lucia he still have his two bags. He ask me if I have mine. "One thing I'll tell you. I want my freight money from the Coke."

"O.K., Carlo." A man going to give you bread. It's a nasty thing where strangers go in a country and you don't receive that person well. You never know what place you're going to fall.

I sail, I sail. I sail all about. Even to Guyana and Trinidad. One time I come to St. Lucia from Trinidad. I was only here for four days before the fire catch.[15] The fire was like the star light— *tweee, tweee, tweee.* It not falling on the small houses so much, just the big houses and stores, stores, stores. It was an American job. There's a trick in it, you see. They want to take up the old wood house and put up big houses. All the town was wood house before, and you could get a room for four shillings a month. You could get a room to rent before you say "Jack

Robinson!" You could stand up in town and watch. The fire went straight so. All the big buildings and the stores—George William's, the sugar factory, the back store, the customs. After the big buildings went, the little houses start to burn. Fire. Fire. It passed Barnard's straight and went down to customs. Whiskey, whiskey, whiskey—all the local stores burn. The fire was a select fire. Whiskey on the ground like sand, pig tail, pig mouth, store shoes, boots, casks were running. You fill your bucket and off with it. The last fire I was from sea and I ain't caught nothing that day, but this time. . . . I see a barrel and I shove me hand, I find a box—I pull the box. When they say put it down, I say, "Uh unh, not me." I take a bag full of rice, pig tail, salt fish. I go home and I put a pan on the fire. I go back down, making trouble. I just take a net, everything. As I reach home an Anse la Raye man come in a canoe and say that he want everything to buy. I tell him to give me fourteen dollars and I would give him the load. I make him take everything—whiskey, gin, all.

The next morning everyone was by the square—all their faces black. They sit down by the square. The rain come, and all the people go inside the church. No house remained. There were some two hundred dead.[16] All those who lost their homes they put in Vigie in the soldier's barracks—black, white, everyone mixed together. Others they put on the Morne.

I go to sea. When I come back I see a big line. Everyone have a basket and a book. You take your basket and your book, and you get your sugar, your rice, your bread, your potato, your corn beef. I watch and I laugh. Me no care. I go home and I just put some rice on the fire, some peas, and I make some fish broth and I eat. Then I go up to see my aunt at the hospital. Her house was burned up in the fire, and when she was running she step on a piece of burnt galvanized and split her foot between her toes. That was my mother's own sister, and they take her to the hospital. I go there and I say, "Good morning."

"Good morning, Charles. Charles, they stick me here." I ask her what happen. "Well, the fire catch as I was running, and my foot get cut."

"I suppose it burn everything you had in the house."

"Everything burned."

I say, "You come by the water and you go by the water."

"What are you telling me about?"

"I come big now. Your brother have plenty people, plenty friends. And you burned and you have nothing. Where is he now?" I was staying at my girlfriend's. "I will see if she can take you."

I go up to see Baby. I tell her, "My auntie is in the hospital."

"Really?"

"Yes. They do some fooling around and they put she up because she have no place to stay."

"She can come here."

I get a car and I go to get her. In a couple of weeks her foot was huge. They say when the guy was cleaning the foot off he wasn't careful enough. She get blood poisoning and die. When she die I go to the police station, and they gave me a coffin for twelve shillings. I go and I take it to the church for the funeral. I sit down in the hearse—in front. Then I go to the burying ground. I see the hole they were going to put her in and I go down in it. It was full of water, so I put four stones—one in each corner. Then they put her straight down, slacked it, and pulled the rope up. I say, "Auntie, you in front and I behind. May God be with you. You was trying to put me in the hole first, but I sure I put you there first. Good-bye," I say. "Bury her now." That night we make the wake down there. In a few days, when the eight-day wake pass, back to sea and sailing.

You've got to have a wake. You've got to make a nice cross and put it on the tomb. After the ceremony everybody is going to stop in front of the cross on the tomb. After you make the ceremony, you have expenses because you have to cook the dinner— that's for your parents or your husband or your aunt, any close relative—and you're bound to do it. If not and you're a woman, your two feet come big, so. If you're a man you get two big stones. Even if the person is a little child—if he has six months—you're bound to give dinner for him. You have to give the priest three dollars to make the ceremony. You have to keep the tomb clean and on the night you're making the ceremony you have to put new flowers. You wait eight days, because there must be time for the dead body to ask you for light. That is the ceremony for you. You've got to light a proper candle and carry it to the priest to light for the dead person.

In old times, the dead used to do the same thing he do when he was alive. Plenty people come, and you singing and cooking food. The person leading the singing for you is going to drink the cock's blood.[17] It's not he one going to sing—plenty people, men, women, all singing different songs. You tend to the dead and you're serious. All the time you crying and singing songs. Everybody going to help you. Everyone comes to your home and keeps you company. If you haven't got a room at home you have to look for a place or rent a place. If you have a big yard, everything is good. Each person brings a basket of food. This one bringing rum, this one bringing a piece of beef, or pig. The first thing you've got to look for is the drum, and the drum will come very early in the night. At two o'clock in the afternoon the other drum will be in the yard already. Two drums, that's the main thing. You do number one, the drum, because he won't leave you alone, he won't let you in peace until he has the drum. You hear singing that day. You tremble, all your nerves come strange, when you hear the drum's sound. That is a rule in St. Lucia. There is no way in St. Lucia that somebody is dead and you don't have that. Sometimes the echo is so heavy that you could be anywhere and hear it. The law cannot stop that. We do the dance. This goes until daybreak. You follow the advice of the people who are singing and bawling—people from everywhere are going up, following the voice. More people, more people, more people. Sometimes they have a drum beating in Vieux Fort. You pass in the ocean and you hear the echo. So long. Straight into Vieux Fort Harbor. You're obliged to go there. You hear the echo and you hear the song. The main man come and tell you good night and he bawl. He singing, and you hear him scream and hear the answer of it. Your head and hair stand up. Every man comes straight to the dead—takes off his hat, shoves his hand, and takes a flower. You see a mountain of people and women sitting on the bench wearing a patch dress. They wear that for the drum, that's their costume. All the time this is going on it is very nice. There are plenty of people, and you have to squeeze to pass. If you don't do this for the dead, you'll have no rest at your house.[18] You won't be able to stay there. You'll have to go to a lunatic asylum. The house is hot, your bedroom is hot, you're bound to be crazy. If you don't treat him nice after he's dead, you don't escape. He could have left you a million dollars, but it would be finished like water. You wouldn't get it because you hadn't kept your promise. But if you take care of the dead and do what you promise, then you is happy. Oh, you is happy. When three months has passed you want to repeat the ceremony yourself for your husband. You would go to the priest and he would tell you yes. Then you invite a couple of people, take them at your house, and you would never feel nothing because he would be taken care of. You going to sleep tonight just like you're with your husband. After he's dead, he's not banished. If you act like a lady, you will see him in your sleep. While sleeping he will tell you what to do. After your husband is dead, don't marry again. Keep your children and live on what he left for you. Don't get somebody else, because he will eat you into the grave and you won't have time to spend your money. He will do it for you. He will trick you, and your dead husband will turn against you and torture you.

I will tell you something else again. There is a woman right here by me. The husband used to work fig, banana. Every night when the boat come in he work. He gather the money. For so much starving, he make a nice life. His house is finish, but it too cold. The doctor say he stop too far from the kitchen. He got a pain there in his stomach. The woman just leave the man inside the house and go and meet a next man. The poor man lay there suffering. He have nobody to give him food. During the time the woman at the next man's, she husband dead inside the house. He have a dummy boy, and it is the dummy boy who cry and go up and call she—tell she the husband is dead. Everybody know how the husband dead through starvation. Now after he dead, big drum going to beat. *Hum.* The big drum going to beat, eh, and the schoolmaster of the drum, he know how this man get it. There is a song which will come out from your head. It tell she, "You know what you lost, but you don't know what you will get. You cause your husband's death. One day you will be dead." She start to cry and big drum start to answer the word. *Butu, butu, butu, butu,* and the song going on.

(*English translation*)

Mama goooo
Ay, Mama gooo
Ou save ça ou pède
Mais ou pas save ça ou
    kai trapééé.

Mama goooo
Ay, Mama gooo
Cé ou qui la cause
    la mô mari-ou, ooh,
Mamaaa.

Mama goooo
Ay, Mama gooo
Mari-ou mô,
Cé ou qui en est cause la mô,
Mama, cé pou ou compren,
Mari-ou mô.
Ou save ça ou pède,
Ou pas save ça ou
    ké jouèn,
Mamaaa.[19]

Mama goooo
Ay, Mama gooo
You know what you lost
But you don't know whom
    you'll catch.

Mama goooo
Ay, Mama gooo
You are the cause of
    your husband's death,
Mamaaa.

Mama goooo
Ay, Mama gooo
Your husband is dead. Alas,
You are the cause of his death.
Mama, you must understand
Your husband is dead.
You know whom you lost,
You don't know whom
    you'll attract,
Mamaaa.

After the nine days, wake again.[20] He repeat it for him, and you know what the next man do? He tell her, "You won't do me how you do your husband. Take the food you have upon my land and get the hell out. Don't touch my land again no more." You know she thin like that now. She cannot go in the husband's house because the dummy boy take his two hands and throw her in the road. He pick up her bundle and send it in the road for her. None of she daughter have nothing to do with her. The same thing you do the black dog, the same thing you do the white dog.

After I bury my aunt I stop in Dominica for seven years. You know what humbug me in Dominica? The mountain chicken.[21] If you like eating frog you could stay in Dominica for the balance of your life. But not me. Every Saturday you're going to see them in the market there jumping. If you eating that you could stay in Dominica 'cause you could get that a lot. They believe in that— the mountain chicken. "Get your mountain chicken!" Every woman passing, they got it. I used to eat at my aunt's—Monday, Wednesday, Friday, Saturday, but Sunday we don't eat there. Sunday I eat aboard the vessel. Saturday night I just take food at the house and carry it in the boat. I catch some little jack fish. I sit down on the boat in the night. I fishing there and all the fish I catch up I put in a bucket and I clean them. Tomorrow morning I cooking good. Everybody eating at my aunt's, but not me. I don't want no mountain chicken. What! He bawling so!

My cousin tell me, "Well, Charles, tonight we're going to catch some mountain chicken. You going?"

I say, "Yes, I'll go with you." We go up high, high on top of the hill in a cocoa tree, and we have two dogs. When I hear this thing scream I was frightened because it bawl so hard. The dogs bound, and it start to jump—and the dog catching them. If you don't have no dog you can't get the mountain chicken. They leaping too fast, man, and they big! When I see them put the frogs[22] in the bag, I watching. Two eyes shining there. We come with a bagful—six of the small one and two of the big. They just put their hand behind their back and take them in the market. Lots of people eating that, but not me.

From Dominica I go into Antigua and bring back coffee. I go down to St. Kitts, to St. Martins, and St. Thomas. At that time I was captain of my own boat. Everybody know me, and I was working and making money. And you know who I going to see in Dominica? The Caribs. I got to stop there. Do you think I want to make a fool of myself? It's the Carib girl I have to look for first. She was the one who give me the pipe to smoke. It don't kill me, it clean me. After I get better I still go back in St. Lucia and I do what I have to do with my sister, but when I come back to Dominica, I go to see the girl and her family. I bring them coffee from Antigua, and when I go to sea catching fish, I bring them fish. Do you think that because I was feeling better that I would brush back the Carib girl and take a next girl while she was watching? What! You think I am crazy? She would take it back the same way she give it to me. It would be very easy for the Caribs. I would be leaving Sunday morning to go to Antigua. She would just take three cashews and some water from the church—some "*dleau béni*"[23]—and throw them in the pump hole, and you know what would happen to me? I would never make land. As I turn my head to go out of the harbor and up to Antigua, I would feel my breath weak and I wouldn't know where I was going. That's a grace they would give you. But it cannot happen to me because I know what they can do. I know they could do that. I take care of myself. The Carib girl come down every Saturday in Portsmouth to meet me. I come from Antigua on Saturday, and Saturday night she sleep on board with me. Sunday morning she would see when the boat leave and she would be certain sure that I would be back next Saturday. Monday morning she would go up in the country and Saturday she would come back down to meet me. She could not give me a hard time because I don't give her a hard time.

When I was living with the Carib girl I get a message to come down here in St. Lucia to join the *Granville Lass*. She was happy for me because she knew I have a good job and was going back in my own country. She give me yams, dasheen, and next time I come into Portsmouth, everybody going to find their own hole—well, I got mine. I pass in the yard like a bull and I jump on the step. Her mother say, "Who is it?"

I say, "The boss. Look out!"

"Charles!" Then everybody come—mother, sister, brother. That time I have two bottles of Cinzano and a bottle of La Blanche in a bag. I dump it upon the table there.

"Have you eaten yet?"

"Sure, I've eaten. But I want your food tonight."

"O.K., Charlie," and the girl come up. "I'm not dead yet."

I say, "I'm not dead yet, neither. I make you a visit to come and see you."

She ask me, "Where do you eat all the time?"

"I've stayed working all the time. I didn't have a chance to come here. I haven't come to stay. I just came to make a special visit."

"Oh, dear me. How are your girl friends?"

"How are your boy friends?"

She say, "I don't have any."

"Well, I don't have any, either."

"I would believe you, Charles. You hurt too much that day, eh?"

"I hurt what belong to me, but not what don't belong to me."

"O.K. Now, what time are you going on board tonight?"

"I'm going on board in the morning. I don't see you for a long time and tonight I see you. Do you think I'm going to let you go free?"

It was all right. Her mother and father know I was the boy friend. Oh, I drink very full. She come and tell me to go and get my rest, to go lie down on the bed. I have some rum in my belly and I sleep. In the middle of the night she wake me up and say, "Well, what are you doing? What's wrong with you? Do you know where you is?"

At that time the rum in me head, and I had not caught up myself yet. When I opened my eyes I saw the next day. Then I change the program—eh, eh. When a man is young he miss no chance. I stop there for the morning. The boy off the boat come and call me. "Charlo."

"Hello."

"Ready to go."

"O.K. I'm coming."

[To the Carib girl] "I don't know when I'll be able to come again."

"All right, Charles."

"I hope you will be wishing to make a baby for me."

"I would be glad. With you not there, I would like to carry a child."

"O.K. Good-bye."

That was the time I was working with Charlie Bristol, and he was making contraband, too. He was working for a white man called Mr. Polymarque, a man from Guadeloupe. We were dragging wine and rum between empty casks. We'd take a load of two hundred casks from Martinique, and you'd get about forty casks of rum and wine and these we'd land in Cooley Town.[24] You meet a low ground just beyond Roseau. They'd roll everything in the savan [savanna]. Rum went there, wine, there. And nobody would pay any attention to that because these were empty casks. I was doing that every day. Sometimes there weren't too many casks, but when you heard it was twelve you'd get vexed. I'd say, "Jesus Christ, you think this man going to send me at this hour to go and take that blasted thing." All the time that was humbugging me. One night as I was unloading I hear, "Put the board across and roll the barrel inside." When I turn to see two men, each of them with a long range gun, my belly cut me. I thought I was dead. I try to shove the boat away, but they say, "No, no. Come back. We want to help you." One was Mr. Polymarque and the other was a revenue officer who was working for Mr. Polymarque. Do you think he was a fool? The government put them there with a gun to prevent anyone from making contraband, but still when he's the watchman, he's making a share. Well, they help us finish the job, and when I carry back the boat I start to quarrel. But Mr. Polymarque tell me, "Charles, don't get vexed. I will fix you up." Captain Bristol would only have given me a tin of corn beef and a piece of bread. Mr. Polymarque was more generous.

One night we were sent to make a certain job. When you come down from Roseau to Portsmouth, just before you catch Portsmouth you meet a piece of savan. You will see a cave there, so, and there was a big hole there full of snakes. Before we could go in there we had to take a big parcel of sulfur, light it, and send it down the hole. There was a big chest of gold down there. We had to put a block and tackle on it and it took all our strength to pull that bitch. Mr. Polymarque and Mr. Bristol were there laughing and drinking. They gave a bottle to the four of us. I say, "Listen, is that thing real?"

"Yes, Charles."

He did not go into Portsmouth. We stop a good while on the beach there and then we pick up and go back to Martinique. When we reach that same night, Mr. Polymarque get his car and a couple of French men to put the chest in the car. Then he say, "This is all O.K. We'll see you tomorrow."

Captain Bristol come and gave us ten shillings apiece. He tell us, "Go and get a drink."

I say, "Who me? Uh unh. I don't want that. Listen, let me tell you something. You can be sure if you don't give me what I'm asking we all going to jail. I going to jail, you going to jail, everybody's going to jail because I am going straight in the station to report it."

"How much do you want?"

"I want five pounds for me. Five pounds for my share. I don't care for the balance."

He tell me, "Here, take it." Do you know, Mr. Polymarque gave him four hundred dollars for the crew to share, and Bristol was taking all. Mr. Polymarque never tell me about that. Bristol take it all and he try to give me ten shillings. God have to beat that man, huh. But Bristol get caught. You know what happened?

Well, he was always going making contraband with the French people, and he carrying three women—his wife, Mistress Carewell, and Madame Almé, and Mrs. Taylor. Madam Almé said that this trip she wasn't going to Martinique, but could Captain Bristol buy her about forty-eight bags of rice. Captain Bristol always landed the rice in big thrash baskets, covered over with limes. When the immigration master come to see, he would think it was limes. But all the time now it was rice. We used to carry cocoa bags, and Captain Bristol tell us there were tannias in the bags—take care of them. Well, the kind of way he tell you it was tannia, you know it isn't tannia. I say to myself, "You is a fool. I will make you understand." I pull my knife and I stick it in. When I smell it—ham. I open the bag. I take three and the next man take three. Then we cover it over and stowed the tannia. When we reach Martinique we land all the bags together. We bring them ashore and put them on a truck. And some men drive it away. I watch them, because that was all contraband they have. Now for this entire trip Madame Almé was not with us, and Captain Bristol was supposed to get her some rice. But he don't buy none for her. He only bought some for Mistress Carewell. When Madame Almé see rice by the wharf she go and get a truck to pick it up. But when she come by the wharf with the truck, Captain Bristol tell her that the only rice he have a chance to buy was for Mistress Carewell. Madame Almé get hot. She get blue because Miss Carewell had got all the sale. She tell me, "All right. We will stop him. Listen, Charles, when you reach St. Lucia, stay ashore. Here's five pounds—stay ashore and do not come back aboard this trip and you will hear the results."

"Yes, Miss." I go and buy wine, I buy tequilla, I buy everything because I know I wasn't coming back. All week I was by the wharf, and you know, when you don't want to do something, the least thing a person tells you makes you hot. We leave Dominica to go back to St. Lucia. When we reach Dominica Channel—it is always rough there—a canoe we were towing burst its rope. Then, *pow*, the boom burst. I tell Bristol he would have to send his mother to go cut it, I wasn't going. I don't care because offshore I don't do nothing. He say nothing. He send two other fellows in the water. When the boat dive, they go back up. They want a rope to tie on their waists in case they miss the canoe. Well, they get the canoe and they tie it short. When we reach Martinique I was wishing things had happened already. We go on to St. Lucia and I unload the cargo. Then I pick up my hand bag and basket.

"Charles, what's the matter?"

"Tonight is Saturday and I'm not watching tonight."

"If you're not watching tonight, you know what will happen."

"Fuck you." And I go. Monday morning they take the boat from Western Wharf and bring it to Conway by the customs to take on cargo. I pass there.

"Charles, what happened. You're not working?"

"No, sir. Did you hear what you told me? If I don't come to watch Saturday, you know what I have to do. I've come to get my paper and I've come to get my money from Mr. Chastanet."

He say, "I not paying you."

"Don't be a damn fool. You will pay me. Even without your paper I'm going to get my money."

I go up to Mr. Chastanet, you know, by the square, and I say, "Boss, I've come for my money. I'm not going this trip."

"What's wrong, Charles?"

"I'm not going."

"You're not going?"

"Naw."

The next morning Captain Bristol was by the wharf. I jump in the whaler and tell him I'm going to sea. He did not go in the afternoon. When I come with dolphin and flying fish, I say, "Give me your pan. Let me give you some flying fish." I take the pan and I give him some flying fish and some dolphin. "Ah, Charlie!"

He have to take wine in Martinique and those empty casks to Cooley Town. He know I could do the job well. "Why, Charles, why are you not going with me?"

"I tell you already that I don't want a man to fire me twice. You tell me in front of everybody." He's a kind of man, if you meet him by the corner and you say, "Captain, I need something to buy," he would say he don't have a cent. But the moment you see he have a woman by him, you could ask him for twenty dollars and he would give it to you at the same time. Good. The next day I go to fish again and when I come back I meet the boat going out of the harbor. I bawl to him, "Captain Bristol, you son of a bitch, you're going to Dominica, but you won't be coming back."

Friday night I was sitting down at my home and I hear, "Mr. Charles, Mr. Charles. Look, a gentleman coming—a car coming."

"What gentleman?"

He tell me, "Mr. Chastanet." I go to meet him.

Mr. Chastanet say, "Charles!"

"Yes, boss."

"Disaster! Disaster, Charles!"

"What do you mean to tell me?"

"Why didn't you tell me before the boat went out? They got my boat."

"What happened?"

"They seized the boat in Dominica. Oh, God!"

"Now, how are they doing that?"

"Everybody is locked up in jail. Disaster. You know what I'm going to do?"

"No, sir."

"We got to take that boat up. I'll pay for my boat, but not the crew. They can stay in jail." That was his idea, but he didn't know the Dominica rule. When he reach he find this case was a sea affair so it have to be dealt with by the treasury. We go upstairs in the treasury, but it do no good talking to the harbor master. He tell Mr. Chastanet he have to pay two thousand dollars for his boat, twelve pounds for the captain, and seven pounds for each man. He say, "I'll pay the money for my boat, but I don't care a damn for those people."

"You won't get your boat so long as those people are locked up there in the police station, because those people were working under the captain's orders. They must obey the captain." Mr. Chastanet don't want the boat to remain in Dominica so he pull out a book of checks (he was a big man—he was the harbor master in St. Lucia) and he sign one check and put it on the desk.

"All right, Mr. Chastanet. I will send the harbor master to take off my galvanized chain upon your boat and put your iron chain back."

Mr. Chastanet say to me, "Charles, you are going with us from now on."

Now Captain Bristol believe that everything was all right. "Charles, what is up? Is everything all right?" "Yeah." He ask Mr. Chastanet if he could take passengers and cargo as before. We load on the cargo but we don't take no rice or dasheen. We take passengers from Martinique and carry them up. We reach St. Lucia and come by the wharf. When we get up I throw the rope, *feeeew,* and put it nicely. I help the passengers with their grips and I go and call the crew list at customs. Monday was payday. Now my job was to get Captain Bristol's pay and carry it to his wife. He have many girls. He was making so much money for all he was doing that he got enough money to surprise the girls he have outside.

I go up to Mr. Chastanet's and I tell him the captain tell me to do as usual. "Do as usual. Well, usual is the end of it today. Here's the envelope for the captain. And here's the next one to drop for the captain, and tell him don't put his foot on my deck again!"

I laugh. When I reach his house I say to his wife, "Madame, here are two envelopes for Captain Bristol, one for a week's salary, one for a week's notice. And Mr. Chastanet say to tell him not to put foot on his deck again."

"What?" Bristol had never told his wife that he was in trouble in Dominica. Madame take out the last letter, open it, and read what Mr. Chastanet said. Then she find out what Bristol do in Dominica. When Bristol come down from his girl friend's to his wife, he believe everything was nice—he came down the road like a big bull. In a week his belly had come flat, flat, flat, and you know he was a big man. When I saw him, I say, "Hahaha, Mr. Bristol. Your pants can't fit you now, eh?" We never see him in St. Lucia again. One day I meet him in passing. I say, "You're going to be back young again, man."

"I thought you were dead."

"I still going on strong. I still alive. Where are you going?" He say he was working on that boat but those men tell me he not even captain. The damn fool and all that he made. Now he's only a crew.

Fishing

WHEN I FINISHED with Bristol I went back to fishing. I hustling. Sometimes those days looked so long. Every day is fishing day, but not every day is catching day. You got two pants, four shirts. Where there is no fish and you feel the shortage you got to sell one to give the child something. You still have one pants. If you come out today—you know the way you leave the house—if you coming with something you feel bright, you have a good mind, but if you come with an empty bucket you not feeling good or bad. When you've got it—going up in the harbor there—you're feeling big, but when you see the quantity of people right by the wharf and you have an empty boat you don't want to go in. I go to sea already and, when I see that I ain't catch nothing, I don't come back up. No. I go in a place in Lagon, a hole up there to windward of the land. I pull the boat up and I sleep there the night. I go and get a breadfruit and I roast it. In the night I get a thing you call a "soldier" [soldier crab]. I see it coming upon the horn. I give one lash, I prick it, scrub it in the sea water, and I roast it. I eat like I have the best dinner. I save a crab leg. I open it and take out the flesh. I rub it up on the hook and I slack it and I start to catch flying fish. When it was about eleven o'clock—dolphin. I catch a few dolphin. Three o'clock I come into the harbor. I feel great. I feel a man. When I come in now, I full of fish. My people were crying. They said last night they don't sleep because people say that they would bring sugar and coffee to make my wake. I say, "Listen, let me tell you something. After today, when you see I go to sea and you don't see me tonight, remain three days. If you see three days and you don't see me, well, then you could make my wake."

When you're fishing you follow no man. You're taking your own mark and you're using your own sense. I go my way, you go yours. A man tell me once, "Why didn't you follow King? Follow him tomorrow down by the Pitons. There they're taking flying fish and you will get flying fish." I was so vexed I turn my back and I leave this same man. You must follow your own sense. Perhaps a man certain sure he going to catch flying fish in a certain place, and you stop in another place and you meet the fish more than he. I do that many times. And sometimes again, if you meet the tide going up, that's what you want. The tide going up outside will take you outside upon the fish. The more you go, the more you picking up fish. If you follow someone, when the man see you catching the fish, he just let go the rudder, and what become of you? Now the man picking up all your flying fish. The man see you catching fish down there, so he just let go the rudder. Look out, for he coming on your backside now and he got all your fish. You could quarrel, you could say what the hell you like, but the sea don't belong to you. That's why I say follow no man.

Yes, you must have sense to fish. All the boats have a bailing hole for the water to run. When you catch flying fish you throw them in the bailing hole. You break his gill to make him bleed, and all the time he there bleeding. Now the limber hole giving you water and the flying fish making it blood water and that same water you send in the sea. All right, you're taking four or five flying fish and you pung [pound] them fine, fine, fine. Put them in the bailing hole and then take three or four buckets of water and throw them in the bailing hole. Next you take some dry coconut, grate it, grate it, grate it, and when you finish send it outside the boat. Now, where this thing going to go, there will be a calm, and Mr. Flying Fish drinking that water and eating the coconut. They come red. When you see they come down, slack your net up and you slack the next net up. And you got a thing they call a "kali," each time you dip it, the kali[1] full. Sometimes you got to throw some out to put the kali aboard. All right. You don't touch the net yet. You bring all the net at one time and then you start to take off flying fish from the net. Every time you're taking off flying fish you're slacking the net, taking off flying fish and slacking the net. Sometimes, before you finish slacking you're done full already. If not, you got the next net there and you got to pull it. When you finish the boat is full of flying fish and you go straight by the wharf.

Ah, this thing you call a fisherman—it's a terrible job. Sometimes you get caught in fog.[2] One time I was jam in it. When we was going the fog was not so heavy, but when we was coming back, one could not see another. When we meet two or three boats at one time, they ask us where the land was. I tell them, "If you follow me you will be safe."

"Ah, you don't know nothing."

"All right." I gone. Quite the next day they were coming in—everywhere. Just like a wild goat. When the storm pass they stand stupid. "Where the land, where the land?" But I gone and you know where I went? I jam right to La Baie [Castries Harbor] and I going to *slack-bam* right in town. When you leave you must remember to check your course and when you return back you must check back your course. But they went like new sheep that go in a pasture. When you let them go they can't come back at the master's house. Anywhere a man going to sail, as you leave you must watch behind your back to see your course. If the wind is blowing hard and gives you a fast drift, you figure the distance you left, and when you leave you know how to get back in. You've got to know the currents. Sometimes you will get three currents in a day. One will take you out early in the morning. Then about two o'clock it picks you up and carrying you inside under the land. Now you don't kill yourself. If you miss the fish, it dragging you inside gradually and you let it go. All the time you're going to see a few fish coming. A good while—some more. You will stick there because it not going against you now. That tide going in your favor and you don't care if you reach at twelve o'clock because you know you will catch fish. But now in the night, the tide going up. You see the boats mad to go in. *Bam,* the tide is going up. When you see the wind fall and give you a little bit of calm, you're going to tell yourself don't worry again because those fish in the bottom, they cannot come up. The wind and the sea is too rough. They strike deep in the chamber. Every fish got a chamber. Don't you think because a fish is in the sea that he is going everywhere in the bottom. No, every fish got his chamber. Blackfish and porpoise sleep together. They doesn't sleep wild but have their hole, just like you. They got fish right down to the bottom. This is redfish—I call that "bottom fish." You got to send down a piece of lead on your line with twelve or six footing hooks right to the bottom of the sea to catch this kind of fish. Redfish is nice, decent, clean fish. Now that's the fishing ground. When you go more far you will catch a different fish, because this fish is at about a hundred and forty feet. It has a round head and its scale is brown, but it is a redfish. They call him "gros zie" [French *gros yeux*]—a big-eyed fish—in Patois. A small, lovely fish, but you have to go far to windward of the land to catch this fish and you have to have a sinker and seven or eight heavy hooks. Any time you hook this fish, what I call the "cutter" will try and take some of it—a shark or barracuda. The barracuda they call the "watchman of the sea"—anytime you hook a fish, he grabs it and cuts the line. As you bring up your fish, he coming up heavy—you hear *gugu.* Catch it—that will be a barracuda. You must use wire or you will lose everything. When you hook a kingfish in the bottom of the sea, when he shakes his head you lose every hook you have on the line, but if all the line is a long wire going down to the bottom, when he gravels he can't cut it.

It was a kingfish that make me lose my thumb. It was before-day morning and I meet a piece of wood in the water. That's what they call a treasure—all kind of fish are under it. Now I was so in a hurry to tie the bait—if I had put down my hand I wouldn't have gotten injured—but I held the bait, like this, and the fish cut me from here. And the doctor had to cut my thumb off to save my life. I was a way out there off the land. At first I don't know I get damaged so much. They take a piece of cloth and tied it up, but it bleed and bleed and bleed and come big, so. After a good while I begin to feel giddy. They carry me straight to the hospital. I reach there about nine o'clock. They say, "Case of ten, case of ten, immediately" and they carry me into the operation room, take off my clothes, and give me a kind of white robe to put on. When I was going under the operation I see a man quite a ways up there, and the old clothes on him.[3] I watching. I lay down, but I watching. I see about five boys on top of my face and then I gone. When I get up—pepper in me hand. My hand burn up twice with fire. I ask for some whiskey, and they give me a pill in a glass of water. I went back again. When it was about three o'clock I got up from me sleep, but my hand still burning me. The sister come and give me a big tumbler and tell me to drink it: milk and brandy. She give me one injection, and I lay down upon the bed again and I get sleepy. When it was about twelve o'clock I was hungry. After I wake up I call her and tell her so, but she say, "I can't give you nothing but a glass of milk."

"My God," I say, "I won't be here at daybreak!" Well, she put a pill in a glass and it bubbled and she give it to me to drink. I sit down there and I don't stop ten minutes before I go back to sleep. In the morning I get up and they give me tea. I make four days there before I come out, and I bet you can't tell me what I done the very day I come out. The hand was done up all the way up my arm. I tell the doctor I feel all right, and he say, "Well, you can go." I put on my clothes and I go up. When I reach by the wharf, I see my captain there. The captain vexed. I ask him what was the matter. He tell me he only have two men and he want to go to sea.

"All right. I coming."

"You can go to sea?"

"Yes. Tell my woman I go to sea." I put my sea clothes on and I go. I go to sea and I start to catch fish. I fishing flying fish. In a good while we see a blackfish. "Blackfish, I tell you!"

The captain say, "What do you say now?"

"Man, pull your line. I tell you blackfish. Pull your line. Hurry

up!" The same time I pull all the line and put it there in a corner.
"You ready?"

"Yes."

I say, "O.K., let her go." As we reach the blackfish I say, "You
fucker. I got to make it." We watch. We down too low. I say,
"Keep up, keep up, keep up. *Boom bang! boodubooduboodu* [noise
of the blackfish]. Hold that, hold that, hold a bomb." I have a
next harpoon—fast—throw the iron. You know what happened?
The bandage come off the hand. It start to bleed. I forced the vein
with the weight I made. When I pull the rope, the rope pull the
plaster off, and you know that plaster was sticked hard. The captain, he have an old patched pants and he pull his feet out of
them. He naked now—all his body was outside and he show
everything. He help me tie my hand. I could do nothing again.
We hustle. Everyone start to use the cutlass, chopping all the fish
to put it in the boat, in big chunks, you know. The blubber was
humbugging us. When they finish, straight to the hospital. I
have an old pants on me and when the doctor see me, he said,
"Charles, where have you come from? You were discharged today." I say nothing. "Charles?"

"I do not go home. I go to sea."

"You mean to tell me you went to sea today? You're foolish."

"Get a pan and send your servant down by the market and I'll
give you some liver to eat."

"You're not leaving here today."

I go into my same bed and lay down. He give me an injection
and he shove the hand in hot water and he take off the blood of
the blackfish. Now I frightened. What kind of fever catch me? I
feel terrible. I don't want to die like that. The doctor tell me I
would get better. "Tomorrow morning you will go home at your
house." The next morning he dress me early and tell me to come
back later in the day. When I reach I find them chopping a
blackfish. People, people, people everywhere. I just come in and
said, "Morning."

"Morning." My hand all bound up like that and I sit down. The
captain say, "Give him a piece."

I say, "Not one piece of blackfish would I give my mother!" They finish cutting and I go to collect the papers. The fishseller weighs each tray on a scale and gets a paper telling the amount. We share the money and I go home, but I don't stay there to get better. I go to Dominica to meet my aunt. I take the loss of my finger to heart and I say it was no use fishing. When I reach my aunt's she tell me, "You is a fool. Lots of people lost a thumb and they living." And she make me something like a little purse to shove my hand in. It have a buckle and when I come to take hold of a line, it protect it. So I go back to fishing.

You know shark? Well, I strike a lizard shark there with a piece of iron with all my strength. After I strike the lizard my head hurt me. I give him the next harpoon. He watch me, so. I say, "Aha, I don't give no more lash." I pull the spade. I give about three hits with the iron spade and I sink it in, so. Then he shake his tail. He shake his tail and I kill the whole body, put it in the boat. They take it in the market. Nobody will buy it—a penny a pound. When they come, the head too ugly. Tomorrow morning when we reach we got to throw carbolic acid on the fish and they give it to the cat. That's lizard shark—no good. Now we got a next shark again. He got two horns—the hammerhead—with two eyes. I catch that already in the fishing ground. I put the slack on my line and the next thing I see I have a big one. It was big! All right. We cut off the head. We throw the head over because it is very terrible. The balance of the fish guts we corn [salt and dry] and we cut up the body and put it inside the boat. When we reach by the market it sell like hot bread. I catch lion shark too. We have a strike and he breach in the air. He breach again. I get the line in my hand. He fell, *budu, budu*. You know what happen? We have a kind of big hook, understand? We did not put the flying fish like this across. I put the flying fish straight. Then I tie it tight and I toss the wire. Now when the shark see that fish in the water like that, he swallow the fish. Then he swallow the hook in his mouth, and it hook him in his guts. Now he crazy. Each time he come to fall, pick up the slack. Don't let the twine mix with his tail, because the tail is sharp and will cut it. He roll like this. I say, "Well, if you going down to the bottom, go down." You know what the shark do? He go down to the bottom and arrive on Daddy's boat, like this. And he eyes don't blink at all. He watching you. I just hold the line. Each time he fall, I pull. Each time he blast, I hold the line. He fall and he get up again. Now I watching so the shark won't fall in the boat—that's all. The fellow so frightened, he left his place and he stand by the gun. I was watching. I say, "Set the gun and put the pin in action. When I tell you 'fire' you will fire." He watch. He say that the fish blast. "Start the engine. Follow him." When we reach I say, "Fire!" He take it right there—*bam! budu*—and he fall, the harpoon right there, so. It have sixteen little one in it. That day I believe I have a lucky chance. But a shark so wicked. You put the fish in the boat and you believe the fish is dead. Remember his teeth. One man left a shark, so, in the boat. Now he catch an albacore and he come to pull to land it. He miss his step and he fall in the lion shark. When he pull back all his arm is gone—because the mouth done lock and the shark got three row of teeth. What you got to do—put the albacore on board, crank the engine, and straight to the hospital. The doctor got to cut all this, and when he come out he hasn't got an arm.

A next man fall in a canoe. He fall in the sea and when he fall the shark get him. By the time we reach hospital, he dead.

Ah, you think I don't suffer, too? I had a whaler to fish with as well as my canoe. A whaler is bigger than a canoe. A canoe turns over quick, for there is no room to save yourself. But my whaler, ah, child, if I reveal what happened to me you will be surprised and you will be sorry. I got my whaler after I came out from Barnard's, but it sink when a St. Vincent man tried to drown me. I left Conway, going to Soufriere to fish. When I reached in Soufriere Friday night, everybody there tell me, "Why did you come here? There is no fish." And when I went at the lady's who was going to put me up, she say to me, "No flying fish here."

I just say as a joke, "Ah, you damn fool. Tomorrow I will give you plenty."

"Carlo, where are you going to get them?" She tell me that she had some sprats corned for months, and nobody would buy them. Now everybody come and buy all. At the same time she was telling me this, a girl come and tell the lady, "Your cousin said, 'Come and send your basket for some sardines.' " She give her basket to the girl, but she come back and say the man had sold all the sardines. "You mean to tell me the man send and call me and then he sell it to somebody else?"

I say, "What are you quarreling for? You will get fish tomorrow."

"Nobody in Soufriere can catch fish, so you think you will!"

The next morning a fellow called "Shampoo" come and ask me where I was going to get flying fish. He say, "Man, if you is hungry, you is hungry. I will give you twenty-five cents to get something to eat, but there is no use trying to get flying fish because you are wasting time."

I tell him to keep the twenty-five cents. "When I come back you can give it to me."

Beyond Canaries I meet a riffle [tidal edge or tide rip] going up, and on top of the riffle was some kind of water grass. I see two flying fish jump on the riffle and I rush the boat inside and I stop the motor. I lower the sail and I shake my basket. Flying fish cover it. I load the boat with fish right in the riffle, and when I come in the same man which tell me he was going to give me twenty-five cents meet me. "See what you bring. You fill the boat with sand. We ain't buy sand here." I don't answer. I just lower the sail and pull in the boat. There was two of us—a St. Vincent man and I. When they see us everybody came to see. "Oh, flying fish! Flying fish!" Everybody came and we sell, we sell, we sell at three for four pence. We sell all the flying fish, and Peter called for his share. I give it to him, and he go into the rum shop and drink with common people. After, he go with a young girl and he sleep. Tomorrow morning he don't have one cent. They take all. He come down but he ain't tell me nothing. I say, "What are you going to cook for dinner? You have some fish there?"

"Me no got money."

"Where you leave your money?"

"Man, the whore I go sleep with last night, she take every cent."

"What?"

"Man, I telling you. I went to sleep with a girl and during the time I was sleeping—when I get up I haven't got a cent in my pocket. And I don't even see the girl. I find the bed empty and me without my money."

I kill myself laughing. "You mean to tell me, Peter, you haven't got a cent?"

"No, the girl picked my pocket. I ain't got nothing."

"Well, what are you going to eat today?"

"If you lend me something I going to buy some farine and I got some fish that I going to eat."

"All right. Here is a dollar, but I ain't cooking here. I'm going to eat at home where I put it up." He take the dollar and go and drink fifty cents rum. Then he come up where I was staying to eat. He sit down there, eating, and ask me if I don't want to go have a drink. I don't feel tired, but I say I feel sleepy and I pick up myself and go into the bedroom and lay down. As he finish eating the last piece of fish he leave.

The next day, Monday, we go to sea. We catch some flying fish and some albacore. I say, "Well, I'm not going back in Soufriere. I am going up in town."

Peter tell me, "No. I'm not going in town. You remain here."

"No, I'm not going to remain here."

He said, "We're not going. Let's go into Soufriere."

"I'm not going to Soufriere. I'm going up in town."

"I tell you, we're not going to town. You can go in town. I'm not going. I will remain here."

"Give me the boat." I take the boat from the fishing ground. When you cut the corner to go in Soufriere right by the sand and the bananas there, I say, "About." And I go about. I was going up in town. He take the boat and went right on the beam with it, and when the flow hit, he didn't slack the main sheet. It was a lucky thing I didn't go by the main sheet because he might have done me something. I was standing up so inside the boat, up on top. I was studying—"Tonight I go to pictures because I got money." I saw that in my mind. He didn't want his wife to know that the whore had stolen all his money, so he told her before he knew I was going up in town that he was staying in Soufriere. The boat went bottom up and then bottom down. I say, "Ah, you sink my boat." That time I was overboard. When the wave pick him up he screamed. I say, "Fuck you. You sink my boat." He thought I was a fool, that I would come and hold him to save him. "You sink my boat. I'm not going to save you." When he go down he opened his hand, so, and I just went *shhh*, and the wave break, *boooom*, over his head. I ain't see him up 'til now. He had a big cafu [heavy sweater] on him, and when this thing filled with water, where could he go? You know this kind of big bird they call "dashee" [perhaps a frigate bird]—dashee cover me because all the flying fish were floating in the water. The albacore went down to the bottom. I lost everything—all the fish money I had in the boat, all the corn fish I did corn, and all the dasheen I bought already.

I have a long bamboo pole about the size of your leg. You got that on board in case the boom break. When I see the bamboo floating I take it and put it between my legs, and I start to paddle the bamboo with my hands. Sea, sea everywhere. When the bamboo dive, I dive. I shut my eyes. There was a man on top of the hill that saw everything, and he ran to the station, and they send three boats. I swam from two o'clock 'til six o'clock when it was making dark. I was naked as I was born. There was nothing heavy on me, but I was weak because too many waves strike me. As the first boat reach me I just told the gentleman, "Turn my head." He lift me up, and I never knew nothing again. They took me to the dispensary in Canaries, and I stopped there fifteen days. I never knew that I was in the dispensary. It was when I got up in the middle of the night. I see my head on a white lady's lap and all 'round me was a big blanket and a lot of big hot water bottles. I didn't know the nurse and I said, "Miss, what's wrong?"

"What's wrong? Don't you know where you came from?"

I said, "No."

The next morning when I opened my eyes my neck was stiff and I couldn't open my jaw. They had to give me a kind of cup with a beak to drink, but I couldn't have any food. They rub all my back and neck with something called chichima[4]—a thing like ginger—you pung it and you beat it in a cup with fine salt. That night they bring food for me—a cup of macaroni with egg. They tell me they can't give me heavy food yet. The nurse ask me how I feeling. I say all right but I was still covered with hot water bottles and I still felt cold. She tell me, "God didn't want you yet."

The priest was sending milk for me every morning, and when I start to eat people from Canaries send me eggs and tea. When the priest come he ask me if I wanted to confess. I tell him, "Yes, father." He said he would come the next morning. He came and I confessed.

All the time I was in the dispensary, what do you think I was studying? My money I lost in the boat. All the time I was there. There was a tourist boat in, full of white people, and they came all about, visiting. They said, "Here is a survivor," and told them that my trade was a fisherman, that my boat sank, and one man drowned. The tourists came and found me on the bed, so. The nurse took the money for me and tell me to shove it under my pillow.

I come out from there on Saturday. The nurse bring me a razor and ask me if I could shave. I say yes and when she bring me a mirror I see my face in a hole—deep, deep, deep and beard all around. When I shaved my face felt light. The priest gave me clothes—and you know the priest was a big priest—the pants I put on me could take two men, and I was just like a sprat in the shirt. I had to shove the hat on my head, so. They tell me to stand by, get ready, because I was going up to Castries at my house. The priest took me down to the boat and said, "You're going with Johnny Monrose. A safe voyage." Johnny Monrose had a coast boat.[5] Jesus Christ, I was worse than a diver with the pants and shirt, and here me going to sea with a crowd of people. I was 'shamed and sat down in the corner upon a bench. Johnny Monrose come up and say, "Carlo, you try for your bread and you almost lost your life. That is no good." He brought me to sit down in the stern. "Have you eaten?"

I said yes because I did not feel to eat. I sat down studying what I had lost—the money, the fish, and the food I was carrying home for my child. The tear come up in my eye, and Johnny Monrose ask me, "What you cry for? God give you your life back. What you lost, God going to give it to you."

I say, "Mr. Monrose, you say that, but I have got a family. Now look, I am going up there with an empty hand and today Saturday. I don't know what we are going to do."

He tell me, "I'd rather you didn't have a cent and God done save your life." When the boat reach by the wharf Mr. Monrose say, "Don't move from there before I come to meet you."

"Yes, Mr. Monrose." Everybody on the wharf saying, "They bring Mr. Charles. Come and see Mr. Charles." Mr. Monrose tell a boy go and get a car to take me up at my home—I was living in Conway at the time. When the car come everyone give me a hand. Mr. John tell the man that he would pay him when he come back, but the man say, "Don't worry. I won't take no money for Mr. Charles." Then Mr. Monrose put me in the car and shove some money in my hand, all wrapped up small. I don't take time to watch it then. I sat down in the car, and the man put me in Conway, right at my house. I go into my yard and I see my people sitting down, so. My wife did not expect me, because they told her that they don't know when I would come up. As Edith see me she come and grab me and start to cry. As she cry she tell me, "Charlo, don't go to sea again." I had three child there—two small ones and the next little one—and nothing for them. I watched those child like that and I grab the little one and kiss her and I go inside. I counted the money they gave me because I was a survivor and it was twelve dollars. And Mr. Johnny Monrose had wrapped up twenty dollars. I changed my clothes and I dress myself good. I tell my wife, "I give you twenty dollars paper. Try your best with that. It is American money. You've got to go and change that and do what you need to do." I put the balance of the money in my pocket.

"Tell me, Charlo, where are you going?"

"I go at Barnard's store."

When I got down to Barnard's, Mr. Barnard said, "Well, well, well! That's what you were looking for. You was working for me. You leave me and go buy a boat and go in the ocean. Now you nearly remain in the ocean. Eh? You like it so? Sit down. What do you say now? See the result you have. You're not going to sea any more."

I say, "Didn't you nearly get drowned?"

He tell me, "Yes."

"And you're still rowing in *Spindrift*."

"But, I'm not going the places I use to go before."

"Well," I say, "there are many ships sinking in traveling, and that don't mean no boats go sailing. I will tell you something now. You tell me not to go, and I'm telling you that next week I will bring a surprise for you."

"What surprise?"

"I don't know, but I'll bring a surprise for you. Remember you tell me not to go to sea, eh?"

"All right. Now, tell me how you feel."

"Not so good yet."

"I understand you lost everything."

"I haven't got nothing at all."

"Miss Osborne."

"Sir?"

"Give Charles twelve dollars."

When I come back my food was rice. Do you know I couldn't eat the rice? My stomach couldn't take the gravy. When the doctor come at my house he tell me I can have soup, flour, pap, and plain rice. So my wife take a fish and boil it and give me the water to drink. I drink fish water for three days.

After a week I go outside and I watch the sea. Everybody was going to sea. There was a boat there that don't have a captain, and a fellow tell me to go and ask the owner if I could have his boat. I went up to the man.

"How are you feeling?"

"All right." I say, "What about the *Christiana?* She haven't got no captain?"

He tell me, "You could take it anytime you want it."

"Anytime?"

"Yes."

I see a man standing there and I went and tell him, "I get the *Christiana.* Look out you're going up tonight. Here is two shillings. Buy stores for me and look for a next man to work the jib. We're going up."

"What time are we leaving?"

"I'm leaving at eight o'clock because it's far to windward of the land, you know."

That night we went up under the land until you pass La Baie. It's just like a gate and when you bust the gate you see the open savannah. You could see here, you could see there, you could see all about, but you're there and no land now. You just lie down, so, and you going on up the road. There is only one thing you can do, go down to the bottom or go up the road. As you go by Gros Islet you reach a place where you hear, *golu, golu, golu* and you see sea, I tell you. It's like a pot boiling. You got to ease your hand, like that. All right. We go up, we go up, we go up. When I watch I find I am upon my right mark. When you find the Piton peak between two mountains that is the mark, the boundary. You call that Grand Sec and when you are up there, there are two things you must watch for. If you turn over, they have a boat that will save you. But if the boat does not come you got to remain there. Or if you see the weather give you a sign, take yourself off from there. If you have sail, pull your boat up and go down. If you have an engine, don't you put no headway in the engine. Just let it go medium because with the riffle and the sea the boat going to dive too much for you.

All right. When I reach the mark I heard *boodu.* I say, "I see something. Is that fish doing that?"

The other man tell me, "Yes, Mr. Charles."

I say, "Look here. Take that biggest head of line you see there and put the big hook on it. Put on a whole flying fish."

He tell me, "Yes."

"Good."

"Bust the jib!" The boy bust the jib and, Jesus Christ, tail breaking in the dark. When it came again I see it, and the thing shine like gold. "Cut me a flying fish." I don't have time to read the mark on the line as we put it over. Before day break we have three albacore. When the sun starts to bust, small fish come up and the big fish go down. All night the big fish come up to eat the small ones. Well, when the big ones go down to the bottom to rest the little ones come up to get something to eat. So we change the line at daybreak and put a small line and a smaller hook under the flying fish belly. You split the belly in half and you put in the hook and tie it. You call that a "turn well." We load the boat with fish.

Now the trouble is this. My wife don't know where I had gone, because I don't tell she I was going out tonight. I had had dinner already, and she believed I had gone out to the pictures. When I go out I don't have to tell nobody. I am a big man already. The little boy say, "Mama, shut the door."

"If I do that, where is your father going to sleep?"

He say, "You will not see my father tonight."

"Where he go?"

"I don't know, but Daddy not coming tonight."

"Look here. Will you tell me where your father go? Do you know?"

"Yes, I know where my father go."

"You aren't telling me?"

"No."

She say, "Give me the knife."

"You can kill me now, but I won't tell you. I know we will see Daddy tomorrow."

She say, "I don't believe Charles would go to sea last night."

The boy, who had come outside, say, "Yes, Daddy go to sea." Jesus Christ. The lady start to quarrel. Now the man who lived next to us was going out and he called to her and said, "Come here. What you quarrel like that for? Charles is a man. He not coward. Death is everywhere. He could be dead by you. Charles has got three child inside the house. He is going to go and get something to give you to eat."

"But he could look for something else to do. I don't want him to go to sea again."

"I bet you tomorrow morning when Charles comes you are very glad."

About eleven o'clock the little boy was outside there watching for his father. "Mama, Papa coming. Look the boat." She come outside with the little child in her arms and watched. She see the boat coming. If the boat have no fish, it go in this side, but if it have fish it go the next side by the marketplace. She see where I was going and come down. I called to her. She say, "Hello."

"Come."

She come and she look in the boat and she laugh. But she say, "You think I friends with you?"

"What I do?"

"What you do! You don't have no son of mine."

I say, "You fool. I bring you fish."

The people there say, "Ha, you was quarreling, but you won't quarrel with what you have in your hand."

I unload my fish and leave it by the market for the woman to sell. But the fish is too much for she one to sell. I take four pounds of albacore and I open the albacore guts. The best part of an albacore is the head and the guts. The flesh is just like common, common food. It's dry. I take off the liver because it's the sweetest—the liver sell more than the fish. I pick up the whole three guts. I give the captain one, the boat-steerer one, and the boy one, because there were three of we. Mine was the big one and I carry it home, put it in the pan and *aahh,* I eat. I send two young bonita to Mr. Barnard for his surprise.

My wife tell me, "You went to sea, Charles."

I say, "If I sit down and say I'm not going to sea, who would give you support?"

"You could get a friend to work for you."

I say, "Not me."

The next night she ask, so, "Charlo, are you going to sea?"
"Yes."
"What are you going to carry now?"
"Make some bakes[6] for me. Give me bakes and fish and full me a flask of tea, but don't give me any coffee."
"All right." When it was not yet eight o'clock the child take the hand bag and the box of line. She say, "Good night, Charlo."
"Good night, dear."
"Sails, make a good trip."
"O.K."
"One thing—if you find Golu boiling, come back, eh?"
I say, "O.K." She was the one who let the rope go. We ain't quarreling again. The next day I hook a little albacore. The sea was so black you could not see nothing. When I look I see this fish—he was red under the water and his eye don't beat. I say, "Jesus Christ, that's a billfish [swordfish]. Oh God, give me strength." I hold the box and I take the first little fish I caught. I put a hook there and one hook there and I make the two so they come together. I throw it overboard and feed it through the line. He take it right away. When he swallow it he turn his back. I put me foot on the rail and I bend over. He bend me back, and I bend again. I say, "You can't break this, sonny. That won't allow you to go too far because I will get at the warp."

I say to the other man, "Hold it. If you see he gives slack, take the slack in, but don't slack back." I went forward and I picked up the harpoon. "Let him come." When the fish was close I sent off the harpoon, right in the guts. He wet, he beat, he wet, he beat. I say, "You can't go away." He so big. When he come we throw the rope. Now we start to give him the lance. When we kill him we take the hook and put him inside. The boat sit down the fish so big, and that boat could carry three blackfish and still it ain't full. We take a rope and tie the tail and straight to market. I can't tell you what kind of taste he have because the flesh was too old. Me ain't want that. I sell it and I catch young bonita and dolphin, and I eat that, but the billfish is too old for me. Let it go to market, it's fifty cents a pound. Lots of people buy it, though.

I've killed many many billfish. Sometimes you're towing and as you see the flying fish raise, *boodu*, look out, your line going to go because the billfish going behind the flying fish you have on the hook. It going to swallow it and you are sure to kill it.

I catch a fish already—his body just like a plane. The back of it was black and under the belly was white. We harpoon that fish, but up to now we don't know what kind of fish it is. The teeth was as a feather. I know people say it was a young whale. When we bring it by the wharf everyone come and see. And it sell because everyone says, "Whale, whale." He going, he going. "Whale, whale, whale," I say whale too—I say it's a young whale and I get it sell—because it don't have no bad head. He was just like a porpoise, but he big. Everybody say it was a young whale, but I don't know. It was the money I wanted.

All right. You know tockle [turtle]? We got three kind of tockle. We got one, his fat green in color.[7] We got a next one, we take his bone and make all kind of nice things—brush, comb and everything.[8] And we got one now, just the color of the land snake. You take his bone—making wristwatch.[9] He come big as that. I harpoon one right behind his tail in Vieux Fort at eleven o'clock in the day. When it was twelve o'clock in the night I was out far below the Piton, beating up. The tockle take me from under Piton and bring me straight in Laborie—without no sail, nothing at all. Everything low down, and he oneself towing the boat, coming straight to Laborie Harbor. You call it "cowette"—a kind of black-and-white tockle. It stinking fresh. When we reach there the thing was big. Seven people give me hand to put it inside the boat. All right. Tomorrow morning I carry it to Vieux Fort to sell. We take three stall, and people selling it. How much do you think for? Three pence a pound. When they see all the tockle there nobody don't want to buy it. So we go and get three barrels and we salt it and put it in the barrels. Saturday when we was going up to Castries, we put the three casks in the whaler and we go up with it. We reach there about eight o'clock in the morning, roll the casks by the market. By the time it say twelve o'clock, you couldn't find a bone of that kind of tockle in the market. Three pence a pound, they didn't want it in Vieux Fort. We sell it at one-and-six a pound in Castries. People fighting—"Give me three pounds, give me four pounds." I gone. I ain't stop there because I won't eat that. I give a policeman some liver off that. He give some to my second cousin. The next day the man call me to come. When I go he say, "Charles, my wife left that for you. Taste that." When I taste the liver, it just like cow's liver, it so sweet.

I say, "Jesus Christ, I think I didn't know. I give that man my fish liver."

My cousin say, "The next time you make all that misery in the night with that tockle, don't let the dumb policeman enjoy the best part of the fish." From that time when we catch a tockle the first thing we take off is the liver.

You've got to have sense to fish, and to fish up to windward of the land you've got to be a hero. You leaving this morning and you meet nice, nice, nice weather. By two o'clock you still see nice weather. Around half-past three you just see something come out to windward of the land. It dark, dark, dark, and it bring sea and wind. If you don't have the sense to get away from it, what become of you? One morning when I reach out there fishing we catch two albacore. A fellow tell me, "Mr. Charles, what's that?" I see the sky come out there, red like fire. I said, "Lift up the boat for me, please." I lift up the boat myself and down the road. When it strike me, it catch me below Gros Islet, but it cannot meet me because I was hugging the land going down. One boat remain up there. The man was a believer. His boat turn upside down. He sits ashore now and he never go out in sharp weather. A coward man live long. There are two captains you know: Captain Goodweather and Captain Badweather. After a breeze there is calm. I won't rush it. Wind raise sea. No wind, no sea—because it's a male and a female. The sea is a female. The wind is male. Sometimes you see a hell of a big mountain. I've climbed the mountain already. The bird up there eating. I go up there and reach right on top of the mountain. I hook a fish. The boat stand up right on top of the mountain. I bring my fish alongside, put it inside the boat, slack the jib and down, so. Sometimes when you're coming down you see one mountain of whiteness in front of you. You've got to go on top of the mountain. Nothing will happen to you. That's God's work.

Listen, I take a boat from Conway and we went in the ocean to fish. As we're leaving by the wharf, a man there says he is going out to pick up a load of dolphin and come back. He thought he was Brother Mighty. When we reach the fishing grounds, you know what that man do? He want to double-cross me, so he go outside of me. He stand up and right between his two foot, *bam*, the thunder hit and burst open the boat. His two foot was in the boat and his head in the water. The Man up there showed him which one have more power. He have a green river knife [large sheath knife] and he was cutting bait with it. He left it right on the top there and when the thunder and lightning bust, it draw them. A green river knife is a dangerous thing to have in your boat. That's the sailorman's knife, but it draws the thunder. If you have it in the boat, shove it in the box line [line box], and use a common knife. It's a kind of dagger and when it cut you, it burns like pepper. The green river knife drew the thunder and both of them in the boat.

When we hear the *bam* I say, "Look at that! Well, boy, we can work no more. Let's go." A man bound to go and help when he see another boat in distress. If a man call you for help, and you do like you don't see him, if God helping that man and he reach shore, he will go straight to the harbor master, and it is you who they come and look for—lock you up and jail you—because he was in distress and you didn't stop.

I just come and take the boat and tie the two foot right there by the timber. I leave their two heads in the water the same way. Don't you touch the body! I went to the harbor master's office and I say, "There you are. You'll find the hole right there in the center of the boat. The flying fish they was cutting is there and the green river is right there in the water and that cause the two men's death. There is your witness." Four policemen and the doctor come down. They find the two men there, and the first thing the doctor said, "The green river killed them—it pulled the thunder and sank the boat." Although we bring these men from the ocean to the harbor master for three weeks they try to see if we going to change what we tell them. They laugh you up, saying, "You caused that man's death." The law don't want to know what you eat, but the law want to know how you dead. If a man come and say, "I going to kill you, I going to do you this or that," the law don't bother. It's after you dead they want to know what happen. For three weeks, when you come from sea, two policemen waiting for we. As we come, we take the fish, put it in the market, and run and give statement again. The same, the same.

When you hear that the breadfruit are ripe I know my time has come, because when the breadfruit are full in the tree the blackfish is a fool. His heart and his head are big with grease and oil and he cannot stay under the water in breadfruit season. Each time he goes down to the bottom, he got to come right back up.

When you going to chase the blackfish, the first thing you do is fix up the rope and put your harpoon on guard. You fix up four harpoons, two on each side and one upon the gun. And you have four extra balls of rope there ready. Join them together. Now those harpoons each has a rope upon it for when you shoot a fish. The moment you bring a fish alongside there may be other fish coming with it, and you don't have time to stop and rig those harpoons. You would be too late. Sometimes you just jump, take up the harpoon, and strike at the same time. *Feeee.* The fish won't tell the next one. But if you don't do that, you will have lost a chance. Now when you strike a blackfish you don't have no right to stop him. Let him run with all the slack. Let him go, and when you got about twenty-five fathom out, you stop him and you make a double turn around the whaler's bulls head.[10] Then you have enough slack and the harpoon cannot lift out. When the captain says, "Bounce," you take off a turn from the logger head and you have it in your hand. There's a man behind you now taking the slack, drawing all the time, all the time, all the time. The captain tell you, "Bounce"—he is the one you're listening to—"Bounce, bounce, bounce." You pull it steady. It's not the fish you're pulling. You're pulling the boat upon the fish. All the time you bounce, it's not the fish you bring. The fish is over there, and the boat is coming behind the fish. When it comes close to the fish you give him the second iron with the gun. Then you hear the captain tell you to battle him. Now you have two ropes on him. He cannot burst that, and you can do what you like. The two ropes would be bound together with a double turn and then passed around the block [the logger head]. They're pulling the fish now. The man behind you is taking the slack all the time. Hold on there. Take a double turn again. Then the fish kicking. He can't go with the two harpoons he's got there. When he comes close to you, you pick up the spade, the spade is broad, like that. You lay him back. *Bam.* When you hit him with the spade you pull it back and you strike him again. He start to "shoo." Now you don't strike him anywhere. You select the place—by the heart, by the liver. He shaking, like that. Make him take it inside. Then the captain will say, "Slack away." He start to beat with his tail now. "Slack away!" When he get a little way off he start to bawl, "*Mooo, mooo, mooo,*" and he dive. Slack away, slack away. Don't do nothing, don't pull him and *shooo,* he dead. Now we have to put him inside the boat. Then you cut the fish in half—you make three pieces. The first piece goes in the center, the next up in the bow, and the next one got to stand and trim. You must make sure it goes far enough aft for the propeller to catch the water. When you catch two and they is two big ones, put a rope under the second one's wing and tow it. It won't sink and it not bleeding. The shark would never come there because it believes it is alive the kind of way it following the boat. If you are stopped there for the night, tomorrow morning it start to spoil and start to drop oil. Shark going to say, "Good morning," and will go and meet it. Sometimes you will catch three at once— the father, the mother, and the calf. You've got to kill the calf first because the mother is bound to be around the child. It's just like a human—the mother crying. The time you hear the crying, *pow,* you have the mother there. You put the calf inside. You pull the mother there. Now the man get vexed. He goes up there and then comes down to bust the boat. When you see him coming, coming down, you watching. "Keep up, keep up!" "Fast!" Let the rope go. "Stop him." "Hold." I bounce him and he's dead.

One time I have four blackfish alongside. I call another fellow who haven't got any and ask him how much he would charge to take two fish beside the wharf. He's going to charge you something, you know. You got two fish dead, and he ain't got nothing. He tell me, "Well, I'm going to carry the two fish for you—one for me, one for you."

I say, "No. You charge for carrying the fish ashore. That's all." He say that he was going to charge me five papers apiece. "O.K." We cut it up and help him to put it in the boat. Then we in front, he behind. The same time he reach by the wharf I paid the money he charging, expressly so he won't touch no flesh of that blackfish. "Congo, here's your money," and they went at their home. But first they come tie their boat to mine. That night I lay down in the boat. I put a lantern on top of the deck and I take a nap with one eye shut and one eye open. At one o'clock in the night everyone get up and cut the fish—take off the big bone—put the fish aside, chop the next one. You're going to discharge the boat which is not yours first and send the fish in the market. When you get your money, you take off the money you paid for carrying the fish first and then you balance the shares. The boat gets half and the men share the other half. The man in the bailing hole gets a common share—he works too, you know—because each time the boat dive it full of water, and he's bailing. The harpooner will get two shares because he is the sticker. The harpoon is his, the coil of rope is his, the cartridges are his. Now if the blackfish gone with a coil of rope and a harpoon, it's not them that will pay for it. You get the trouble. You got to refund back the harpoon you lost, the pole you lost, and the coil of rope tomorrow. The boat steerer gets a share and a sixpence more a pound. Sometimes he come out good. The sticker won't keep company with the crew, but the boat steerer must be your friend. I want to take good care of my boat steerer because he could humbug you,[11] you know. You got to feed that man with a long spoon but good. When you tell him, "Keep up," he might not keep up, or if you tell him, "Stop her," he might give way and the fish would be gone.

Anybody could humbug you if you're not careful. Sometime they humbugging you in the step of the mast. They put "something" right in front there. When you go to fire the harpoon, it don't fire or the rod which is in the stand kicks back and throws you down. That's why you should never put the gun in front of you. You stop by the side of it so that when it kicks it don't catch you. Anyone can tie you.[12] They will come and fix you up in the night. That's why, when you come in the morning, the first thing you've got to do is to wash the boat from forward to aft with graisse lotion [fat]. And you have a kind of bush called Chardon beni,[13]—it have a prickle in it—you pung it and put it in the lotion. Then you wash the boat from forward to aft and throw the balance of the lotion inside the boat and leave it there, so. When you start to work, nothing can stop you. When the blood comes inside the bailing hole, you're bailing both of them together. That makes a nice ship. But if you're a damn fool you will have to take your wife's sheet to make a sail. You've got to have science [obeah] and you've got to have sense to work at fishing. Every day you go, every day you go, and every day you cry. You know you have three or four children in the house and a wife, and everybody brings fish but you can't get one. You ask yourself the question why. Because somebody put something on you. Now you got to take your wife's bed sheet to make a sail. She makes a sheet out of bags of flour cloth, but she makes it like a sail instead. Then you take the sheet and put it to soak in something[14] in a basin. When you dry it, don't squeeze it out and then nothing can happen to that boat, nothing can happen to it atall.

Sometimes they come in the night and chop your rope and carry it to the burying ground, or they will beg you for a piece of fish. If they carry that fish to the burying ground, you won't catch nothing. You is finished. You may as well carry your boat there—unless you is wise. You could feel a hundred fish and you won't catch none. You will lift up the harpoon and hit upon the fish, but it will bounce back. Something's wrong. Sometimes you fall overboard. The fish is so close to you, you can already see the dead fish. You see something pass like a shadow and overboard you go. When you go by the market, if a man asks you for a piece of fish, go to the lady who sells it and tell her to give it to him. He can't do you nothing because he buy it.

One time I went to sea for three months and I can't get nothing atall. For three months I was suffering. I nearly get jailed. One night I was so hungry I took the tow line and I climbed a coconut tree. I cut a bunch of coconuts and put them in the boat. I was starving. I say, "How could this be? Every day I going to sea and I don't catch nothing. There's a man tying me." I check myself. I remember this fellow told me, "Any day you come I will give you a slice of fish so you get your dinner but you won't catch none. Hahahaha." He laugh at me. And that was true, he was always full of fish, but I cannot catch none.

I went to Vieux Fort by the Indian man[15] He have a drugstore. I call him and asked him if he had something. He told me, "Yes."

I say, "All right, I want three shilling worth."

He tell me, "No. It's a dollar a drop."

"Give me three dollars."

In the night I go and wash the boat. I wash the harpoon, wet the rope, put some in the bucket of line. I light a fire and smoke everything—open the sail, open the bait box, smoke the boat inside, and smoke the boat outside. I make a tea and all the crew drink it. At one o'clock we leave and I meet the same man in the ocean. I tell him nothing. I give him no chance. I cover him with my sail—I was on top of he. I just take the water of my boat, smell it, and sent it down to him. One man say, "I smell something that's smelling sweet."

When it was time for daybreak I had three big albacore on board already. I went up and I reach a piece of wood on the sea. I tremble. There were all kinds of fish under that piece of wood— dolphin, kingfish, bourse. I lower the sail down and load my boat with fish. Then I set me sail straight for Castries and tomorrow morning I by the market there.

One time I went to sea and we strike two blackfish. We towed one alongside. As we reach Vieux Fort we start to cut the next one up and put it aboard. The owner of the boat, Captain Durocher, brought a bottle of rum. "Here is a bottle of rum, Charles. Drink your full and I will share the money with you after."

How the hell will you know your business if you're drunk? I told the man, "No sir, when we're done, share the money. Everybody going to have their money in their pocket, then we can bust the bottle, but before that, no."

"Oh," he said, "You are a ringleader. I will put your ass ashore. You don't make me ruin my boat. I say to drink."

"No!" I pick up the bottle and put it aside. "If you believe you is a man strong enough, come and take it." Nobody moved, but he said he was going to put me ashore. That night I meet the man at the rum shop and he told me, "I have a new man better than you. I put you off ashore."

I said, "Thank you. Do you think I would come in your boat?" You know what I did? I said, "You son of a bitch, I'm going to fuck you up." I went into the police station where he have the tub and the harpoon, and I threw my "message" on the harpoon and in the tub. When everybody was ashore I went in the boat and I scatter some in the boat too and I said, "Tomorrow you're going to see your ass." After that I went and meet the Indian man. I tell him, "I understand there is a boat in the harbor that no one will take to sea because the captain said it would never take fish again. I want to take that boat."

"What, that boat?"

"Yes."

"All right. I will give you something for it."

I went down to the boat. It have a lot of rock under it. I get my crew, and we take some coconut husks and we go down to the shore and scrub it. I take the sails and the nets and I strike my light. We smoke the boat inside and out, and every man get the same thing, too. Everybody smell it good. I took the medicine and put it in a galvanized tin, and everybody wash their hands and wash up good. Then I make a cup of bush tea full of maweepoui.[16] We drink that—that was the bread for us.

When it was one o'clock I hear Durocher corking[17] his boat. He was shoving out. I laugh. I meet him out there by the lighthouse and balled up his wind because my sail was a bigger sail. I watch him good. Up the road. The tide was going down like a river. I beat up because I knew my mark. You've got to go up high. As you open the corner to Dennery, you slack off—then you're going up the blackfish line. When day break I meet an old salt fish barrel. There were some fish under it—salmon, dolphin, shark—all that. We catch a young bonita. We chop it all up—that's to make friends with the fish. The three men I got there, like three tigers. Every man got a hook. We lay the sail down flat. Nobody can see we. The boat is a big boat and we load it full, then down the road. When I reach by Laborie I saw Mr. Durocher towing. Now he under me, and I coming on him. He stand up there, so, and I come close to him. He put his head so and said, "Oh, damn, oh damn, Charlo."

"Yes."

"Give me a broth."

"Uh unh." I say. "You have a pan there." He tell me, "Yes."

"Well, give me a pan." I full the pan with gravy and boileen fish,[18] but I don't give him one of these fish I got in the boat there. Me? You know what he going to do with it? He would take the same fish and go to the burying ground.

When I reach Castries it was eleven o'clock in the morning. We put the fish in the market, and I took a dolphin and a kingfish home to my wife. I gave her some money for the children and then down the road. Tomorrow morning before day break, I was in Canaries. I saw Durocher there with Police. Police was standing with the harpoon, but the fish was coming to me. Police say, "Keep up, keep up, keep up." As Police throw the harpoon, the fish just do that. I lean back so and I throw the harpoon. You want to hear cursing! Durocher cursing Police. "You cause that. You cause that. You tell me you a damn good fisherman, you're a damn good sticker. Charlo, come there. Look. You way outside the man." You know what I do now? I cut the fish and make him bleed. If you scatter the blood no more blackfish will come.

I took my fish into Vieux Fort and hear what Durocher going to tell me. "Charlo, I got money. Take a car to carry the fish to your wife and come back down. I going to be waiting for you."

"Me? Uh unh!"

"Tomorrow, Charlo, you come from here and go to sea, man. We be sure to kill a blackfish."

"I not going." The next day I went out and I get two blackfish, but not in his boat—in my boat. We catch some dolphin and when we leaving the fishing grounds and coming home, we meet the blackfish.

Durocher was from Cannouan and he had two boats. He used to be dealing [with the Devil]. One time when I was working for him and we wasn't catching any fish he told me, "Well, we're going to St. Vincent. We ain't catching nothing. Do it my way now. I carrying you somewhere."

"Yes. All right."

We left from Vieux Fort at eight o'clock going down to St. Vincent. Sea! Sea! Sea! We in a whaler, mind you, like a calabash, towing the other boat. Nothing atall. He steering, I working the jib. You know what kind of water we take. When we reach St. Vincent he said to me, "Charles, you know this thing I telling you about. We're going to see about weselfs tonight."

"Yes. Right."

"See that place up there. We got to go and find out what we can find out. Don't mind how high it is, mind the crowd of people we're going to meet up there looking for their business. When you reach Belair, up on top of the hill you're going to see a light. That's the Shouters[19] and that's the place where they make obeah."

We climb, we climb, we climb. The hill steep and then we come down, so. A woman sit down there cross-legged in a hole, a candle in her hand. When they see you come, if they is against you, they tell you, "Go, we don't need you here." And they chuck you out. The woman is a fortune-teller. She has a black candle with a lot of different red and black pins upon it like a vessel's mast have rigging. And she has a looking glass which has got two faces, front and back. When you come there you say what you want. It's not she taking the money, but the man inside the office will carry it. When you give the man the money, then she will talk. She pulls the money from the looking glass and she calls you. "Do you know that woman?" You're bound to. "Yes." "Well, that's the person against you trying to get your bread. What are you going to do with her, kill her? What do you want to do?" If you want to kill the person, she will kill her right there. She could be on a chair at her home but she would be dead right there. I said, "No. I will take care of her. Just fix me up." It was a woman called Marie Saint who lived next door to me. She was the one who was doing all that and I didn't know. I used to give her fish. Sometime she would call me and tell me to give her three pence of fish. She took those same three fish to the burying ground and no more fish for me again.

The fortune-teller gave me a vial of "will power"[20] and told me to wash my boat with it and to take my wife's bed sheet, soak it in the will power, and use it for a sail. Durocher get himself cleaned too and before we reach in St. Lucia, both of we was loaded with fish. When we went to Belair, we got coconut, pears, and breadfruit. I told him, "Those things you get, you going to throw them away, you know."

"Don't be so foolish. We're going to take them to Vieux Fort."

"All right. We're going at daybreak. When you see me lower my sail, come and meet me." By the time he reach me when I lower my sail, I got blackfish already. I throw away the fucking breadfruit. You see, when you is a stranger, and if God sees you're not afraid to interfere, it's all right. You got to take a good step for a piece of bread. You must believe in God. But God tells you, "Seek, and you shall find. Knock, the door shall be open." There is nothing in this world we have that God didn't put it there. But you sit down there and pray from Monday to Saturday and see if you're going to get it. God helps those who help themselves.

Mr. Durocher overdid it. He deal with the Devil and rub his boat too much to get fish.[21] When you rub your boat too much the Sea Devil will come. Many, many people lost their life to him. *Bam*, you're gone. Every day is fishing day, but not every day you carry back your life. When you deal with this man, twelve o'clock in the day has no right to catch you on the ocean. And you have certain things you mustn't carry in your boat.[22] So long as you deal with the Master you will never leave the wharf and come back empty. You always pull fish and all the time your net is going. But don't let the day by you, for the Sea Devil won't let you be. As you see you are halfway, cut it off. Do without it. If you continue, you won't live long. Captain Durocher lost a boat. He had two boats and the Sea Devil took half. Yes, you got to be wise to go to sea and catch fish, but you mustn't overdo it. Don't make the boat too hot! You will leave this morning, by nine o'clock you full of fish already, but always you're asking the time. The Sea Devil comes first as a small, little fish. The second time he come big and he come to turn the boat upside down and to take a life. He just passes his head, so, and lifts up the boat. He take the man he want. That happened to me already. There was a fellow that say to me one day, "Let's go and load the boat with fish and come back."

"How you going to do that?" I say, "I going." Every day he was going and catching fish, but he never went until the afternoon. We went out far, to windward of the land, towing. He got one, I got one. Before the line slack we got another. We got four albacore, three kingfish and a young bonita. We were in deep sea water when I hear *boom!*

I say, "Chine, what go under so?"

Boom!

"It must be some stone[23] that's gone too far."

"That cannot happen." I hear blowing. "Chine, LOOK AT IT! THE SEA DEVIL REACH!"

"Charlo, look in the box!" I found the bottle in the box and threw it overboard. That was what he wanted. I never go to sea with that man again. And you know his job now? He send the boat to sea and when the boat comes in he picks up his money, he repairs it, and paints it, but he don't go to sea.

You think the ocean is nice? The ocean has got no friend. It got all kind of fishery [fish]. The whale is nothing. It's got all kind of fish—dangerous fish. When you go to sea, if you want to make a farewell party, you go clean. You can do things to catch fish without interfering with this man.

"Watchie"

ONE DAY I went to sea, fishing. I left at five o'clock in the morning. About four o'clock in the afternoon I was coming up. I had caught seven albacore. When I get up near Marigot I see a boat shaking in the water. I say, "Let me go and see what happen to that boat." I went and I meet Mr. Malcolm Peter, the owner of Peter and Company store, upon a spree in a launch. Everybody drunk, the boat can do nothing for itself. Mr. Malcolm had bust his head, and all his hand were bruised. All his shirt was dirty with blood. "What's wrong with you?"

"Charles, come here, come here." I take my rope and I tied the boat. He come jump in my boat and sit down between my legs. I carry the boat up to the harbor master's office, and they take Mr. Malcolm to the hospital. He got his wounds dressed, and the next afternoon I saw him. He told me he would give me twenty dollars and a parcel for what I did. I say, "I don't need that today."

"Take it."

"You know what I want? Every day is fishing day, but not every day is catching day. I would like you to get a job for me. Any kind of job. I will take it."

"Tell me, really?"

"Yes."

"All right, I will make inquiries for you. I promise you."

Three weeks I go to sea and I ain't catch nothing. I get vexed. There were no fish. Now I went out and when I come back I hear a woman tell me, "Mr. Charles."

"Yes."

"There is a white man there in a car. His name is Mr. Peter. He tell you to come down to his office anytime, as long as you come before four. He say that he been looking for you all about the country for five days."

"Is that so?" By that time I was hungry. I got nothing. I go down with my hat and my sea clothes. I pick up nothing. I go down. When I reach I see three men sit down there, coming for the job. It was a watchman's job.

"Charles."

"Hello."

"Go to the office. Mr. Malcolm wants to see you there."

I knock three times. "Hello."

"Hello."

"Where have you been? Out fishing? You say you're asking for work for your payment. Well, I'll tell you. You have a long payment. As long as you need a job and as long as you're a trusting man, you are a watchman." And so say, so done. "Hamilton, look, give Charles a key and a Coke. Show him what to do and go. Miss Riley, give Charles ten dollars and charge it to cargo. You got to take duty tonight, you know."

"O.K., sir." I go and buy a pound of rice, a pound of potatoes, a quarter-pound of peas, and I fill me belly full. Up to now I have work.

I was living by myself. Edith had died. It was nothing bad. She used to give paper by the closet [public toilet] in the market. That was she work. Now she got plenty friends—that what kill her— and after she work she go and take rum with them. When I call her and talk to her she said she didn't have to take my advice. I say, "O.K." Yes, she had money. When she come to get paid, she don't want to eat 'cause the rum cut she appetite. "You working and you a big woman. I cannot watch you." I go to my work. She fall sick. She going to the hospital. She taking doctor's medicine and she still going to the rum. I wasn't there when she die, but I come when I hear she die. I left here on Saturday to go down to St. Thomas with a load of wire. I put up onions already— everything to make black pudding for Christmas. I kill a pig.

When I come back the pig was there, nobody done touch the pig. They bury she there. I had seven children with her. It was for she that me take nine months and four strokes of the nine-tails. After she died I stopped, seven years with nobody. I say, "I want no woman." I stayed in my home. My daughters tend to my clothes. That's all I want. I cook. I eat. I went to work at Peter and Company and I stay there. One day I put pig tail and peas on the fire. The thing burn like a black piece of charcoal. I say, "Oh, all my food done burn." That same day I say, "Shit, I got to look for a woman." God must have put her there. She come and sit down on the step by Peter and Company, crying, about eleven o'clock at night. I hear and come out. I walk to her, "What happened to you?" She told me that her sister had put her out. She had nowhere to sleep, so every night she was sleeping with a man, and every night the man want to ride her. When she say no, the man made her get up from there.

I say, "Where's your mother?"

"She's dead."

"Where's your father?"

"He dead." She tell me that the mother went to buy tobacco one night, and when she coming back in Canaries by the family they throw poisoned pig shit in the mother's face. That killed the mother. And the father, they give him poison too. Pieces of skin was coming out of his body and it stink. Then I say, "Well, Ann Marie (her name was Ann Marie Morris], I tell you something. I don't have no luck. My wife is dead. You want a home. I take you at my home. If you play the fool, I put you out. How you make your bed is how you lie down."

She tell me, "Never."

"O.K. Come. Get up. Come up with me." She get up with a little thrash basket. That was all she have. The next morning when I go up, she come with me. When I reach I open the door. "The door is open. Come in." She come in. I place the key in a tin, and I say, "Look where the key." I tell her, "Go in there. Open that box, open that. It's full. You're going to see beef— cook it." I went and took off my clothes and lie down on the bed and sleep. I never touch her 'til Saturday night. It was not like I say, "You come and make a certain thing with me and tomorrow morning you go your way and I go mine." But I did not do that. I did not interfere with her.

She tell me, "Nobody would do what you do. I sleep there with you and you don't even touch me."

I say, "I don't touch you. You is mine. If you were passing I wouldn't let you go free, but you not passing. I know we have enough time for it." She laugh. I never rush a woman. What is for you is for you, but if it not for you, you could cry, you could bawl, but you wouldn't get it. After there was a time we didn't used to let a day pass, but not today. That's right, that's right. You will find when you are newly friends with a girl, Jesus Christ, sometime before the watch tick . . . perhaps sometime you're more in a hurry than the person. But when there is one year, two years, three years—brother and sister.

When Ann Marie first come and she was new up at my house, there were those who think she would come to pictures with them. One man call up and ask her if she want to go. She tell him, "Listen, I come up to Marchand with my man. I don't want nobody's man. I got mine. I know I is an ugly woman and I don't want nobody to laugh when Charles is passing. Yes, he's an old man, but I know when he and I going down the road, he lift up his hat high." When Ann Marie going in town she go like a racehorse making a race. She just going to make she message and come back. You can't stop her on the street. If you tell her you have something to tell her, Ann Marie will curse you.

I was renting a house then, but the owner called me to pick some breadfruit for him. The rain fall in the night, and when I go, Jesus Christ, the breadfruit is wet and slimy. I went and told Mr. Sam Boyce that, and the man said, "If you don't want to pick the breadfruit, come and pick some mangoes for me." I went and picked the mangoes. "I have a big piece of spice and I want you to take it for me." I take it for him. Saturday, when I go down in town to go to work the man give me notice to leave the house. It wasn't just because I didn't climb the breadfruit tree. He use that as an excuse. Mr. Sam Boyce wanted to take the house from me and give it to a next man. I was paying ten shillings a month, and he get in a man who will rent it for five dollars a month. Now this man was working another man's property, and Sam Boyce was going to give him some cattle to care for for him. He kept them for two years, but when Sam Boyce sold one he only gave the keeper a few dollars. The man get vexed. Now he had four other cattle of Mr. Sam Boyce's and you know what he do? He go into the bush and he cut a kind of withe—a Carib kind of vine called babara.[1] He pung it until he have two baskets full and then he go and bar up the river with bamboo. Then he set the baskets in the river to foul it and just how the river going down, just how he killing the fish, or the cattle that drink from the river. He kill all four of Sam Boyce's cattle, and they stink so quick they can't do nothing but bury them. The man stand up and tell Sam Boyce, "The same thing that bit the white dog, bit you. You take all your money and I get fuck all, but you won't get no more cow to hold a rope with." That man didn't have no conscience. He could have killed two, but don't kill all. He kill all of them.[2]

Sam Boyce give me notice I had a month to look for another house, but when I come home Fati [Ann Marie] tell me she can't make a month there. Sam Boyce was making coal and pulling coal. He tell the girl to come and help him pick up the coal down there in the bush. When she come there he put a curse on her. He say he could use her and I wouldn't know. The girl took a bag of coal to carry up and didn't come back. She was vexed. She curse and she pick up everything, shove it in a corner, and say we must move and leave the man's house. "What about money?"

I say, "I will try." I went and see Mr. Bushell, he was my boss at Peter and Company, and I told him the situation. I say I need some money to go and get a room. He tell me, "Well, go and get a room for the time being, but look for a house and I will get it for you." When I came back I had twenty dollars and I say, "Fati, I want to go see if I can get somewhere." I beat everywhere in town, but I cannot get a room. I come back and I sit down.

"What's happen to you, Charlo?"

"Fati, I could get no room."

"Well, give me the money. I am going to try myself." She tell me, "You don't want to leave this man's house."

"No, don't tell me that. I want to leave."

The next morning she start. She come back at two o'clock in the afternoon—hungry and with no hope. "Charlo, what we going to do? I want to leave that house because the man treats you in the worst way. I don't know what to say now." She start to cry.

Now there was an old lady called Mrs. Alcindor, and when I go to sea I bringing fish for the lady. I would go up the hill and say, "Ma'am, look what I bring for you." She have a house she was renting. But the woman who was living in it found she was too much by herself—she want to be closer to the road to see people. So she left there and rent a house close by the road. Now the lady come tell us, "I hear you want a room. I have a little house up there and I would like you to come and see it. If you want it you can take it and you won't need a house." I went there and I say, "Yes, there is a few board it want on it."

Ann Marie tell me, "Take it. A bad sleep—a rough bounce—is better than none."

I say, "All right. Give it to me. How much is it?" She tell me ten shillings. I say, "Well, I'll pay you for three months."

Before I have two months, she come and tell me, "Charlo, I can't fix the house and I will have to sell it."

"Well, I don't know how much you want for it."

She tell me, "Two hundred."

"Ma'am, you know I haven't got a cent. Now where will I get that money?"

She say, "Well, pay me by the week."

"Uh unh. I pay at one time." And that is how I get it. Mr. Bushell helped me. The lady is dead now, and I the one there. I fix it all up. I take a couple of pieces of wood and I dismount some boxes and I stop the hole. During the time I was fixing the house, the woman that had moved closer to the road tell a friend, "Don't mind what Charles is doing. He will fly, he will leave the house." I don't say nothing, I just do like I didn't hear.

Later I come to know Mrs. Alcindor was a "duppy woman." A duppy woman deals with the Devil. She can turn all different animals and she can fly in the night. The night she want to fly she going to put the powder in a glass and she going to throw the essence in the glass and you going to see it start to boil. If she want to turn a dog, she will turn a dog. You can get the powder in doctor's shop and what you want to turn tonight, that is what you drink. Then you go behind people and humbug them. Everybody in Marchand was miserable. When somebody is behind you for the whole night she will be on top of your house. You can't sleep no way. You are miserable in the night. There were two of them in Marchand—two sisters—and everybody up there was miserable. Now they have gone everyone is in peace. Marchand has come quiet. You think Marchand is nice?

When we had a couple of weeks in the house a kind of red ants covered the house in the night. And she sent another kind of thing too. It walk like a crab, a blue thing we call "zacakorn" [scorpion], and it got a thing to sting you. I can't see it, but it come and wound my wife at night. Finally my mother came and told me it was Mrs. Alcindor who was doing me this. Then my brains come natural and I find the thing right in the corner there. When I bust the piece of board I take it off. It want to run. I say, "Not today. You gone." I fix it up and I am not bothered again.

Behind the house we have a bamboo tree. In the night we'd always hear, "Meow, meow, meow," and we'd hear, "Bowwow-wow." It was something that was set for us, to make us go mad. Now Fati went with some other girls to look for coconuts and she pass from that and turn crazy. When they carried her to the police station she made the same noises like the cat and dog, or a pig—"ruh, ruh, ruh." All right. After she had got down in the lunatic asylum the dog and the cat come to me now. They come doing the same job for me now. I hear the cat under the bamboo tree, "Meow, meow, meow," "bowwowwow." I say, "Yeah! Good. Who send you going to receive you" and after you get your share of the person. I went down in town and I get my message and set my trap. The cat dead, the dog dead. Now the spirit of these two animals turn against the owner, and she have the building above me and she say that something come there Saturday and beat her and everything.

Oh, my wife has passed a lot of trouble, you know. She give me three children. The first one is Simon, the second one she give me is Zander, and the third is Angela. Two to help me and give me food. The last one to wash a piece of pants for me and give me a bread. After she was confine with Simon the sickness take her. For three months she just sit in a chair. You got to put a bench under her feet and two pillow under her seat, and she sit there night and day. Her foot is cripple, she cannot stretch out. And after, she running and doing like cat and dog. You know who did that? Ann Marie was confine, and the clothes from the hospital she left for a woman to wash. It was this woman that do that. She crippled her through those same clothes. Those clothes she washing[3] is the main clothes of the body. That same person that take the clothes to wash take the girl's panties and fuck up Fati. She take them and put her astray. When I realize what happen I start to make an egg[4] the woman can't find, and when I see I didn't do no harm with it, like the wind I carry Fati to the lunatic asylum. She make three trips there. When they believe she wouldn't be back in the house, I come up in a car with my woman. Ah, now you mustn't chase away a dog that bites you. Make him come.[5] The woman come. She tell Ann Marie she glad she come out from hospital. Now she's a woman that like sweet food. I make Fati cook chicken and give her a plate of food. "Fati could make good food, eh?" She so raven, she eat the food. Now only a little five dollars you got to spend for this from the doctor's shop. You call the powder in French, "poude voltiger" [volcano powder] and "poude brisée," that's "fighting powder." You put a bit of those two powders in each of the food and give her to eat. That's your payment. She can't get nothing to help her. It can't come out. Well, it's not Ann Marie's sickness that she have. She got she own sickness. Ann Marie send back the sickness. Sometime she well, sometime she bad. The other morning I see she by the door, and she start to root like a pig. Somebody say they carrying her to the doctor. I just stay there in my rocking chair and say, "You son of a bitch, you, you caused my people to go crazy." She was trying her fucking best to make my wife lame and lunatic the balance of she life. That's because she find my wife was too bright.[6]

When Ann Marie was in the lunatic asylum I still working at Peter and Company. A woman charge me three dollars a week to keep the child [Simon] at night, and in the morning I got he behind my neck going up the hill with him. Rain, thunder, lightning, I take the cloak, I cover him, and I going up the road. The two of we inside the house. I cook, I wash his clothes, I bathe him and take care of him. When I see the boy's eye start to have cold in it and I see he coming small, I say, "Well, if I not dead, you won't be dead neither." I open up a carpenter bench and I put some cocoa bags behind it. I cover it nicely, open two bags there, and we sleep. Simon was a small little baby then. He didn't even have four months yet. He was too small to sleep on that bag. I beg the woman to come up and try and get him to sleep. But he come big now. He has made his First Communion.

If sickness was something they selling in the market, people would never go for sickness. When Ann Marie well I glad for her, but when she sick I troubled for her. I got to tend to her. I rub her from head to foot. Me too, when I sick, she tend to me like a child. I train her in bush, and if I didn't train her to be a doctor, you wouldn't see me here now. There was that time when I was working at Peter and Company when they give me the bad tea. It was Enid and a next man. It was expressly through jealousness. They were jealous because Ti Son come there every Thursday night, meet me and give me drink and give me money. Enid tell the other man, "Look, Mr. Charles have a son." She had a son with him too, but the boy say he was too awful for a father. I take food at her house—wild yam and salt fish—and they make a tea for me with poison in it. I never think—I was friends with the girl, so I drink the tea. After I left she house I go down to Peter. When I reach by the square I went at the corner where they have a rum shop and I take a little nip. That's what the poison was asking for. When I reach by the lawyer's I just feel something passing me and I fall. I use my bowels, I puke. It was a lucky thing my wife was at the cinema. Somebody take a piece of bag and put it under my head and went and call my wife. When she come she say, "Ah, Charles, they got you now." She get a car and carry me to the hospital. There was a cooley man—an Indian man that came there in the night—and he dead that same night. I don't dead yet because I have something below the tea[7] that is stronger than that. The poison and it fighting. I use my bowels and the poison come out. Now tomorrow morning at daylight the man come with two women and a bottle of rum to bathe me because he hear the man which come in the hospital last night there dead. Now I come back alive! Enid and the man come and see me. I never chase them away. I come out from the hospital and I never tell them anything, and now . . . she belly big, so, her two foot swell. The man left her. You see, I give her something to drink, too.

A next man Enid have, a black man called "Boy," I make nine months and four days in hospital for. The man holding my work—he have my work, hear, and he never come see me, except to find out how I stand. When I come out of hospital I say, "Well, you damn well going to pay for it." I come down. He's so foolish. He going to poison a bottle of wine and he going to bring it down to me. He won't drink none, but he going to make me drink it, so you think that is safe? He come and say, "Carlo."

"Hello."

"I understand you going to take your work this week."

"Yes. Next week."

"Oh! All right. When you're taking your work, you tell me, I coming there to meet you and take a drink."

I say, "Sure." That same man going to try and get my job back. The next week he come with a bottle of wine.

"Hello, Carlo."

"Hello."

"I have brought a bottle of wine." We go in a rum shop, but the man won't drink his wine. He get something else. Two or three friends come in. The man talking so, he never notice that I throw out what he give me to drink in a tin there. But he drinking steady. I ask him if he would like a nip of stout with me. He say, "Yes," so I went and throw a little of his wine in that and I bring it to him. The fucker—*glug, glug, glug*—he drink the whole bottle. In a couple of days he was sick and went to the hospital. The doctor tell him he can't get any better, that he have to go outside and take medicine. He go up to Dennery at his family, but his family won't have him. They tell him, "Where you make your grease, go and meet your own there." He go back and stop by a shoemaker man. The man say his house ain't a hospital, and he dead there. The fucker, and he wanted to kill me for my own work.

I worked at Peter and Company for nineteen years, and then Mr. Moyle call me and tell me, "Charles, how would you like to work over at Mrs. Ganter's?"[8]

"O.K. I will try and see. If I like it I will stay there."

Mr. Moyle say, "They is all right. Nobody don't trouble them."

He send me here before they open, and I have been here ever since. Mrs. Ganter just like a mother to me.[9] Yesterday night I tell Mrs. Ganter, "A man could say what the hell he likes about black people, but I tell you, black killing me. Give me white people."

Mrs. Ganter tell me, "Don't say that in front of black people, because they won't like you."

"I don't give a damn what I say, Madame. I tell you the white people is the rising sun. Without white people you don't eat."

One day I was coming from sea. I had been fishing steady. As we come in Conway the wind kept breezing, breezing. I take the fish and drop it by the market and I come by Mrs. Ganter's. I see Madame there. "Charles, do you know we expect a hurricane tonight? Be careful and get a good rest. I got two men coming to help you."

I say, "Madame, I'm hungry. You know, I just from sea."

"You've had nothing to eat? Would you like bread and butter and a cup of tea?"

I say, "Something like that."

I went home and when it was three o'clock I start down. Rain, rain, rain. I say, "Oh, God!" Everybody pumping, pumping, pumping all night. And wind! You hear *Whooooo* and water everywhere. By morning the rain had stopped and I left to go up at home. When I reach by the bridge I see a man coming to meet me. "Mr. Charles, your wife is confine and the child inside the house. She haven't got a nurse yet because she was too frighten and there was too much rain. I am going to the hospital now to call the nurse and get a car." By the time I reach up there, the nurse got the child already. I meet the nurse inside there. She say, "You is Mr. Charles?"

"Yes."

"Your wife make a girl."

I say, "O.K." Mrs. Ganter say the child's name is supposed to be Dorothy—we call her Angela—but the child bawl just like Dorothy.[10] She never want no pillow or no blanket 'cause when she born she stop there for half an hour before the nurse come. That was the last child Ann Marie give me and she's a nice little creature. I like children. I'll tell you the medicine of a child. If a woman born in this world and she haven't got a child, she is no use. She got to have babies. Maybe she have fourteen—if God give you a son or a daughter, you have a next fourteen. If your husband die today or tomorrow, that boy going to give you a penny and that girl going to give you an old dress. Some women who are in the family way take pills and kill the child. Sometimes they drink bush. We have a kind of bush living by the river. It is a vine and has a little yellow flower, call it St. John Bush.[11] If you make a tea from the leaves it will turn red like blood, and when you drink it you will see your courses come. Your belly could be three months and it gone. The child destroy. I got that kind of bush by my home, but Ann Marie never take it. She put it on the fire. She like baby. One day when you come old, you'll find your daughter or son will look after you. Yes, the time is hard, but God give you finger to scratch it. The more you pet a child, the more the child like you. The kind of way you raising her, the kind of way she come. The first set I bring with a woman was

seven children and I must have seven outside. I lost three
though—they died small of typhoid. Then I make three with
Ann Marie. That's seventeen. I got a daughter in New York. I got
a son married to a white woman in France. I got a boy in a
banana boat. I got one in Demerara. I got another son in England, and I have a daughter married to a Cannouan boy down in
Vieux Fort, Septima. When she was small she was worse than
Angela. She didn't want to know her mother atall. The mother
take the child and carry her to Vieux Fort. She phone me from
there, "Come to Vieux Fort and take up Septima, or Septima will
die." When I come I see bones and skin.

I say, "You take my child and carry her at your mother's house
and you see her state now."

"Well, take her and carry her up." I take the child and take the
boat. Me don't sleep in the house, sleep in the boat. Tomorrow
morning I get my load and carry it up. Oh, the child glad. She
hug me so. When we reaching Soufriere, I buy two-pence coupé
[cut cake], and the two of us eat. When I reach in Conway I put
her up there in the house. A couple of days Septima pick up and
start to come fat. The mother come up now. She say, "Septima,
you take your father in your heart and you didn't want to stay
with me."

Now Septima come a big girl, and she marry Chairman. This
thing happen so funny. When I was a watchman by the wharf for
Barnard, the boy used to take care of me, tiefing salt beef and
bringing it for me, "Daddy, Daddy, Daddy, take this." And the
boy come big. When I left the watchman's job, I come to go to
sea. He come and ask me if I would go with his uncle, that same
George Durocher. Up to this morning, up to this afternoon, the
uncle begging me to come and work with him again. Well, the
boy liked me so much, I say, "O.K." He tell me we're going to
spend two weeks in Vieux Fort and come back. I say, "Ah, I sure
when I reach I going to get some coffee."

"How you going to get coffee?"

"I got my daughter in Vieux Fort."

He say, just joking, "I going to call you 'father-in-law.'"

When I reach I just push the door. "Well, Daddy, I saw you when you were coming and there is your coffee," because she know I a man that like coffee. I drink, and Chairman watch. I say, "All right, you meet my daughter—eh, eh, meet daughter." He speak and I left them there. When I come back for dinner I see the food he bring—more fish and some lovely mangoes. I say, "Eh, eh, Chairman. What you mean so quick?"

He laugh, "Uh, uh."

Then the girl come tell me, "Daddy, Chairman say he love me." Chairman watching me, so—you know Cannouan people are bashful.

I say, "All right, Chairman. I know, old man. I can see. I don't tell you no but my daughter is not going to swim. If you can shove a ring on her hand, well, you could get her. But no ring, no love."

"Yes, Daddy. Yes, Daddy."

"I not going to shove my daughter in a kind of yam before I know the end of it.[12] We'll go to Cannouan and see your mother and your father. All right?"

He tell me, "Yes. We're going next week Sunday or Monday." And we sail over to Cannouan in a whaler with no engine. In Cannouan a man going to carry you at his home. He going to give you a properly good dinner and treating you nice. But one thing, make up your mind to swallow. Wow! Before the bottle empty, next bottle. And they're bringing soft roast corn, and don't talk about fish. They treating a stranger nice and kind, and the food good, good.

When we get back to St. Lucia I tell Chairman, "When you ready you let me know." And when that thing take place, Chairman and Septima come up to buy dry stores and a nice dress. They tell me in two weeks' time. I say "O.K. When you're ready let me know." And the day they were married, I reach there about three or four o'clock in the afternoon. I get myself ready. At five o'clock the wedding start. I took my daughter to the church and I delivered her to the husband. I went to the table and I take a shot of wine. I wipe my mouth and I say, "All right, Chairman, you is second." *Bam*—I gone. What! You think I was going to eat some food? If that cake have a dot of poison, it not catch me. And now when you see Septima you going to see so many pickney [pickaninnies]—she have about five now and she married.

I have a son, we call him "Ti Son," who is a greaser on a banana boat. He have a big house here, back by the bridge, and his wife is there. When the man come to try and cut my guts and try to break in here, my son come right inside there and call Mrs. Ganter. He tell her plain, "If you don't give my father a gun, this is the last year he will work here. I'll put him at my house." Mrs. Ganter told him that she couldn't do that. The government won't give her a license to do that. "Well," he say, "if he can't get it, make up your mind this is the last year."

Being a watchman is a dangerous job, you know. That night I made my rounds and I come here by the office. I just hear a knock and when I turn my head I see a man stand up there. I have time to say, "What you doing there?" and *feeew*, with a piece of glass, the same glass he had removed. He swing it across my belly to cut me, but I duck and get away from him. He run and when I step up there he gone in the night. If I was a slow man you would never see me here today. I went and call Mr. Ross. "Come quick, Mr. Ross." He say he putting on his pants, but I tell him, "Never mind the pants, just come." We phone the policeman but they couldn't find the man. The policeman told me, "I wouldn't take that job without a gun, Mister." The other night the watchie over at Peter and Company had his arm cut. But I have my two friends here [he reached down and patted the two cutlasses that lay beneath the bench].

And I will tell you something else, and I will make you keep your mouth shut now. Here they have dead people buried. Eh? You doubt me? Any time of the night I will hear, "Charles."

I say, "Hello."

"Everything is all right?"

I say, "Yes." Peter and Company got it down there, Chastanet got it, the bank got it, everybody got it. When they're digging the hole to make the foundation of the property—building the store or the shop—they work in the night late and they buy plenty rum. They have a big basket of bread and a big tin pan full of corn beef. That's the time they are going to snatch one. When they leave him in the hole, that's the watchman. Right here, many, many, many nights I hear, "Charles, everything is all right?"

I answer the call, "Everything is O.K. Yes, it's all right." You have to be a hero to do this kind of work. When you see a man like me doing this job, you know he must have made his name before. You got to be responsible. I was a secret detective, you know, long ago here. There was a policeman called Burton and he tiefed a blanket from the police station for a woman. Now he have two women—he bring the blanket for one, but he had nothing for the next woman, so she get jealous and go to the station and report him. He was in bed when the police come and arrest him. They find the blanket and carry it to the police station. He gets six months. After he get out he gives the sergeant one solid bang and runs away from the country. They cannot find that man atall. Sergeant Thomas tells me if I get Burton I get twelve pounds. So I say, "O.K." I went up in the country. There was a certain fellow who used to come down every Saturday to sell farine. I ask him if he's seen Burton.

He tell me, "Yes. You mean a tall, thin, fairskin fellow, way up on top?"

I say, "Oh, good." And I go tell the sergeant I know where the man is. "But I not going to chase a dog that run when I go."

"Are you sure you know where he is?"

"Yes."

"Charles, are you going for him?"

"Yes."

"I know you got the guts to go." So I went. I take a horse and I went up in Marquis and I find him up there.

"Good afternoon."

"Good afternoon." I come right in front of him and in one hand I have the handcuffs, in the other I have the gun. I say, "All right now, Burton. Are you going down with me in the station or are you going to remain here?"

He say, "What a choice."

I say to the man he living with, "Mr. Jean Pluie, come here. You is the road constable. Here's your handcuffs. Put Burton's two hands behind his back and handcuff them. Hurry up!" He handcuff Burton and he threw his own hands behind his back. "Now you come this side." *Click. Click.* I handcuff Jean Pluie the same way to Burton. You know why? He have a map. He have a right to arrest anybody. He didn't have no right when a man commit a crime to keep him at his house. I take them down the track and there are two cops waiting in a car at the bottom. I say, "Hahaha, Burton. Got you!" And I tell the cops that Pluie is the road constable and he got Burton at his home. He knew what Burton had done and he should be arrested too.

They say, "All right. We take him." They give him six months. Now Mr. Burton go to court in session.[13] They give him ten years and ten stroke of the cat-o'-nine-tail. He take five and cannot take no more. That caused the policeman to die. He stayed a couple of months in the hospital and he died. What really kill him was knowing that when he got out of prison he had to see the next wife. That was humbugging him.

That was how I make my name. Today if I dead, I going to be dead with my shoes on. I'm not going to be dead at Marchand neither. When you see a person dead in Marchand that is the time they tief you most. When you're crying and those people come and see you, you think those people come to see you, but they come to tief. Uh huh, uh huh, yeah, they come to make lavéyé [a wake], yes, plenty rum and they're singing, but they're tiefing you too. The first thing I know, I won't dead in Marchand. I don't dead in hospital neither. I dead in town. If I feel sick and go to hospital, I will take me up from hospital. I going to be dead right before you take the big bridge over there, because that my son's building. I got my room there, and before I bury I going to sleep in my room on my bed. Everything is there. I have my death suit already. I can't wait until the last moment to make preparation. I got the shirt there and the suit. They bathe me and dress me and I will look great upon the bed. I will be all in black in my death suit. I'll look great.

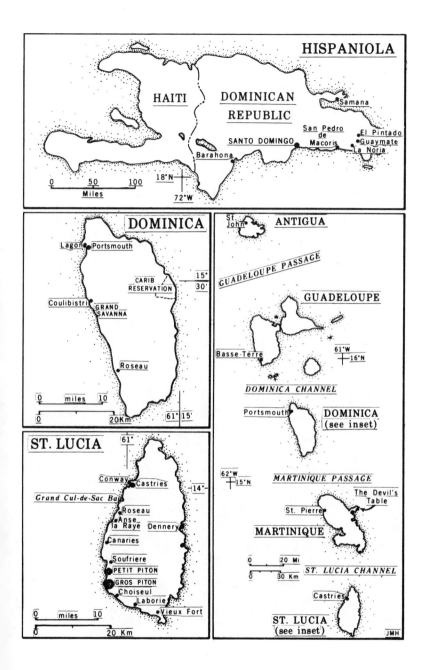

The Pitons, often used as "marks" for the fishing ground

Loading cargo, Portsmouth, Dominica

Charles warning our son, "What you plant is what you reap"

Preparing the harpoon

The market at Castries

Charles's wife, Ann Marie, and Bruno, before he was "done in"

In front of Charles's house

Returning from fishing, Conway, St. Lucia

Charles relaxing at home, son Simon on left

Part Two:
Conversations

THROUGH THOSE EVENINGS as Charles sifted his life memories he often assumed I fully understood what he was telling me. In many, many cases I did not. Sometimes I would question him at the time, or if he was in the middle of an involved story I might return to the subject another night. I had a good working knowledge of West Indian supernatural belief, but I couldn't always follow Charles as he fluctuated between what I had always considered to be two distinct worlds: the natural and the supernatural. What did he mean? My mind couldn't always grasp what he was saying, nor could I always rationalize some of his apparent inconsistencies. But I wanted to understand, and to do so I often had to be led, step by step, something that was almost incomprehensible to Charles. He was bewildered at my lack of understanding, still he answered me as best he could. It is hard for anyone to explain the obvious and the familiar. My academic mind wanted definitions, and that was what I sought. Definitions as such were often exasperating to Charles. They were after the fact. He was interested in coping with the situation, not belaboring it. As I listened to his tales evening after evening, I began to understand. Inconsistencies didn't seem to matter. They were almost irrelevant. The emphasis was on living life, and this was done in terms of both the natural and the supernatural.

I have already made the point that once my husband had left the scene an almost immediate change was evident in Charles's attitude toward me, that now as a single woman I was vulnerable to countless dangers within his society of which I was ignorant. On the first night after my husband's departure Charles was relating the story of how he was poisoned when he was working at Peter and Company. From there he launched into a long harangue on how careful I must be of such situations, and he suddenly produced a bottle containing a number of leaves soaking in a clear liquid. "I tell you. You got to get this thing they call 'en tout cas'—that will help you if somebody give you a bad rum to drink. That is your life in your hand, 'cause you don't know which place you might go to a party. You don't know. The party you go to—many people die like that. You go to a party and the next morning you're dead. If somebody poison you, that will save your life."

I looked at the bottle as Charles uncorked it and wondered what it contained. "It's not poison. I wouldn't poison you. Watch." With that he tilted back his head and took a good sized gulp. "You taste it." There was no hanging back. I took the bottle and followed his example, trying to show no discomfort as fire rolled down to the pit of my stomach. Jack Iron, a raw form of rum, seemed to be one of the chief ingredients, but aside from the fire a bitter taste lingered in my mouth.

I stifled a "Wow" and said, "Thank you"—then asking the obvious, "Do you put rum in here?"

"Sure. You got to put rum in—let it soak. You take this and buy half a bottle of rum to put in it."

"What about you?"

"Don't mind me. I could fix up my bottle. That's your bottle now, I tell you. Take care of it. If your body feel funny or you find something go wrong with you, just take a little spoonful and swallow it. Then you on the level. If it wasn't for that bottle you wouldn't see me today."

"You mean you had taken a spoonful of that before you were given the poison that night?" I asked.

"You know that! Anywhere you go—if you are invited to a party, before you leave your home—take a dose of that—you, your husband and your children. Then when you go, you are properly rigged. Anything bad they give you, you puke it back. Take good care of that. This is what you call 'en tout cas.' Nobody knows this. If I tell you where I learn this, you would be surprised—from Santo Domingo you go down to Haiti, and I spent a month and fifteen days with a fellow called Antonio in Haiti."

In the ensuing evenings I still continued to record the life of Alexander Charles, but he also began to teach me. He was worried at my obvious lack of knowledge in what he considered the basics of life, and in the absence of my husband he took on the role of my male protector. "I don't know if I will dead this year, but I know before I dead you got to get something in your head. I cannot let you go like a man to fight in a war without no gun." That trip, the night before I was to leave for home he arrived with a number of "messages," as he termed them. The first was a little bottle of a sweet-smelling red liquid. "This is for the morning time, when you get up," and he proceeded to show me how to put it on. Carefully he rubbed his face, under his arms, and then clapped his hands together. "Do like that," he cautioned me. "Watch me, watch me good. I call that 'The Lady's Power' or 'will power.' And you keep your mouth shut. Don't tell nobody about this. That's your protector. Nobody can harm you with this anywhere you go. Don't allow a soul to get that. That cost money.

"Now, something else for you. Remember I told you about a bush? Tell me what it is, about the bush for the baby." I wracked my brain. I knew it was important to remember the name.

"St. John's Bush," I ventured cautiously.

"That's right. Janie, you forget nothing." He was pleased. I had passed and I secretly heaved a sigh of relief.

"I tell you about that. Now I show you how to try it. Tomorrow morning when you're making tea, put two leaves and let them boil. When it properly boil pour it into a teacup and it will come just like blood. That's what I was telling you, but don't let nobody know your secret and your business. When you reach you put that in your grip in case you want to use it some day. You don't know when that might be. Even dry, that leaf still doing the job. So long as you got it. But a child not a ha'penny bread. It is easy to take, but hard to make. It could cause plenty trouble, plenty suffer, before the child come out. If this one die you don't know the next one you're going to get. But keep that.

"Now this, this is the balance of your stuff." Carefully Charles unwrapped three little packages in newspaper. "Don't you waste it," he cautioned me. "I give you plenty extra. When you reach home in the night at six o'clock, just hold each of these in your hand, put a little bit of each in your coal pot and light it. You close up your house and the smoke go inside your house and you will feel very nice and comfortable with the smoke. Nobody will know how you get it or when you get it. Shove your finger in there. Squeeze it, smell your finger." I poked at a white, powdery substance gingerly and Charles let out a hoot of laughter. "You see how it smelling?"

"Yes, it's sweet."

"Now look at this one." It was a kind of brown, resin-like substance with a bad smell. I wrinkled my nose and he nodded. "Now this." I looked at the third ingredient and tried to memorize it. This was a kind of crystallized material. "That's a parfumé[1]—smoke for the house. They call that in Patois, 'parfumé.' When you go in the doctor's shop[2] you ask for 'parfumé.' They say, 'What kind you want—is it for boat or home?' You say it's for home. They charge you seventy-five cents for each parcel. Put all these in the fire together, just a drop of each. Sit down right in front of the smoke and let it go. In a good while get up and when it finish smelling, open the window and everything. Leave the ashes in the pot until tomorrow morning. Then scatter them on the step you're walking on."

"You mean outside the house?"

"That's right. Scatter it upon the step. When you're coming out with no shoes, you mash it, and when you're coming in you mash it up too. Right.

"Now this is in case you got any scratch upon your feet during the time you're in your garden." He produced two round white pills which looked rather like aspirin. "You take this and put it upon a piece of board and you take an empty bottle and you squeeze the tablet. You will make a powder and that powder you could just put on your foot. Then you're cured."

I started to thank him for his "messages" but he cut me short. He had heard somebody coming down the walk. "Come on, come on, pick up your business." And he helped me stuff it quickly into a paper bag. "What you got to do now—secure that just how you secure me in your heart. That's your property now. When you reach home, you're comfortable. Nobody knows your business. Nobody can ride you. Nobody can play you tricks. Nobody can make you change your mind to do something. You're under your own control. That's what you want."

That was my first experience with protective magic. I wasn't quite sure what I had been given, but I realized all these things had great significance for Charles. For the moment it was enough that he believed in them and that he cared enough to want to protect me. I was touched at his concern and we parted on a warm note. From thence forward the door was open, and our conversation turned more and more to bush and magical medicine.

When I next returned and we were once more by ourselves, Charles told me, "There's something else we've got to talk. What remains of what I gave you?"

"I still have some will power."

"How much do you have?"

"I have about that much," signaling about half a bottle-full with my fingers.

Charles was very pleased. "Good. I glad you take care of it. What about the powder?"

"Oh, I still have some powder." He was satisfied.

"Good. That's right. Well, you and me going to go ahead good—like a daughter and a father. I save you a great love, child. I don't know. I don't know if I dead this year, but I know before I dead, you got to get something in your head. You got to get something learned because Captain Beck coming old, as Captain Beck coming old, you coming a big girl. You don't know what may happen. If you know your right hand and your left one, your heart cannot get beaten, because you know what to do if anything happen to you. That's what you got to remember. You see today, you're going to see tomorrow. You don't know what will happen. But if you learn sense—if you know something—all that could happen to you would be good. Know how to carry on your work, how to carry on your house without you asking anybody anything."

From then on Charles began to instruct me in earnest. "Ah, child, the best thing you got to do, you got to get a book and I going to fill the book for you. The day you knock your toe you will know how to tend to it. It better you learn it and you know it before you're drifting between two logs." After he told me a particular cure or remedy he would tell me, "Now write that down." At first he was chiefly concerned with protective medicine and magic. He would bring me a leaf and tell me how to make a tea, explaining that this was to "melt the blood inside you caused by any blow" or that was good for stiffness or something else eased "cutting in the stomach." I began to ask the names of the different plants and ingredients and encourage him to teach me more of his knowledge of bush medicine. I didn't want to move too rapidly, for I suspected he had a deep knowledge of magical medicine and perhaps even obeah, and I had hopes that slowly some of this would be revealed. And so it was—bit by bit. As time went on I realized he was not only thoroughly grounded in bush and magical medicine, but was also familiar with obeah, black magic, and the invocation of the dead as well. He was willing to teach me or tell me anything I asked about bush or magical medicine, but very reluctant when it came to the blacker arts. At first I was careful never to press Charles, never to ask him a question that he wouldn't be willing to answer, but gradually as our relationship developed I became less cautious. Sometimes I could prod him into a discussion almost in spite of himself. One thing was certain. He had become my protector.

One night my husband and I went out for supper with another couple who were living in St. Lucia at the time. I returned early because I didn't want to miss an evening with Charles. He was there waiting for me. Although I hadn't seen him before I left, he already knew where I had gone and he was very disapproving. For the next half hour he regaled me with the evils of going out for the evening. He started in full swing.

"A man find you so nice. He find you is a beauty and he is the one to have you. He will invite you to a party and that the last party you will be invited to. From now on stop it. If you are invited to a party always refuse. When I hear you going out for dinner tonight I worry. If you did tell me that last night, I would tell you so. Party is nice, yes, but party is bad too. When you cook at home you know what you eat, but not at party." To appease him I explained that I had taken some en tout cas before I had left. "Ah. Before you leave?"

"Yes, like you told me."

"The same thing I tell you—when I teach you before—you got to take that before you go anywhere. If you go gamble a meal and you eating food that is not good, it not staying. It come back. You puke the last of it. Next time say, 'Well, I'm sorry. My time is no more party.' Tell him plain, 'Your party and mine different. My mother and my father is my party. There's a difference. I'm not going out to no party. If my husband going out, O.K., but I am going to stay home from now on in St. Lucia.'"

I said rather weakly, "I didn't really want to go tonight."

And he answered, "I know that. Somebody told me that you were going to a party but you have to come back quick because you want to speak to Charles. A white woman tell me so. She say, 'Come here,' and she tell me, 'I see your friends.'"

"My people?" I say.

"Yes. She say, 'Your people say they're going to a party but they won't stay long because they have to come and meet you.' All right. I not your husband, but from now, party altogether out. Excuse yourself, say 'I'm very sorry. I couldn't go because I tend to my own child.' And if your husband go, let him go, but don't you go. There are many things about it. You never accustomed to drink rum. They dope you at a party. In a couple of months you will be a total drunkard in the street, and everybody will grab you and go and do what they want to do with you and let you go. You will lose all you have. This one grab you, the next one grab you. Every night he beat you. You have three, four customers and you don't know nothing. Stop it. Don't let me hear about no more party. You could cook on the boat. You could drink on the boat. If you want to go out, eat first and then go. When you come back you know you're safe. Don't talk about party. Party make you lose your life. In a party they spoil you,[3] you know. They poison you too. When a person give you a glass of rum he shoves his finger in it. He let the nail grow long and he put a little powder under the nail and now that poison is there for you. You're going to drink there—you're gone. The only thing that could save you is the Master—en tout cas. When I dead you have to call my name every day for that. You got to show the whole people that a young girl like you is a good girl. You don't pick up friendship like that. Cut it from now on. I'll make you put it in your head tonight. I know what I tell you. You sit down and you see too and you check it. You will find what I tell you is quite fair. Ah, poor you, you don't know, but I older than you. I know.

"Now I'll tell you something else. From the time I leave here in the morning until I come back at night I chewing tobacco. Tobacco burn—taste it. I tell you taste it!" I wasn't too thrilled about the idea, as I'd experimented with chewing tobacco as a child and hadn't savored it. I stuck it in my cheek, trying to ignore it.

"Now, that's tobacco. That's a medicine."

"Really?" My mouth was getting hot and I was wondering how I could diplomatically get rid of it. There was no way.

"Sure. If you got tobacco in a corner of your mouth, you safe. Any man give you a rum in a rum shop, you drink it and it meet the tobacco. As you drink it, spit it out. The moment you swallow the juice of this you will turn man to beast. (I was beginning to believe that.) You are so serious, nobody will call you as you passing. They will see your face is strange—that you vexed."

"Oh, the expression it gives you?" I was wondering what my expression was.

"That's right." Charles chortled. "When you go down the road you should always have it there. In a good while you're going to see your two foot come light. You going down—you pass straight. 'Come here.' You pass. You go down to the wharf, you go down to your office, you go anywhere you want. Nobody can stop you and nobody can control your brain now. I'll pass you some schooling before you go, because you don't know nothing."

It was shortly after that that I said good night to Charles and made my way across the railway onto another wharf. As I stood there in the dark I took imaginary aim and spewed my chaw in the water. I heard it splat somewhere beneath my feet and stumbled off to find my bunk.

Almost every night Charles would bring a leaf to show me. He would make me feel it and smell it and repeat the name after him and always he would tell me, "The schooling I passing tonight is: if anything go wrong with you, you not bound to ask anybody. You not bound to go to no doctor. You can tend to your ownself." On a typical evening he told me, "I will bring you three things tomorrow. Vin chassent—that's the one if anything wrong with you, you cut a little piece of it and put it in the water to soak and you drink it. And miyuk [manioc] chapelle.[4] It's just like a cassava. You take a little bit and you grate it, put it in a glass. You'll see a big froth. Drink it fresh, fresh, fresh and it will make you have a nice appetite to eat and you'll have no trouble with your body. It's a cooling. And the next thing again—if you don't feel good, you feel sleepy—you buy an ounce of tobacco and a bunch of seasonings from the market—onion, thyme, garlic, and chichima. Tomorrow I will show you—you must bathe yourself. You got to take care of your body. Nobody will do that for you."

"And that will keep your body clean?"

"That's right. I will bring it for you. Many people don't know that. Just take those things and go and bathe in the sea. Rub yourself all over and throw the balance behind your back. When you come back you'll feel better. And no doctor—nothing at all. If your husband feel himself no good tell him, 'Come on, let me give you a bath.' You ain't bound to tell him anything. You show him you is a doctor."

Charles chuckled. I took the opportunity to ask what might be good to give my husband who was suffering from the "traveler's complaint." I wasn't sure he would take it, but I thought I might at least make the effort to bring him a local remedy. Charles was obliging. "Oh, I will bring it down for you—some bush to boil for him to drink. First you must give him a dose of senne with a grain of salt. You know senne? That will clean him up, take off the cold—that's a cold he got. Something he eat was too cold. Then in the morning when he get up you got to give him bush to drink. You never hear of those bush, maweepoui, charpentier, faydo blanc, jampana, guava? You take the leaves and boil them together and you give it to him to drink. Then everything will go. Sometimes it's a cold, sometimes it's something you eat or something wrong. You call that a cold. How long he got that?"

"About two days."

"All right. Tomorrow night I'll come. Look out for me. I'm coming down early." And true to his word, Charles arrived with his "messages" the following evening.

Periodically Charles would check to make sure I still had an adequate supply of en tout cas, will power, or the ingredients for the parfumé. I took these opportunities to question him more fully on what these things were. One night he told me, "Janie, I saw the woman for the en tout cas today. She tell me she going to bring it for me next Friday, because Christmas she didn't come down into town. I say, 'O.K.' That will do no harm—that will be better, because it will properly soak when she come down. I will put it strong for you."

"Does she make it then?"

"She bring the worm for me. Yeah, and a bottle."

"It's a kind of worm?" I asked, silently wondering what I had been drinking.

"Yeah, a kind of worm for that personally. It's a tree making that worm. It's a tree and it have a vine around it. The worm have two horns, something like a buffalo.[5] Now I might have it before the woman, because I got that behind my house growing. That's right. One day I was passing behind the house and I see one like that on top of the leaf. I say, 'Ah, how do you do?,' put it in a bottle—a big bull, a master. It's a master of medicine of people going to kill you."

I was still trying to get specifics that I could relate to. "What kind of a tree is it?"

"Twef is the name of the tree. It's the tree making that medicine. That worm come upon the tree leaf."

"And you get the leaf and the worm?" I remembered there had been a number of leaves soaking in the rum.

"That's right. The worm on top of the leaf. You could drink the leaf just as well as the worm, but it's stronger when you got the three worm in it because the worm just like a cattle."

"What do you call the worm?"

"Sheenie[6] twef."

"Sheenie twef?" Like so many of Charles's names, it sounded awkward on my tongue. "And the tree is twef?"

"That's right. Now tell me. How is your next bottle?"

"You mean the red stuff—the will power?"

"That's right."

"I have about a quarter of a bottle left."

"Well, I will bring you some more tomorrow." And sure enough, the following evening he presented me with another bottle.

I was surprised at its color. This time it was a clear kind of liquid, but I thought it had the same strong smell. "It's a different color."

"That's right. This is the one that's the strongest for the home. The other is different."

"It smells the same."

"Who tell you so? This one is a different scent. It stronger. That's the oil of rose. Smell it good. Look out for it. That's a flower."

I suppose I must have sounded dubious as I said, "Well, I had the red stuff before," for he answered rather impatiently.

"I the one who give you that. I know what I give you."

Now I was the one who was becoming exasperated. "Well, what *was* that?"

"That one I give you before? That is oil of rose and red lavender mixed together."

"Oh."

"But this one is pure—without anything. The oil is a very big man. At sea you got to use red lavender with the oil to cut off its strength. If you use the oil willfully, you want to see the Boss[7] too quick."

"Is the essence of rose different from the oil of rose?"

"Sure they are. The essence and the oil are two different things. The oil is stronger than the other." He was laughing at my ignorance. But I still didn't understand what the oil of rose had to do with the Sea Devil.

"Why does the oil bring the Sea Devil? Is it the smell?"

"It instruct the fish. That's the power it have. If you going to use that for fishing and you put it in the palm of your hand, you got to use it tonight—rub your hand from tonight."

"The night before?"

"Yes, and you don't touch the boat with the oil. Just take that same hand you use and you're keeping fish steady. If you use that raw, the very same day you see the Boss coming up there."

"You mean if you don't water down the oil of rose?"

"You got to cut it off with cool water. Just put a drop in the water in the boat and wash down the boat."

"But if you use it strong then you see him coming?"

"That's why I tell you, the oil and the essence."

"Use them together?" I was getting confused.

"No, Sir! The essence by its ownself. The oil, you got to cut it with the red lavender."

"Oh, that's right. Yeah."

"And still make no mistake to put too much, because you're going to hear something going to bounce the boat—*boom*. They give you a long time to catch some fish. Suppose you leave here at one o'clock in the night. You going up on the fishing ground. You reach there about five o'clock or about half-past three in the morning—away to windward of the land. You got six, seven, eight, nine, ten, and at ten o'clock up your centerboard and go down there so. Don't stay. Twelve o'clock will catch you in the harbor, but don't let twelve o'clock catch you to windward of the land. You could meet the fish like sand—pulling. You've got to have your watch in the bottom of the line. Know the time of day. Good. All the time you're killing fish steady. Before you send your line in the water, fish there. People are not catching many, but you catching steady. But don't stay there 'til twelve o'clock because he going to bounce you—*feeew*—he going to blow. He blow. Well, if you've got the bottle with you throw it in the sea water or if you have it in the box, it is worse. He want it because you have it there. He'll just pass his head there, so, and lift you up in the boat. He come back again. He want it. What you have there, send it in the water. As you send it—*tap*—he go down below for it. Yes, this thing is good for fishing, but don't carry the bottle. Send the bottle over. Do what you have to do ashore, but leave the Boss at home.

"You could do all this kind of thing, but don't carry the oil of rose on the ocean. The same thing if you have a shop—if you want to get sale more than anybody else. You get up about one o'clock in the night. Just sprinkle that same oil of rose from the door of the shop to the street, the same way people are going to the market, the same way the shop block up with people. You haven't got enough things to sell."

"So it works both on sea and on land?"

"What? Are you mad? It work everywhere. If you are using the oil of rose and you go in a hotel—let's say you go in the hotel looking for a man—when you have $1000 the next girl don't even have a dollar. That's because you have the protector pulling men for you.

"Ay yay yay, Janie. You want to kill me. I going so deep with you. You take the oil of rose, shove it under your arm—shove it both sides—and then the man sleep on this arm—you know a man like to shove his head under your arm. What become of you? When you tell that man to go home, don't talk about leaving because the last cent he work for, he give you. If you left that man, he still come to see you. He going to forget his mother. His own mother going to beg him for a shilling. He just get paid. When you reach, you're going to tell his mother to come to you and you will give her a shilling. Because the man doped. The smell under your arm of the oil of rose turn him stupid. He know he love you. He don't know what to do with you to satisfy himself. He will sleep under your arm for the whole night. He's happy. Tomorrow he go and work. When he come for the evening, he kiss you. When he get paid—straight to you. It's not his fault, Janie. Next morning you got to tear up the envelope. Tell him, 'Take this, put it in your pocket to give your friend.' You think oil of rose plain [simple]!

"In Guadeloupe there's a man called Germany and he has a boat they call *Ballatar* from Martinique. He meet me by the wharf where they were selling fish. He ask me a dolphin. I take the dolphin to him and he tell me sell him three. I sell him three. He find he was so glad with the crowd of people that was there that he tell me when I finish, 'Come in the morning by the boat *Ballatar*.' I told him my name and he say, 'I going to meet you.' He say, 'Carlo, I will tell you something. I'll bring a present for you on Saturday, so look out for me.' I come Saturday. When I was in the ocean fishing I see the boat coming in from Martinique. I just say, 'Pick up the hook and hurry up. Fix up your line. Put away everything. We ready. I want to get in. Hurry up. Clap the mast on. Make your tow bait.' By the time I had fix up everything, I see him there coming. I know I ready already. And the way he coming, he just pass to leeward of me and I was to windward of him. He have engine, I have sail, but I don't care because I see him. I send me line to him and he do me that. When I reach by the wharf I tell him I glad he come in front of me. He ask me what I have. I say I have one albacore and some flying fish. He tell me he want eight pounds of albacore and two dozen flying fish. I say, 'O.K., we'll go in the market for you to pay me two shillings'—50 cents a pound. He want that fish to carry to Martinique, understand. O.K. When I reach, he say, 'Charles, look, just take a little bit in your hand from tonight, and tomorrow morning don't touch it no more. Pass your hand over the line and look out.'

"When I see this thing, I say, 'Well, I leaving tonight about eight o'clock and I going up to windward of the land because I hear they have a lot of albacore.' I have a good calabash full of flying fish—tow bait—put three hooks, each one got a flying fish on. He give me a paper bag and I make a flying fish there ready with the line. I put it in the paper bag and I slash it through the paper bag. Then the sea water going to tear off the paper bag and the flying fish is going to go in. Jesus Christ. Albacore! Put it aboard, loose the line from the wire, jump on the next one, slack it. When day break I going down with seven albacore. I say nothing. The whole week—only oil of rose on my hand . . ."

"Not on the line?"

"Nothing atall. Only on my hand."

"Was that the first time you ever saw that work?"

"I didn't know nothing, Janie. It's true. I give the man the fish, and Mr. Germany call me and told me about the oil of rose. He bring the bottle that have a pot under it like a barrel. You see, what you plant is what you reap."

Another night Charles was questioning me about the parfumé he had given me and I was able to ask him the names of the different ingredients. As usual he prefaced his remarks with a warning to pay attention.

"I warning you, if your head is hard, make it to open. Ay—you must listen good to what I tell you. Now, this thing I told you to burn for smell. You will take some, put it in a piece of cloth and pung it. Then put it in a basin and throw water on it and you mark your house with the same water in the basin. My wife do it every Monday. If you want to see peace in the house you must do this. She do it this afternoon before I leave. I was sleeping on the ground. She tell me, 'Get up, go on the bed sleeping. Give me room to do my work.' She take the basin, scrub under the bed, everywhere, and I don't even move because I know I cannot say no, because she do it for both of us."

"You said she punged all the powders together?"

"Yes, all together."

"What powders do you pung?" I was after their names.

"The same ones I give you."

"But what's that called?"

"That for your home—to clean up your home."

We seemed to be talking at cross purposes, but I persisted risking his irritation if he was trying to avoid telling me the names. "Yeah, but what do you call it?"

"Oh, that name of the thing. Well, you've got l'insens [incense], benjoin [benzoin], and la mienne [myrrh]—all that you mix together. You burn some and you scrub with some. You smoke the house but you've got to scrub the floor."

Ingredients of a parfumé

"Is l'insens incense?"

"That's right. The Church using that. Why the Church using that—to chase away bad spirits. Don't you believe bad spirits don't come in the Church. That's why you burn it in the house too. When you sleep nothing can come and take away your sleep and humbug you. Sometimes you hear a rat on top of the roof of the house—*brdrr, brdrr, brdrr*. All the time the rat up there, you cannot see it. It's making the noise, disturbing you, and you say, 'It's a rat,' but that time it's a human being turning rat. The rat comes at six o'clock until six in the morning. Do you think you can sleep? If it's a rat, then why—when you put your fish on the table and you don't cover it—why don't the rat come and take the fish and go with it? That's not a rat, it's a human turning a rat. A rat tiefing everything he see. In the night I sit down, so, and I see a rat come out. What she come out with? Two sweets of chocolate in her mouth. A rat will come in the house if you have coconut there. He take it and carry it off to eat it. But that *brdrr, brdrr, brdrr*—that's something different. You cannot rest yourself, you cannot sleep, and tomorrow morning you sick. That happened to George Alliman. It was a 'mice' that killed him.

"George Alliman was in the bedroom sleeping. The mice go in the bucket of water and fall there. He making noise, he fighting to come up in the water. He do that expressly to make George Alliman come out from the bedroom so he'd have a chance on him. The wife tell her husband, 'George, I cannot sleep. Go and save the mice.' George get up from the bedroom to come through that door to go and kill the mice. It throw him down and cut his tongue from his mouth. Was it a mice? It's a mice, eh? It's a mice. Another person turned it.

"Now remember there is a different smoke you make for the boat. I will bring it for you. The smoke and the bédaf."

"The what?" I had never heard him speak of that before.

"The bédaf."

"Bédaf," I said, trying to pronounce it right.

"Yes."

"What's that?"

"When I give it to you, you're going to see," Charles told me elusively. "That's for the boat."

"Do you rub the boat with it?" I prodded, trying to elicit some information.

"You wash the boat with it. Dash it inside, dash it outside."

"Is it a leaf?"

"Um hum, it's a leaf, too."

"Just as long as it's not a cattle's tongue!" Charles had told me that a cattle's tongue was a science. "You go up and you cut the cattle tongue, and you beat the boat in the morning at daylight—early, early, early. You beat it just like a child and throw the whip in the sea and that boat will take no more fish."

He laughed. "Bédaf is bound to cut that. When you're leaving here you can't expect to have good luck, without you got your things working for you. Smoke it up."

"With the same bédaf?" I was still confused about this bédaf.

"No, bédaf is for the deck—when you're working—you have it in a bucket."

"But you smoke something else."

"Yes, that's right." I finally had it. Bédaf was something different that you scrubbed the deck with while you smoked the boat with the parfumé. Apparently it was a kind of leaf which was punged first. Then mixed with some water it was used to bathe the boat—or, as it was called in Patois, "un bain." What Charles called "chardon benit" was supposed to be the same thing. As I later learned, the parfumé Charles used for the boat was one of four parcels. The first three contained l'insens, la mienne, and benjoin, as for the house, but the fourth was a bad-smelling substance Charles termed "safétida [Asafoetida gum]."

He continued, "You smoke it and you take the water and you wash the deck. All those boats you see by the market—every morning, every boat they wash and scrub, to clean them to go in the ocean. Remember the smoke is for the inside of the boat and the water—you just take a piece of old bath towel. You wet it and pat it, head to foot, for'd to aft. You don't know. Something could happen very easy. You could be leaving there, and they go and do what they want to the boat. If you don't clean yourself you're just there like a dummy. I cannot let you go like a man going to fight in the war without no gun. Where are you going to get? You don't see where you come from. When you reach you find there's a better man than you.[8] Each time you do something you miss. Each time you miss. But not with me."

"No, you've certainly tried to help me a lot," I said appreciatively.

"There is one thing I think, Janie. I will tell you, I believe God did send you right to me. The two are we so," he said, placing two fingers together. "Before I die, I believe you have to get half of mine."

"I hope so," I said earnestly. With that he threw back his head and gave a great laugh. For the rest of the evening we talked of other things, but I knew that our relationship had reached a new depth.

Shortly after that Charles brought me some bush to learn to identify. "Look, this one has a long leaf—break it and smell it. It's a different smell." He went over the different leaves with me and then said, almost teasingly, "There is a powder. I don't have to give it to you, but if I give you that, would you try it?"

"What powder?"

"Would you like this thing? Would you have use for it?"

"What kind of use for it?" I asked noncommittally.

"If your husband was treating you bad and he have a different woman, this powder good for you. But your husband treating you nice. I see the kind of way he treat you."

"Yes, he treats me nice," I said backing up a little, but I was still curious about the powder—even if I didn't need it.

"Well, that's why I wouldn't give you the powder."

"What's the name of the powder?"

"What's the name of the powder?" he laughed and clicked his tongue at me. "You call it obligé."

"Poudre obligé—like powder of obligation?"

"Yes. It mean in English, 'you're bound to.' You do like you don't know nothing and you put it on the ground where he walk or put it upon the table. He's doped. Nobody could ask him any money to borrow. Without you say yes he cannot give it. He just get pay. He cannot touch the money before you through with it. A man going to call him and say, 'Please, I want you to lend me a shilling.' He going to say, 'I have money, but you got to ask my wife.' When he come in he going to say, 'This man ask me a shilling, do you want to give him?' And this powder is a terrible powder—obligé, poudre obligé, in Patois. I could have get that today if I wanted to. But I studying. Not to say, I cannot give it to you."

"No, I know, but I don't think I need it."

"If you told me, 'Charles, so and so is the case,' or if he have heart to do you any wickedness or carving up."

"No, he's good to me."

"Well, I won't give you that. But if he make you suffer I'll do worse."

"You mean there's worse than that?"

"I say I will give you worse than that." But Charles was through with that discussion for the night. Suddenly he had another thought. "I forget something. Jesus Christ!" And he was up out of his chair quick as a sprat and off to the storeroom where he stored his things 'til morning. He returned, carrying a little matchbox full of a greasy, clear substance.

"You don't help me know things! I bring that and you don't help me to remember. Suppose you were leaving tomorrow morning, and when I go in my bag I would have to meet it. You cause it. Here you are. It's very distinguished [powerful]."

Before I thought, I asked, "What is it?"

"Jesus Christ, what's wrong with you? This is the boric ointment I told you about last night—for a scratch on your skin or any kind of thing. You keep that by your ownself. Half the time the doctor say he going to tend to you but he going to make it worse. Well, now you have no damn right to go to any bloody doctor. You think I try to kill you? There was a man here they called Mr. Jongue. He take up with a girl, and she get jealous. The man go make an operation and he deaded. Mrs. Jongue sell everything and get the hell out of St. Lucia. She say, 'They kill my husband and they think they going to get me, but they won't.' The first thing I tell you, the doctor watching you. They do things that make it worse. You just go visit the doctor. That night you put on the medicine. You bawl like hell and you suffer more. Bush medicine is the best. We have doctor. Mr. Jongue send for a doctor, and what that doctor do him? Shit! He go in the hospital, and why didn't the doctor give medicine to cure him? The thing start to rotten on the man's leg and he dead. Bush medicine is the best. Me don't want no doctor. Me go to the doctor for four or five days, but me don't want doctor. Me go to the doctor, but me don't take what he give me. When he give me the bottle, I just throw the job in the cocoa and I do my own medicine. I born in nineteen ought one and I sick in my home. 'Charles, go and see doctor.' Yes, I will go see doctor, but when he gives me medicine it don't mean I will take it."

Sometimes in those evenings I would start our conversation off with a question and Charles's talk would range far beyond the question. One night I asked, "What kind of berry is it that people rub a two-pence with?"

He answered, "It's not a berry. I will tell you. If they have a bad disease on them, they rubbing the money on the disease."

"And they put the disease on you?"

"They throw it on the ground and you pick it up."

"And you get the disease?"

"And they cure and you get all the disease."

"I see. I had heard you should never pick up a coin."

"You never cure. Just like that they have a kind of disease. All youself is *bump, bump, bump*. You take your money. You rub it all upon you back and you put it in the road. A person pick it up, and in two months, you clean, but in these days that person would never know how to make the cure.

"Next thing I tell you. Your husband got two women. He have you and he have a next woman. Good. This woman now going to fix sheself up, and when your husband come and live with her, she spoiled. Now he going to come to you. Then the moment he have relations with you, tomorrow morning fire around the slit. Trouble. You cannot shake your leg. You cannot sleep. Fire. Fire. Tomorrow morning, fire. That mean to say poison she drink. He pump it. It inside him. He not drink it, he going to pump it and let it go for you. The woman drink the medicine. She fixed she-self up. All the time he pumping, he drawing. Now tomorrow night he not go over there. He come this side and he going to deliver the juice for you now. Fire. Both side is sore. The doctor come—trim this piece, trim the next piece—and you just like the chair. When your Rosie [menstrual period] come, you have to burn up. You have to burn up every day because the hole is wide open. Wind could get through there, and germs. Well, the doctor scrape you, still this cannot help you because it still sore. That is why a woman got to take good care when she have a husband and the man running about. Because it is very seldom that you will be cured. All your panty and skirt is wet because what he sowing, now dripping and it is not inside, it is in your window. This thing coming out. If you have somebody that can help you, you will be cure.[9] Now, what to drink to cure this?"

"I don't know."

"You will go to a good doctor's shop and ask for salt of nitre."

"Salt of nitre?"

"You will take salt of nitre, put a drop in a glass of water and you will pour water into the glass to full it up. After you drink this salt of nitre, in a good while you're going to feel you want to piss. It turn just like milk. You cut a lime and squeeze it in it. So it is, coming down by the bump. Everything is over, but it is not everybody know that. Now that medicine from Puerto Rico, from a man you call Agousto Labille. Look at that. How I know all that, eh? How I know all that?"

"I don't know."

"I pay for all that. When you reach home you should put that down in your notebook. If you write all these things, then any time you knock your toe wrong and screw around, you know you can go back in your book and mark what Charles say. In Patois it mean 'sel de nuit.'"

"Sel de nuit?"

"That's right, darling."

"Salt of the night?"

"Yes, that's night salt. Now in Patois, 'sel de nuit.' If you go in a doctor's shop you will ask a shilling of sel de nuit—an ounce of sel de nuit. They're going to give it to you. Then put a little bit in a glass and swallow it. If you put the glass full of water, drink all. When you're going to pass water—*shhh—ew*—and you piss sweet. No burning again. But before you drink that, three drops of pee and the tear come out from your eyes. You feel to pee, but cannot pee—three drops, it coming out with blood and a little bit of pee and burning you like pepper. But as you drink the salt of nitre, when it come out now, you see the kind of sweet way it coming out—*shhh*—you wash away captain to cook. Yeah, you wash away, but don't you go and mix yourself with that same person again. Never. He could give you a hundred dollars. Never, because you like you health."

Charles was not going to relinquish his role of gynecologist right away. He continued to warm to his topic. "There is a kind of a thing like a vine called 'shasse pawelle.' You boil it, and it mix like blood. That is good when you have pain in your courses [menstrual cramps]. You drink that with a drop of salt. See, sometime you not dealing with your husband, you're dealing with somebody else, and the last person you deal with have a long foot. When you come to see your courses now, all your belly hurting, so you boil that and drink it the same way as the St. John root."

"What's it called again?"

"Shasse pawelle. Now you say the name."

"Shasse pawelle."

"That's right," he said approvingly. "I'll have to get you that. You take two leaf, put it in water, let it boil properly—just like wine—and a drop of salt. Then you see your courses. When every day you're watching for your courses, but you don't see it, you know something go wrong."

"So you drink that?"

"Yeah, you take shasse pawelle. You take two leaf, put to boil, some salt and you have to drink it like a cup of green tea—hot. When it's about seven o'clock in the night, you feel all your panty wet and you know what happen already. You don't jump because you is the one who make it come. Be upon your guard, because it going to come. Be on your guard. It is so damn rude if you not. As it come, the headache and the bellyache hurting you and you can't sleep again because it come down. But it going to come a lot stronger the first time. And tomorrow night it calling you—it coming like a train—but then it nearly finish. I will get it for you. Why you want it?"

I thought to myself I would be curious to see it, but that it was probably better if I didn't pursue it, so I said, "No, I don't need that."

But it was Charles who gave me my opportunity. "But you could get it. It good for you to keep too. Huh! You say you don't want that, but sometime you don't know."

"Well, that's true." I wondered if I was weakening too fast.

"You say that, eh—that you don't want medicine. Maybe you have too much in your house, but you don't know. You never know, if you have that in a corner and there comes a time and you don't see it—that's the time you're going to pay twenty dollars or forty dollars for it and make people know your business. You could tend to your ownself without that."

"Now another thing. You know what you call 'red lotion'?"

"Red lotion?"

"It's a powder. Call it 'potasse.'"

"Potasse? No, I haven't heard of it."

He was surprised now. "You never see red lotion powder?"

"Do you rub it on your skin?"

"Nah, you put a little bit of red lotion in a basin and you're washing yourself with it. You could go anywhere you go tonight. As you come back you put that in the basin and wash yourself."

"And everything's O.K.?"

"Everything is tight, as if it's never been touched."

"What?" I wasn't sure if I was following him.

"You come back tight."

"Oh." Yes, I was right with him.

"Like you never touched nobody. Your husband come—the trouble he get . . ."

"And he wouldn't know?"

"No. He wouldn't know nothing. You just like a person who stopped for months without that. He cannot find that out."

"I've never heard of it."

"You want to see it tomorrow?"

"Sure."

"Tonight you get yourself caught up with somebody else and when you reach home—look, blood. By the time you wash it, and the moment you piss in it, it turn to water."

"It turns to water?"

"Yes, as you piss in it."

"And then nobody knows it's there?"

"Nobody don't know what the hell you do. If you going to throw it away, somebody going to see you use red lotion, but if you throw it after you piss in it, it turn." Then in a conspiratorial tone he said emphatically, "Janie, I will give it to you tomorrow evening. If God help me tomorrow morning I will get it at the drugstore. And when you're done piss in the basin, you're going to say Charles was right. Tomorrow night sure, I going to bring it. Red lotion powder. It good for you—keeping the inside of the body fresh. You'll see it tomorrow. The same way you just put it in a glass and you take a spoon and you do it, so, you see pure blood. That good for woman and man too. If a man got a bad sore and he washing his instrument—that good. And that good for you, too. You put it in the water and you're washing yourself with it—*ohoo*—and you come back a maiden girl. You find that. Nobody can find out nothing. You got to have sense. If you have that in your room, nobody can find out nothing. You don't care if you go in the world—as you reach—you put that in the basin, wash up yourself, and come back a maiden girl. If you don't got that, he going to find out, because he going to know that you shouldn't be that way. And he going to come and ask you. You're frightened because you know you shove your hand in the ice. But if you know what to do, you don't care. The moment the person drop you there, you going to go into your bedroom, take off your clothes, and do your business.

"If you is a woman and you there like a bloody fool in a room at your house, you no use. The Haitian tell you, 'If you don't know how to keep yourself in a house, you're not a woman yet.' Well, that's right. You got to know, if you get a scratch, how to tend to the scratch. If your toenail cut you, there, you say, 'How that get cut?' You tend to it and tomorrow morning you're cured. Perhaps that was not an easy scratch—there's some scratch that are wrong and you tend to them in a different kind of way. You got to be wise.

"Red lotion is a poison too, you know. If you put a lot, it won't do the job right. But if you put a little grain on your finger and you put it in the tea, the moment he swallow it, it cut his fucking heart, and the quicker it do the job."

"But if you put more in, it doesn't do it?"

"Nah, because it will make the person puke blood, and people will have chance to know what it is. He will die, you know, he won't be saved, but people going to see that it was poison you give him because he going to puke blood. When the doctor come to test him—he dead stiff, you see—he dead stiff. Well, the doctor just holds his pulse, and the poison come out of his nose like that."

"The doctor just presses on his pulse?"

"Yeah, because he stink, and it come out his nose."

"Is it just that one kind of poison or any kind of poison?"

"Any kind of poison, so long as he dead by poison."

"No kidding."

"Any kind of poison so long as they give it to you." He repeated, "Poison is easy to get. I could make you see now. Tomorrow night I could bring you a parcel of poison from the doctor's shop. I'll give you a parcel of poison tomorrow night. And you will keep that parcel. It should be in the bottom of your grip as you're traveling around. The minute you put it on your tongue you won't know any more. If you want to get poison, I will show you how to get poison perfect. You will open a little place in your parcel like that, and get some rice, and beat the rice, and break the poison powder, and put it somewhere where you see mice and rat—where they could meet it. When tomorrow morning come, look upon the pan. You find the pan is clean—not one that eat that food live. Everyone dead—you're going to see. And the same with human. You living here. You haven't got no chicken and fowl, and dog humbugging your peas—humbugging you in your garden. You take some food—some potato—you mash it up and you put the powder there and put it in your garden. When you come you find your food is gone. All who eat that food cannot live. No one, not a human. It's poison."

I was interested in pursuing this conversation and I remembered something I'd read to prod him along. It may have come out somewhat garbled, but I found it served my purpose. "The Indians have a special kind of corn with a red stripe in it. Have you heard of this? This is when you want to do harm to somebody. You put the corn in a yellow flower and you put it where a person's going to walk. The birds won't touch this, but the person will walk on it, and the poison will go into the person."

"That's a worm."

"A worm?" I asked in surprise.

"The worm will be in the center of the corn. You'll feel a crazy way in your foot. He will come up to your leg, and you suffering from your feet up to your heart. And if you not a fool, you know how to dress yourself so that doesn't need to destroy you."[10]

"I also heard you might be able to get somebody who knew how to suck it out of you, but the problem was if the person didn't really know his business he'd suck it into himself and it would kill him."

"He not bound to suck it. The kind of worm—he have a prickle in his tail—and this worm, they call it 'gounouee.' "[11]

"Gounouine?"

"Gounouee. Now this worm from cassava water. You make farine. When you put the farine upon the press to squeeze it, you just making a little swamp, and through that swamp, it cause a worm from this farine water. Then you collect a few, put them in a bottle with the same muddy farine water—just like a big vial."

"And that water's poisonous, isn't it?"

"Poison. Poison. Everything inside there is poison. Good. You are not bound to put that in corn. You put it in any kind of paper or just scatter the water in a package where the person walking, so long as the person not using shoes. The bare foot mash the germ from the water, and the worm going through his skin."

"Oh, and it will go right up to his heart?"

"It going to grow. It turn a worm in his body."

"How do you get rid of it?"

"Right. You take it out and send it back to the person now. That's what you got to know. Then you going to take senne, you going to go and boil the senne and drink it with a dose of this same medicine I gave you with the worm and the two horn."

"The en tout cas?"

"En tout cas," he nodded. "You're going to work it out from you with that. After you cut it from your bowels, you throw it on the floor. You're going to take it back and put it on the same road where the same person passing and send it back to him. He will never get better. He will stop until dead."

"It comes out through your bowels, then?"

"Yes. The worm—everything—come out, because you got the thing to make him come out. If you cannot make him come out, you will always have a wake at your house, because when he reach your heart you're dead. Your mouth will stink before you die, and you're suffering the whole night. Sometime the worm going to travel to your brain, and you're suffering. You go to have an operation, but the doctor cannot help you now. Only what I give you will save you. If you know your work—en tout cas—then you will be cured.

"There is one they call 'British Gun Boat.' You never know that one?" I shook my head. "No? You meet him in the ocean."

"British Gun Boat?" I was trying to figure out what he was talking about.

"Yes. Do you ever see a kind of thing in the water—you know, like a prawn in the sea—and he all kind of colors. He got green, he got yellow, and he just like that in the water."

"A kind of jellyfish?" I was groping.

"Yes, just like that, and underneath he have splinters like a sea cat."

"Yeah."

"And if you touch this . . ."

"It stings you," I finished. "Is it a Portuguese Man of War?" I guessed.

"Yeah. This one have little fish under it."

"Uh huh." His description sounded right.

"Lot of little fish, and all the little fish is poison, and he got a lot of those legs, like a catfish. The moment you see him rub on the flying fish line, watch out. When you take your hand to take up the line, he shock you right there on your hand. He give you two buttons [boils or swelling] right there, so. You got to sit down right in the corner. You cannot fish no more. British Gun Boat, they call that. And he just like that—blue—and you see, when the tide going up, he going up with the tide and when it coming down, you will see him. And you get that. You just take a calabash. You pass your hand under it with the calabash and you bring down your bottle already. You throw it in the bottle and cork it with the sea water. You got that? That is a criminal poison. You destroying people with that. They cannot be saved. Everything in the bottle poisonous—the fish is poison, the thing is poison, the water it soak in is poison. And take good care not to let the thing touch you when you getting it for the bottle. You keep that bottle corked under your bed for the whole thing is a criminal poison. You can kill thousands of people with that. Nobody could save from that. If you have a person who is your enemy, and he have a drum of water which he and his family drinking from, you just have to take a little bit and the whole bloody water is poison. It kill everyone. If you have a plantain tree—a fig tree—you just go and throw a little bit of your water in the root of that plantain or the fig or the cane. The last cane he have is poison."

"You mean if you eat the fruit it's poison?"

"Oh, Jesus Christ, the poison. That water you threw in the root will make the fruit grow. It's beautiful plantain, but it is poisonous. Same with yam or tannia. You throw the water upon there, and if people went and dig it in the night, they digging their own grave. That's why you hear a man fixes up his garden, and then people go and tief the food and die. You swell, you have a big belly, like that. You call that in Patois 'ou mangé.' It means you go and tief and eat poison food. Many people get so in St. Lucia. Sometimes they go and tief people's food and go and sell it in the market. Then those people who eat it, dying one after another. That's from the ocean. You know how much a man got to pay to get that poison? Twenty-five BWI[12] to get a vial of this British Gun Boat. So long you could get that, your enemy is fucked."

"And there's nothing you can do for it?"

"Nothing you can do for it? You see people with belly, so, and he can't work the mouth and the hand. It come, so. That's why I'm telling you—man know, man could know, but sometime man don't know nothing for fixing that—and it's very simple medicine to cure you. Me don't need anybody to learn me. Me don't ask. Me don't beg. I sit down at home. People come to me. When a person come home and he want to get something, he come in upon the plum tree root and sit down there and talk. Don't you worry—not you, not you. You meet me. It's God send you. And I don't believe that anywhere you pass you ever had anybody call you to talk this kind of thing. What! Are you mad? Where you going to hear that?

"If I get a lash I know what to drink for it—to melt the blood inside. You got a kind of thing like ginger. It is just like curry, call him 'chichima.' "

"Oh, what you put in your rice the other night." He had showed me the chichima then.

"You pung the chichima and you boil it. It melt the blood inside of you and make you use your bowels. That's why I telling you, up to now I got chichima tree at home and I never cook my rice if I not put chichima in it. My people too—they put it in chicken, beef, everything."

"What is it, a root?" It had looked rather like a yellow carrot to me.

"No, it's not a root. You know ginger? It's just like ginger, but it have a different color. I will bring it here tomorrow night. I have it right under the house there. Sometime when you see my wife cooking fish, it give the fish a good, good taste. It's a medicine. That good for the inside. If you get any blows you don't know, you just take your own medicine.

"I not the only one I cure. One day I meet a man who sit down, so. He have on a suit but you couldn't see the clothes. I say, 'Why you so?'

"He tell me in Patois, 'I have no taste to clean myself. I don't know. I was working good and right now, I can't work.'¹³

"I say, 'I see that already.' I say, 'You got money?'

"'Yes, I could get money to give you if you want to help me.'

"'Well, bring five dollars tomorrow morning.'

"He say, 'I going to bring the money for you.'

"'All right. You come and meet me by Peter store right down there.' When he come I tell him, 'Take off you clothes and go and bathe there by the bay. When you come back I give you something to drink.' He come back and he drink it. I say, 'All right. You go to bathe for three days and you come back.'

"He say, 'How much you charge?'

"'Nothing. It's not so I get my payment. When you finish, and according to how you find yourself, you will come to me.' He stop a week. Two weeks I don't see him. Then one night I sit down and I see a man coming—cocoa brown hat, nice black shoe, khaki suit—a Yankee man coming. I say, 'You come in front of me there.'

"'Yes. Well, Mr. Charles, you see how I change. Christmas I pass at my home. Tell me, what you cure me with?'

"'I don't cure you. How can I cure you?'

"'Well, it's too long you don't come and see me, man.'

"I say, 'No, no, no. Not so. I don't know it's so. I know you're working. When I see you I will see you.'

"'Well, you will have a shilling in your pocket each time I see you.'

"'Yes, man.'" He open a bottle of brandy. I take a shot.

"'You want to take one again? Take one for the road now.'

"I say, 'Uh unh.'

"There's a nice big captain and he have a vessel. He dragging molasses to make rum here. Now there is a boy who strike his hand and mash it up. The hand come big, like that, and the boy holding the hand. I tell him, 'What's wrong with you?' He say he was working in the molasses and the hand . . . I say, 'I know what happen to you. Come. We will go inside there at Peter store.' And I just hold the hand. When I hold the hand, he breathing hard. I say, 'No, no, no. Don't worry. I won't hurt you. I'll just stroke it and then tomorrow morning you come down to see me before day. Give me your hand.' I take it. I stroke it and I say, 'All right. You're going to sleep. Tomorrow morning before I go, come and see me here.'

"Tomorrow morning he come. Tell me, 'Old Man.'

"'Hello.'

"'Look me.'

"I say, 'Your hand is good now.' He give me the hand, and I cracked his fingers. I say, 'All right. You can go now.'

"He say, 'How much?'

"'I'll leave that to you.'

"'I'll come down this afternoon.'

"This afternoon he going to bring a next man to me now—a big buckaloo, a white man—the captain.

"'Sir?'

"'Yes.'

"'All of these hurting me. All that hurting me. Me can't sleep in the night, I so painful.'

"I say, 'How long you get that?'

"'This year in St. Kitts I get a draft.' The man got flesh. I hold his hand and I rub it good.

"He say, 'All right. I going away tomorrow night, you know.'

"I say, 'All right. Before you go tomorrow night, you come here.' And he come right there, so. I say, 'Now you could go. I want to see you when you come back. Tell me how you feel when you come back.'

"He tell me, 'Yes.'

"At Christmas he come back with a load of molasses. He taking the molasses in St. Kitts. When he come he tell me, 'You have a basket?'

"I tell him, 'Yes.'

"'What size?'

"'A good size.'

"He say, 'Give me.' He put in two bottle of whiskey and he full the basket with tockle flesh—corned tockle—and covered it over and leave it. When I lift it up, it's heavy.

"I say, 'What that?'

"'Leave it alone. Don't trouble it 'til you reach home.'

"I say, 'Don't worry about that, because my wife have to bring it up. When she come I going to give her that to carry up.' Fati come. I say, 'Fati, look.' I tell her, 'You hold that basket right up to the top. When you open it, be sure to take it off at home.' Fati carry up the basket. When I come in,

"'Charlo, look, tockle and whiskey.'

"That was the first boy who give me that. He give me five dollars. I take it because he was a poor boy. He tell me to charge him, but I did not charge him. He bring the whiskey for me and the tockle. He don't tell me nothing, you know. He just put the thing there and then he go back.

"Now Christmas morning the other man come down. He tell me, 'My shoulder is all right, you know, Watchie. Now, how much you charge?'

"I say, 'Well, twenty dollars.'

"He tell me, 'Twenty? I will give you twenty and make it twenty-five.' We go down in the casino there. He buy a bottle of Mount Gay and two Cokes. I drink two shots and he tell me, 'Keep the balance and I will send breakfast for you.' Now I going to get two breakfasts. My wife have to bring my breakfast, and he going to send a breakfast. Now what he bring? Tockle. Me don't trouble that. I eat my wife's and I tell my wife carry the tockle up. Hear what she tell me, 'Well, Charles, you're bound to make good.'"

"And you just did that by stroking?" I asked.

"Yeah, I know what I do. Yes, I stroking, but what about this? Got to say the prayer. Yes, it's many people going to come to me now. They can't walk right. I just put their two foot like that—I don't pull it, I just stroke it. That night you sleep and when you going to get up, you just do that to try it [in pantomime Charles stepped gingerly on the ground]. You couldn't do that in the afternoon, but you could do it now.

"There is a Mr. Winston on Marchand Road. He tell me he have a foot and so many days he cannot put shoes on. I say, 'Let me see your foot. Put it right there, so.' The foot was big as that. I say, 'How you get that?' He say that he don't know, that it come first like a little button. He tell me all the medicine the doctor give him did no good—that thing still hurting him and scratching him. I tell him to meet me. I went and got my things—some lint and some boric ointment—the same thing I give you in the matchbox. When I meet him all his foot had started to come black. I say, 'Well, I think you have a nice foot.'

"'I don't know, Mr. Charles.'

"I say, 'You don't know! I won't tell you nothing now. I will tell you after I tend to the foot.' I took a piece of lint. I put the boric ointment on it and just pat it on his foot. I say, 'Leave it so.'

"Tomorrow morning he say, 'Mr. Charles, are you going to loose that?'

"I say, 'Let it alone. I will come and take it out. Don't you tell me when to take it out.' The whole week pass. The lint come off itself, and he cure. The sickness, it curing all the time, and when the lint fall, the sickness cure.

"His wife tell me, 'Mr. Charles, Mr. Charles. I think I don't know what to tell you. I don't know what to give you. Come. Come. Come.'

"I say, 'That's all right.'

"'Take it. Take it. Come and take something.'

"Janie, this afternoon I coming down to work, and a girl running, running. 'Mr. Charles, Mr. Charles.' And then I see the girl coming and running. The girl grabbel [grab] me like that, 'Come, come, come. Come in the rum shop and I'll give you a drink.'

"'O.K.!' I go.

"She say, 'What you want, Charles?'

"I say, 'I only want one thing. I want a shot of whiskey.'

"When the whiskey come, a next man come. He say, 'What is Mr. Charles to you—the kind of way you treat him?'

"She say, 'That is my father.'

"'Oh, I didn't know, Mr. Charles. Excuse me.'

"I say, 'You get fucked! Why you ask this question?'

"'I see the kind of girl. The girl running when she see you.' He gone. He come to hang around to see if he going to get a drink.

"I drink. She tell me, 'Charles, come. What do you want me to give you? He give me a hundred dollars for my Christmas. From the time I leave you, this man never give me any money. But this man come now, since you give me the article and I use it. The man give me a hundred dollars. And that man never give me money before.' She say, 'Charles, I come and meet you.'

"I say, 'No, no, no, no. I don't want anybody to come and meet me.' Uh unh. I tell her, 'Go. There is only one thing I want you to do. See me nice, pay me respect, and if I die, I will see if you going to follow me in my funeral.'

"'Merci, Mr. Charles. Take a next drink again.'

"I say, 'Yes, I think I will. Give me the next one. I will take it.' And I drink it and come here.

"I help many many people but I won't help no black man. You know why? I help black people already—mostly St. Lucians— and I ain't find no thanks. The thanks I get is prison. Just this week a woman run to me—her father die. She running to come and meet me to help her. 'Jesus Christ,' I say, 'It is not me. I am not the man.'

"'But they tell me to see Mr. Charles. You tell me that you are Mr. Charles.'

"I say, 'Not me, not me.'

"One day I sit down here at Mrs. Ganter's and a man come quite to me. He ask me a question. I say, 'You asking the wrong person. They tell you to go to the wrong person.'

"He say, 'It is you, they tell me.'

"'Uh unh.' I tell him clear, clear, that it is the next man that was in the job before me called Labadie.

"'You not Ti Son's father?'

"I say, 'Yes.'

"'Well, it is you.'

"'Fuck you.' He even tell me he give me twenty dollars. I say, 'No. It's not me.' I know it's me.

"He say, 'You will get me something, I know. I come to you. You bound to get me something. I paying you.'

"'Who? Me?'

"'It is you they tell me.'

"'It's not me. It must be Labadie.' He gone. Why he come to me? He have to go in a fishing test to see who can take the biggest, nicest fish for the prize. He want to get something to get the nicest fish. He come the next day in the night.

"He tell me, 'Look the boat. Go with me.'

"I say, 'No, I not going.'

"'What are you doing? Can you win the thing for me? Can you do the boat for me?'

"I tell him, 'Let me see the line you have.' He show me. I say, 'I am sorry. I cannot do that for you because I don't know nothing. It was Labadie.' He never come back there again. He vexed me. He doesn't catch fuck all. One day a cattle tail won't chase fly. He forgetting, my dear, but I didn't forget. Many a time he meeting me after work with a car and he passing me, *vroommm*. He don't give me a drop. He don't know he want me one day.

"A man, Fordy, come on my step at my house up there. He sit down, like that. 'Charles, they send me for you. You will help me, please?'

"I say, 'Who send you?'

"'Tao send me.'

"'Yes.' He sit down by the door on the step, crying. I watching him.

"The man don't even take tea. He put three papers—three dollars—upon the table. He say, 'I don't have no more.' He tell me he will give me the balance when he come back on the banana boat Thursday night.

"'Take it back. I don't want it.'

"'Take one?'

"I say, 'No. I'll do it for you for the sake of Tao and because you're from quite in town and you come up the hill at my house. I know Tao—know what he send you for.'

"He say, 'Well, give me the money.' He call Simon. 'Take that,' and he start to cry.

"I take a bottle and put some in a glass and give it to the man to drink. Then I tell him, 'Well, you go and take two baths in sea water and take an ounce of tobacco, and the tobacco going to make you feel a fever—and buy a bunch of onion and go.'

"The man glad. The night he return on his ship, I was sleeping. He woke me up. Fordy tell me, 'Here, Charles, what I bring for you.' A nice pair of white moccasins. He tell me. 'You hold these, and this is yours too.' He bring four shirt right there, so. He bring two for me and two for Fati. In the morning I put everything in the basket and tie everything up. He come up there with me. Tell me, 'Now I feel all right. I had no taste to work, and the woman do what she want with me. Bawl me like a child, and I cannot do anything. She spit in my face. I want to go and I cannot.'[14]

"After I make him get away from that woman, Fordy don't pass me atall, atall, atall. Sometime when I see Fordy, I got to cut a street. He run. Yesterday morning I was going up. I was quite by the little trail. Fordy come up and he had a nice little shirt for the girl. He run, he tell me, 'Look, I didn't see you. Here's a dollar, go and buy yourself a drink. Are you going up?'

"I say, 'Yes.'

"He say, 'Let me help you.' He take the basket and the bag on his shoulder and he go half way."

"What, was the woman working something on him?" I asked.

"Yes, to compel him to bring her money. As he work, he bring it."

"Oh, like you were telling me the other night."

He nodded. "That woman did him a lot of things. She tell him off in front of crowds. In front of people she tell him, 'Your mouth is my towel.' The man is shame. A tall, big man like that.

Now after Fordy come up, Clara ain't worth a cent because the same thing turn on she. Yeah. He fuck her up.''

I hesitated a moment and then I asked, "What did you give him?"

"That's poude brisée."

"Poude brisée." I tried to say it. "What does brisée mean?"

"That's a war, a fighting powder. When you get that at the doctor's shop and you give it to someone, they ain't bound to do anything else. If you put it under anybody's house you're vexed with, and she living there with the husband—no peace. That woman and that man always fighting, one on top of another. That's a row powder.

"Since I gave Fordy that, the man dressing nicely. He walking high. But if I didn't give him that, he'd be nothing.

"Now, Tao, the one who send Fordy to me, I help him too. Tao's woman got two men. Tao below and Ti Son[15] on top, and she a red-skinned girl called Rity, is the biggest boss. Tao got to work and bring money for her. Ti Son got to work and bring money for her. When Tao come and tell me this thing, I say, 'Now, Tao, I'll give you something to put in her rum. You will put a drop in the bottle Rity have, drinking her rum. When she finish drinking she will go on her bed and sleep. You will take off the ring and bring it for me.'

"He do that. 'Here is the ring.'

"I say, 'Rity said already she didn't love you because you is too black and too ugly. The one she loves is Ti Son.'

"He tell me, 'Yes.'

"Now Rity is a girl taking any man she want, and he can't leave her. I say to Tao, 'I'm telling you plain now. I'm going to leave Rity for you and I will take my son off. My son won't have anything to do with Rity. He won't speak to Rity. He'll have nothing to do with her.'

"He said, 'You will do that?'

"'Yes. Rity will be with you. Rity going to take any man she want, but Rity cannot leave you. You got to work to support Rity, and Rity working and supporting you too.' I take the ring and soak it in medicine from the doctor's shop—soak it properly—until everything spoil. Then I pick it up and put it in a paper. I call Tao and I say, 'Tao, do you know the ring?'

"'Yes, that's Rity's ring.'

"I say, 'Good. Come with me.' We go right to the corner down by the Basin.[16] 'Stand up there. Look the ring—send it away.' I say to the ring, 'You depart and you will be staying. Ti Son will be mine,' and I throw the ring in the sea. I say, 'Now Rity is your one alone.' Now all the time you see Rity go back, Ti Son not with her again. She go friends with a man called Antonio. Tao such an ass. He hold Rity's bag like that and carry it aboard, and Rity tell he she going with Antonio to St. Martins. Antonio is a good, good friend of mine. I try to tell him about Rity, but he won't listen. He come from Portugal and he works on that white boat that carries ripe bananas and green plantain. Every morning when I leave here, the window wide open expressly for me. I jump on board.

"'Charlie, come have coffee.'

"Antonio is a good, good person. You know when a person is kind. He having a lot of trouble with his engine. He went to make a trip again, and what do you think happened? The enemy was close to him and humbug the engine again. The engine stop in the ocean. Now what he do? Antonio leave a man inside the boat, and two of them went to go and get help. The tide took the boat. Quite the next day about three o'clock in the afternoon he make shore at Anse la Raye. All Antonio's pants cut—his backside, his hands cut. The next one say he give up. He will dead. He not working no more. He give up for God. Antonio say, 'No, no, no, no. We're going to put ashore.' When he make Soufriere, he reaching the station to get help. They give them something to eat and next morning they send them in Castries. Antonio reaching town, but everything he have in the boat. No clothes, no nothing. Where his home? His home outside on the ship. They sent a plane out, and it saw the boat four hundred miles from Guadeloupe to windward of the land.[17] And there was one man in it—a black fellow. The man didn't give up. He got food but he can't eat he so frightened. When the plane see him, they send a man down on a jacob's ladder and they drop him in the boat and tell him, 'Take courage, someone is coming tomorrow at two o'clock to tow you to St. Lucia.'

"They send a cable here to tell Antonio they find the boat and that the boat would be here tomorrow. Antonio come up at my home. 'Charlie, Charlie.'

"I say, 'Yes.'

"'I have heard today. They found the boat.'

"I say, 'Yes, man. Don't cry, Antonio. Don't cry.' Because there was four thousand dollars cash in that boat—brandy, whiskey, gin, cigarette, and everything from St. Martins.

"The next day at three o'clock Antonio come, 'Let's go down.' He say he want to go every second, but he will wait for me.

"I say, 'All right.' We go about four o'clock, and when it was six o'clock the boat was right in front of us coming in. Antonio watch, like that. He so glad he cry. He go aboard. He find the man left in the boat is a navy man. He a navy man, yes. He give me shirt, he give me pants, he give me hat. We put the boat by the wharf.

"Captain Looker—he was the man who was humbugging the boat all the time. He making the same trade with them. He was in Antigua. When he finish he go down to St. Martins. When Looker reach in St. Martins, Antonio done finish there. Well, he humbug the engine. Where is he now? Where's Captain Looker now! Easy to do, but easy to catch! Every day you steal, but one day one of the guards is going to hold you. You going to tell the man, 'Mister, it is the first day I is there picking up yams'—that is the first day! You damn well taking it every day, and tonight I catch you and I will hold you here. Looker was doing that many, many, many times, and God help in the day to catch him in the bloody engine room. He say he was resting there and something fall in the engine room. What you think? If it was a pipe, he would have got the pipe. If it a box of matches, you get the box of matches. If it is a wallet, you'll get it. What you going to do with the man? Antonio don't tell him anything. Just tell him, 'What

you lost there, take it and go,' because Looker a man who is always working with a gun, and perhaps if Antonio had hit him a
lash, he would shoot Antonio there, 'cause Looker don't care
nothing. He's a short, big-bellied man. He's a cruel, cruel, cruel
fellow. Antonio tell him, 'Well, when you find it, come up.'
That's all Looker want. I was over there working. 'Charlie, come.
I meet Looker on board.'

"I say, 'I tell you it is Looker doing the job, but you find it out
so you know.'

"This thing now, it is not you who do harm to anybody. Hear
me. You harm nobody. There is your box of matches, there is
your pipe. Every day you are using your pipe. You set that pipe
on the box of matches while the pipe is full of tobacco. Listen
good to what I tell you in parable. I don't give you young man's
word, I give you old man's word. The pipe is ready, full. I so
anxious to snap the pipe and go smoke the tobacco you have, I
don't check the tobacco. On top it is very nice, but what about
below? That's when you say the pipe is low. After you finish
smoke this, one below there and pass it through your mouth and
it come down through your nose, what about this? A couple of
days your throat come big as that. After it burst you can't live.
You don't kill nobody. You just put your pipe on the ground. You
didn't come tell me, 'Charles, here is a pipe.' Your pipe was
there, and somebody took it. But you know why you left it there.
Every day the pipe disappear. But it is clear. You didn't hit me no
lash. The pipe was on the ground. You always accustom to the
pipe disappear. Well you set your pipe. It's clear. You didn't hit
me. I strike my own self. You have no blame. What! Looker went
down there to see about the engine but he tell Antonio what he
handle, done gone. Antonio know that he open the pipe to the
exhaust. So Antonio push a gas into that pipe, and that gas was
poison. That the same thing I told you the other night. If you
going to interfere in this kind of stuff—Jesus Christ!

"I'm going to make you keep your mouth shut. My uncle—he
is a big man. He got land, he got a big factory, mill to make
syrup. Right. He's a big man, eh? He got shop and everything.

He don't know his backside from his elbow. Good. A man tell him, 'Come and give me a hand today to help me cut some cane.' Well, he go because the man got cane, and he got cane. When he reach at twelve o'clock, he done catch something already long ago. When they say breakfast ready, he say he don't want no food. He go and get his breakfast at his house. But he done catch something already. When it was the middle of the night he find a scratch. He scratching. When he start to cry, he start to scratch all his face and all his face start to *pumpo, pumpo, pumpo.* They had hit him long ago. When he can't bear no more he send and call me. I went up and I find him in the chamber like that. I say, 'What's wrong?' He tell me he go and give a man a day's help, and look what happened to him. I say, 'Good.' I went in the drugstore. I take the horse and I come back up. I take the face and I wipe it. I wash it and put the plaster on it. You know this thing in the sea—it always big like that—on top of the water. When you have nice water it's full of them."

"Jellyfish?"

"Yes. Well, that's what they put on his face—to eat up his face. All the thing is scratching. When you're bathing, don't let that thing touch you, because it will humbug you."

"Right." I had been stung by one once and I didn't relish the thought much.

"Well, that's what they put on his face. How he get that? He don't even know."

"Was he drinking or something?"

"No, No. He not bound to drink. What, drink? Not drink, man. The man's smoke do it."

I was startled by that. "Oh, what does he do, dry the jellyfish out and then . . ."

"He smoke. After he smoke the jellyfish—he don't put it inside. He push it out. He have the pipe."

"And you dry the jellyfish then?"

"You dry the fish. The fish is poison and that's what he smoking inside the pipe."

At the risk of interrupting the story I asked, "What uncle is this? Is this your mother's brother?"

"That's right. He dead now. Not that that kill him. He come old. All right. When he come home and called me to say come and see him, I ask him if he know why that happen. He tell me, 'No, the galé.'[18]

"I say, 'Well, you send the galé back.'

"Send back what?" I didn't know what he meant by galé.

"I send it back."

"How did you do that?"

"I saw the road he passing. Then you scatter the jellyfish, and it worse now. It worse because you walking barefoot, like this."

"And you put the powder . . ."

"In the ground. The same road he passing."

"And the same jellyfish?"

"Send it back to him. Then his two fucking foot start to eat up. I say, 'Send it back. Send it back.'

"If you is a drunkard, I make you give up the rum. Make you so you don't even want to smell the rum. Well, if I love you I will tell it. I charge you. Sometime when I go to bed I don't got one cent, and in a minute when I wake up in the night I got fourteen or sixteen dollars. For what? To prevent a man from drinking rum. That's a medicine now. Sometime people from around the coast come up here. I never tell them the price first. I tell you when you pay, you're going to pay me according to the way you're going to find yourself. Then you come to me, tell me what happened. How the thing goes. When you come, you telling me how you is. Then I going to give you the price.

"A man come from Vieux Fort. He came. I gave him the medicine. The brother I cure and the brother send he. And look now, he is the boss of carpenters at Chastanet. If you see the man, you would never think that man drinking rum. The man is thin, like that—a red fellow. And now he has a woman up there. I run away from the man. When I see the man, I go away. I don't want him to see me. He too grateful.

"There's a fellow, he was drinking, and the wife bring him for me. I charge him forty dollars. He have a rum shop. He tell me he pay me now. I say, 'No, me don't want it.' I give him the medicine, and he go. I tell his wife, 'If you see your husband don't cure of drinking rum, don't you give it to me.' But I know he won't drink. The fucker. When he go down to get the medicine and take it, and then he go in a rum shop and he taking a drink—he puke, he shit and he never drink again. And his wife come Saturday and meet me down there by Peter.[19]

"She tell me, 'Here's your money.'

"I say, 'Thank you.'"

I couldn't resist any longer. "Who taught you that?"

Charles had been waiting for that question. "I knew you going to ask me that. Kindness."

"Kindness again, eh?"

"Kindness," he reiterated. "I'll give you a little vial of rum like this, and you carry it home with you, and the man who is your friend and who drinking too much rum, you bet him that you can make him stop drinking. He will tell you no—you can't do that. You tell him it's a sure bet. 'I present you with something.'

"He will tell you, 'You cannot present me with nothing. I will drink. You will be wrong.'

"You will go inside your bedroom. Get out a glass and tell him, 'Now you drink this with me. Drink it.'

"He say, 'Ah, what kind of mix is that? It drink sweet.'

"You going to say, 'Well, that's the kind of rum I drink.' Next time you drink rum, you know what's wrong with you. Any person that drink that medicine and then go and drink rum, he will puke and shit. Well, the same rum he drink cause him to do that, and he will shit inside his draws—all the things shit, and he will lie on the ground here for half an hour. When he revive he won't drink no rum. Call that sweet spirit of nitre.[20] Yes, sir. Sweet spirit of nitre is a master. I will tell you kind of way you deal with sweet spirit of nitre here. A woman will invite you to go somewhere tonight 'with me—now.' Tell me, 'Charles.'

"'Yes?'

"'Man, we going somewhere tonight and have a good time.'

"I say, 'Yes.' And I don't want to go. I told her yes, I'd go, so I go and take a swig of nitre and put it in a glass of milk—two drops—and swallow it with a glass of water for drinking. In two seconds I got to hold my head, like this. Until daybreak I done. It give me a dose of sleeping medicine."

"And it puts you right to sleep?"

"Right. I close everywhere good and I went and swallow that. And I have to take my hammock. I didn't go nowhere. Take a dose of sleep in the head. Just by your ownself. When you go in bed, you're dead. You not waking before daybreak and you not going nowhere. I used to do that common. So long as you invite me to come and go somewhere—I tell you yes. You come and find me. Everywhere close. I douse the light, put it in darkness. You can't come inside if I close my door, because I had a yard at that time. After I close the yard you can't come inside and I don't want nobody."

"And when that stuff is concentrated you can't drink rum?" I asked, trying to make some sense out of what he had told me. I didn't quite believe that he went for long periods of time without a shot of rum.

"No, I didn't drink rum. After you drink that you can't drink rum. Are you mad? That's why you drink it. That's why you drink it. That's why—if you spend the whole time drinking rum."

"Well, what happens if you drink the nitre tonight—and then two nights later you have a drink of rum?"

"Nah. Don't drink rum. You have to stop about two months before you take it. Not rum you're going to drink neither. You take a little drink of sweet drinks, but not rum, because you cannot stand the smell of it. You got to stop a long, long time before you go and put rum in your mouth—about six months."

"Oh, really? Before you can drink the rum?"

"You cannot bear the smell of rum. The sweet spirit of nitre got some kind of way—something for the rum—and you cannot put it there. The same thing if you using this kind of en tout cas and you drinking rum. But you hardly could get drunk because once you have this inside of you, as you drink rum you go and pee the same time. It wash away as you drink. When you use en tout cas, make up your mind and drink the rum quick. If you don't go quick, you piss on you. You wash it away—turn it to water inside of you. The whole Christmas, you think I don't drink? I drink, but I know if I don't pee when I get a shot of rum in rum shop, by the time I by the market I got to go in the piss house and piss it out. This afternoon I take two shots. Who knows? I come here sweet. My mouth don't smell nothing. Because why? I drunk en tout cas already. Do you think I going to leave home without that? I know already I'm going to drink rum, so I go up in the chamber, lay down on bed, take a drink, cork it back. And when next I meet my wife, she don't know I been drinking rum. If you want to get a good reception at home, that's how to appear. Go up sweet, and if I take any friend who drink, she smell the rum.

"I stop all who drink. She was a drunkard, you know."

"Your wife?" No, I hadn't known that.

"Sure. When I take she, she was a drunkard."

"And you gave her some sweet spirit of nitre?"

"I stop her. She didn't used to stay in the house in the night. She used to go and get rum. I cut it off. But I never tell her what I do. I never tell her I going to give her medicine to drink rum. She always crying she feeling bad, she feeling bad. I know why— because when she say she feeling bad, it is rum she want to go and drink. Well, I give her medicine and I put it in a glass of water and I give it to her. When she come to drink rum, she don't want it. Now when I come I hear, 'Uh, uh, uh, uh, you stink of rum. You stink of rum.' I glad. When a girl drinking rum, that is not good. When she drinking rum, child, she belong to everybody, and I can't understand it. The women in St. Lucia, before they ask for a shilling, they drink the rum. The man know already you're drinking rum. 'Janie, just come. You taking a drink? That's right.' You go and drink. He know what he want. He going to give you two. He going to give you three. You intoxicated and off you go. Sometime, perhaps, he is a good soul. He will try to put you somewhere where people will see you and give you a hand and carry you up to your home. Sometimes he would drop you at home. But there are those that leave you the same place on the spot. One morning I going up and I see a girl lying in the grass there, her dress quite above her head. Just how he finish with her, the same way the person left her there. I say, 'Hey, hey, levez, levez, levez.' I pick up her panty and go down to get her. A black girl. What cause that? Rum. I won't tell a girl not to drink. She could take a little shot, mix, and go back to her home. But now they don't do it like that. You know what they say now? 'I have a good time.'"

Always Charles was teaching me, giving me advice, and telling stories to illustrate his point. Always he was warning me against apparent reality. It seemed that he was trying to ingrain a kind of mental uneasiness within me, a constant distrust of life in general. Often he would quote from the Bible to support his points, and he loved to use parables to illustrate them. In his world of suspicion and distrust there were some positives like the oil of rose which would nullify any evil done to the individual. Among these was Charles's belief in a bodyguard. Even this could be a bit illusory. One night he was admonishing me, "The Lord tell you, 'Seek you shall find, knock and it shall be open.' Don't lean like a person that don't have no life. You just like a person that don't have no life. You just like a cow that going to the fatting house to kill. You is human. Don't believe in all those people you see there. Everybody have their guardians."

"Do they all use different bodyguards?"

"It's according to the kind of trade you have, the kind of things you do. Yes, you have a bodyguard, but the least thing you do, it go from you. The least thing you do, tomorrow morning you don't see it around your neck."

"A bodyguard that you put on and in the morning it's gone?" I asked with surprise.

"Gone," he reiterated. "When you don't obey—when you break the rule."

"Oh, you have to do certain things, and if you don't do them it goes?"

"It goes. You lost it quick."

"Gosh," I said for lack of anything better. He laughed at my apparent surprise, and went on.

"You could tie it, you could pin it inside your shirt, and the least mistake you do, tomorrow morning you cannot find it. You supposed to have one master, not two, and if you don't bring this one on your neck respect, you lost it."

"Respect?"

"When you got that you got to keep yourself straight. When you got that in the day you have it. In the night when you finish saying your prayers, take it off from your neck. Put it in the chamber upon the shelf there. Tomorrow morning when you finish praying you put it back. But you can't keep that on your neck and go and make vice with that. You don't get up tomorrow morning. No sir! You must bring him respect." He reiterated, "Put it there tonight, in the morning when you get up you kneel down to pray, you cross yourself, you pick up your guard, you kiss it, then you could travel—going to church, going anywhere. You have your bodyguard. But don't believe you got that and can break the rules. Bring it respect.[21]

"They have a cross, and in the center there's a piece of glass. When you shut your eyes and open that one, you see a big glass and you see a big reading inside. That's a bodyguard. The only way you could get that is in St. Thomas drugstore. In Santo Domingo you could get that, in Haiti you could get that. All kind of way—black, all kind of color. Made just like a little cross. And they have a round ring. They sell it to you, but they tell you take care of it. I got one, but I get it lost. It was when I was sick. Somebody take it. It won't be any use for the person. Nah. No use. No use. Me don't want that anymore. At that time I was ignorant. No. That good for you, but nothing can come across you as long as you use the will power.

The will power is a very funny thing. The moment you speak—the person find you just like a lion. Any woman. Any man. You could be in a crowd. You could rush in a crowd and just say, 'Stop it.' When you say that, everybody come quiet. A fight break out and you come and say, 'You stop it.' You won't have chance to say it twice. You have your will power. That's what I put on you. You cannot see what you are, but they—when they watch you—they see you big. They find your voice is big when you talk, because you speak with will power. What you say goes. Nobody can stand it because you frighten them. You not destroying no one, darling. You going to protect your own body. I don't find that's anything. You're using your common sense. You could do anything. You got to defend yourself. Your own sister going to pet you, talk to you, carry you somewhere. You don't know if she will give a hand for two thousand dollars to try and destroy you. You go like a fool because it is your sister. Yes, but when you feel the trap, you grieve. You don't know nothing. How could you get away from the trap? But if you have your left on your right hand, you don't care. When she believe you trap, now you going to hold her and make her know what kind of woman you are. That's what I want you to understand. Put that in your head. Trust no Shilo [Shibboleth]. I don't mind that you give your sister a thousand dollars, but still don't let go your heart. And never let her know this. When she come and meet you, remember this. Ask yourself question. You study. Good.

The story of two sisters is what I going to tell you now. There were two sisters, one was a poor girl. The next one was married, and she at she home. The last one now went to marry, and she married a rich man and higher than her sister's husband. Now she go and pass a day at her sister's, and the sister set a trap for her right in front of a chair. She would squeeze a button, and the sister fall in a pit. A pipe would be open, and the water would drown the girl. That's the trap. The girl come and sit down there. A piece of carpet cover the width of the door. 'I glad to see you, sister. How you feel? How your husband treat you?' The girl say, 'Oh I am happy. I got my everything. My husband treating me nice.' 'What about your home? Do you have any children?'

"She say, 'No. I haven't got no children yet. I got my servant. I got my driver. And I have a black dog.' When she was going to her sister's, she put the dog on a chain and left it at home. The dog was rushing to follow her and broke the chain but she didn't know it. All right.

"The sister ask the girl, 'What about money?'

"She say, 'Don't talk about money. If you want a thousand I

could lend you it, and when you have it you could give it to me as you can. I'd be glad to back you because I satisfied I have no more money than you.'

" 'True?'

"She say, 'Yes.'

" 'I glad to hear that. You say you will lend me a thousand, and when I feel to give it to you . . . '

" 'Exactly, when you able to give it to me, give it to me. I don't need money because I got more than you. I will tell you now. All the money . . . '

"*Blam*, right in the hole. The sister say, 'I know your husband cannot get you anymore.' She opened the pipe with the girl there in the hole and she cover the door over with the carpet. When that tank was full, she was going to pull the chain to wash the girl into the sea. But little did she know that the puppy burst the chain. The puppy run and make the round of the building and pull the piece of chain that was outside there, so the girl come up in the water without drowning. The dog swim with her and bring her to shore. The little dog carry her right in the detective department. He just knocking the door with his paw. As he do that they open the door and let him inside, and the lady all soaking wet. The lady start to report to the detective what's wrong and what happened. Now the other sister was so foolish, she going to go and watch the water to see if the tank is full, because she know she going to get the girl properly dead. By that time the girl was in the police station. Now the dog go in front, the detective behind. As they reach the woman start to pull the chain. 'Don't do that. I have your sister.' And they carry her to court and they give her lifetime in prison. And she there on a juking [scrubbing] board, washing for the jail."

I suspected that this dour warning was spurred by my sister's arrival the previous evening. I was not supposed to take any relationship for granted. And as if one story was not enough to admonish me, he launched into another.

"A sister take a scissor and stab her own sister for a man right in St. Lucia."

"Really?"

"Really. She stab her own sister for a man—that bitch! You know she spent twenty years in prison and when she come out, she stepping like a person who was back from the States. Her job was a cook in prison, and when her time up she come out with some money because they paying her. She went in there a young girl. When she come out, she come out a woman—fat and big. And she come out with money. She just paid passage to go up to Trinidad to make that she home, because she knew well her whole family would destroy her. But she smart. She smart. Her brother would have destroyed her. Her name was Bernice. Bernice's mother was a duppy woman. One night she coming up and twelve o'clock meet her right by the market. You hear, *blaaww*. Bernice mother fell down there. They have to get a kind of armchair to take her inside her house. When she start to talk, she say, 'Not me one. Nancy too.'[22] When she have a month, Nancy was bawling. Nancy bawling too, 'Oh, let me go. Let me go, I tell you.' That time I was living in Conway. Now I thought there was somebody coming to rob the house. I jump the window to go and see, and when I get inside the room I saw the woman's eyes red like fire, and she in a corner there, bawling and groaning. Now I call for help. I go down and call Dr. Meyer. Dr. Meyer come and he only do 'Shooo—she is a duppy woman,' and left. Tomorrow morning the prisoner come down and take her."

For a long time I'd been confused as to exactly what a duppy woman was. How did she become one and what did she do? I decided it was time for some clarification. He looked at me as if I were crazy as I asked for specifics. After all, how do you define the commonplace? Still, Charles was patient with me.

"You want to be a duppy man or a duppy woman to get property, to go do this, to go do that, to go get car, to get everything. And you want your son to be a chief of police or to be an officer. Well, you got to go and give the Devil your soul. You got to get a bamboo tree seed,[23] and that's not easy to get. If you don't have dealings with the Devil you cannot get this thing and you got to have heart to get that seed. You understand? The seed is power, and to get it you've got to stand the digging. If you got heart and you want it, well, what you find is what you catch. To get that seed you got to buy a new white sheet and a white cock. You go to four roads[24] and open that sheet under the bamboo tree at twelve o'clock midnight, sharp. And why you come under the bamboo tree with a white sheet and a white cock? To meet the Devil and to tell him what you want. You're bound to feel the heat when he coming. He come very strong and very terrible. 'What you want me for?' He drinking the blood of the white cock. You got to be rough like him and you got to stand the digging, because he not coming soft. He coming with power. A nice, well-built man—well dressed, all in white. He actually in the four roads, eh. He will often be out on a nice moonlight night—a nice, well-stepped man, taking the road in the moonlight. You will believe that there is a ship in the harbor and that he is a navy man. He dressing like an officer aboard a man-of-war with brass buttons—a nice, good-looking white man with a panama hat. One day a girl meet the white man going up the road. She says, 'Mister.' He stand up. 'Can you tell me the time?'

"He say, 'Neeee . . . ' that sort of thing. She drop in the road and she couldn't even talk. You see she was a common woman and she see the gentleman passing. She think she could make some money from that man, but the gentleman make her see that he don't want her. *Neeee!* she dead. The man blow a blaze of fire[25] from he mouth for her. If the fire come out from the mouth it bound to shock you. The woman bawl and scream, and everybody run. The man done gone, and she there dead. When you see a person pass in the night, never call him. You don't know what it is. Never! If you see a man walking in the nice moonlight, well dressed, all in white, don't say nothing. I'll tell you what happen to me one day. I came out from Martinique at twelve o'clock—right by the wharf. I see a white man standing up there with an umbrella on and a nice panama hat. Poor me don't know nothing. I just wait there. 'Mister,' I say, 'can you tell me the time?'

"He say, 'When I was from Hell, it was one o'clock.' I run to the ship. [Great laugh.] He just go up in the sky with the umbrella and he gone. I run and tell Captain Bristol, 'Look, look, look, look at that. Look the man going up there.' The captain could not see the man. Only me could see him.

"The Devil will come and he will speak to you very rough, and you ask him what you want. Then you will be a duppy woman or a duppy man and you'll never belong to God again. This seed got power to do any kind of thing. You could turn any kind of animal—any kind of beast you want—with that seed. You can humbug anybody. You can kill them or drive them mad. Jealousness can cause a lot, and jealousness can cause a duppy woman to put out your brains. These people will cripple you. You mustn't call them a duppy person—never open your mouth—or they will cripple you, make you stiff so you can't move. When a duppy woman come old, she's disfigured. She still turning a cat or dog—that's the way she can destroy you. She still could hurt you and harm you, going up there on the top of the building like a rat and preventing you from sleeping in the night—*Grrr, grrr*. But she cannot fly like before because she old. A duppy man or woman will suck your blood. If you have a baby there now, and you give that same baby to an old lady to mind for you, in a couple of days, that baby dead. She suck the little child's blood to make she come young. I had a little boy[26] I gave to a lady to look after. There is somebody who come and give me the hint: 'Take off that child from that woman, because the woman going to kill the child.' She used to suck the child right in the back, and when I call her, she move the child and put him in his place. I never tell her one word. Tomorrow morning when day break, I just pick up my child and I walk home. And look, the child save now, and the child a good little child. And you know what become of the woman? They find her right in front of her door with a hole in her back. The door was wide open. She could only reach upon the chair, and she dead with the hole right in her back."

"Is that how you kill a duppy woman? Must you stab her in the back?"

"No, no. It's not that. She tell me, 'Give me that little boy you have there. I like your little boy.' And she sucking the little boy's blood to make she come young, you understand? Then on that night she could fly, because she have the strength of young people's blood. But what about the payment to the boss? A promise is a debt. If you don't pay he will come for his own. He want fresh blood. The Devil take her. He pick she up and carry her. All that time she wouldn't bleed—she wouldn't dead on the journey—but when he drop her, then the blood come, leaving a trail, and she is dead in the house with a hole in her back. That's the way. When you got this kind of thing in your body, you cannot be in peace. You cannot rest one night at home. When the time is up you got to go to the Master. What's the use? Take little and live long. When you make an agreement with blood, well, if you can't give the blood when the time come, then you got to pay for it—one of your daughters, he'll ask you. He give you all what you want, and now he wants your daughter. If you cannot give the daughter, well, he take you. When your time come you could fall anywhere, and everyone would know what kind of things you'd been doing.

"Sometimes when you come old you begin to regret what you've done. Your face will be disfigured and you will be ugly. Because why? All that medicine you drink to turn the different kinds of wild beasts. Everybody will see. Then you will be sad, and you will want someone to take that blood off of you. You will just want him to stick you to make you bleed. After you bleed, you is no more duppy woman. But you got to get somebody you can trust. You will tell this person, 'I have been dealing with the Devil, but see now, I want to stop. I want you to meet me at a certain place and just cut me a little bit. You'll see a dog, and you just give the dog a slight cut.' You see, she the dog. You call that in Patois, 'dégagé.' But you got to select a good friend of yours. Suppose you tell someone you come tonight and you don't know his heart. If he is a man with a conscience he will just come and stick you and that's O.K., but if he is a wicked man, he will kill you.

"That happen to Mistress Alcindor,[27] the duppy woman up by me, who I got the house from. The time came when she feel to rest because she too old to be doing things to people, but the person she get to stick her, stick her too hard. You got sting and you got sting."

"Oh, is the hole in the back when you sting a person too hard?"

"Yes, she shove the knife way in. Not a knife—a long thing, like that.[28] Mrs. Alcindor give that person some money too, before she do that. That woman is paying for what she do to Mrs. Alcindor now. Because why? She is the one that make the baggain [bargain]. If someone ask you to do a favor, and you do the wrong favor, well, this is going to kill you. Them two make a bargain. Mrs. Alcindor said she was going in the kitchen like a dog and don't stick her navel. Just make the blood and don't hit her hard. Ah ha. Where the woman stick her, she shove it right into her guts. Bad girl. If you take a job you get paid for it. Now when she get up, even to pass water, she bound to watch Mrs. Alcindor by the side there. There is Mrs. Alcindor watching her, like that. Jesus Christ, you would give up, won't you? It won't take a month until you're dead. That what happen to that lady now. Don't you believe your soul die. When it come out from your body, your breath is gone, but it can still make your revenge. What you plant is what you reap.

"When Mrs. Alcindor dead, her head come small, small, small and her mouth, red like fire. The priest would not receive her in Church. No ma'am. The priest give her all that coming to her at she home and take her and bury her. And she was a duppy woman and yet she taking communion every morning."

"So the priest knew?" I asked in surprise.

"Of course the priest knew. Everybody knew. You can tell by a way a person is dead. She not dead by she ownself or God's sickness. She dead by what she do.[29] You got many kind of dead. You got dead by accident. You got dead by sickness in your bed. When your soul come out from your body, you going to see a tear coming out from your eyes. Then your tongue going to come small, small, like a thread line, and your mouth will stay closed. Now if your soul ask for something wet, then your mother or your husband going to take a spoon of water to throw in your throat. As it going down you will see the tear coming out both eyes, and then you're going to pass away. You will dead a nice death, and your face will come like an angel because you belong to the Lord. Your soul is tame. It didn't talk for nobody to say what you do—what you don't do before. Nobody come to give you a tea to stop your tongue because it didn't call nobody.

"If you make a good life, you will die nice. When you meet your father your eyes will close and your face come nice, nice, nice. But if you make a bad life, you will pay for it. Everybody going to see. You'll die with a rage, and your eyes are wide open. Nobody can come and close them."

"Will they give you a tea to stop your tongue?"

"Of course. He or she going to come step forward to give you a certain tea to make you keep your mouth shut—not to call anybody's name. And that tea means death. They will take two leaves and join them together, and that two leaf—one is gros deetin, a kind of leaf that's thick, and the other is maweepoui— Jesus Christ, you're going too deep with me, girl—those two leaves will stop you talking. They will boil this tea at home and will bring it in a cup. And there's a next thing again. A kind of seed that stay by the river, called 'zhebe zie bourrique'[30]— jackass eyes. Well, you take that and put it in the tea awhile.[31] All these things I tell you tonight I could make it, but you don't need those, because your trade and this one is different. You working on the sea. All this keeps you from calling the list, because those people you're calling, they're alive. It's not your fault, you know, for calling their names. It's your duty to call people's names before you die. That's right. You make them know who is ill, who is not, what this person do, what that person done.

"Before Mrs. Alcindor dead she ask me to burn everything she had there. After she dead and buried I burn three trunkful—and nobody knew what was in it. She tell me not to open it—pull it in the flat and burn it right there. I take some coconut leaf. I cover it all over and pour a bottle of calgon oil on it, and I light the fire and it burn. When a person tell you don't open the trunks, don't open them. So long you see you catch the trunks afire. Don't inhale what the fire burns in the trunk or you will be dead or loco. When the fire catch you could hear the essence in the trunk and the bottles bursting—*boom, boom.* That's why she tell me not to open the trunk—because that will be poison. You see, Mrs. Alcindor was like a crooked woman. That house— nobody dare touch it after she dead. Nobody would stop there or live there. You could see the bed there up to now, and it not today she dead. It's been a couple of years.

"Oh, St. Lucia got lots of duppy people. I was taking care of a horse, and every night a duppy man came behind that horse. Every night, every night, *bububu,* about seven o'clock in the night you'd hear this horse coming up the hill to go behind my horse. There was a Mr. Samuels down the road, and I went at his house and I told him he mustn't let go his horse every night like that. He told me no, it was not his horse. His horse was in the stable every night. It happen again, and I warn him again. He tell me, 'No, Charles. It's not me, cause my horse is in the stable.'

"I say, 'Remember this. Your wife is sick, I climb the coconut tree. I helping you, I bringing things for you by the bay.' Still every night at my house the horse humbugging me. I say, 'All right.' I went in town and I get a pound of lead. I pick up some bamboo with a small mouth. After I let the lead melt, I roll it up and throw it in the bamboo, and it take the same form. When you pull it you find the lead like a bullet. Then you take the lead in the night, scratch [scrape] it, make it fit the gun, and take it to the Church. You know the holy water when you're going in? You take some, put the lead in it to soak. Next morning you set your gun. Put the powder first, ram it hard, and put the lead in. O.K. I ready. I say, 'Tonight is the night.' The horse coming up on the hill now—so powerful. He make the rounds. I watching him and when he coming out of the stable, *pow.* The horse bawl *'OOOOOOh.'* People living in the next side say, 'Oh, they catch you tonight.' He run down from the bush, pass under the cocoa tree, go down in the next hill and onto a flat place. He jump a river and all the time he bleeding. He was a man they call Coe, a black fellow. Tomorrow morning I get up and I follow the blood. Mr. Samuel call me and say, 'Now, Charles, what do you say? You was calling me every day, saying my horse, my horse, my horse. Now you see who really done it.'

"I say, 'All right.' I follow the blood, and the blood go right to the next side over the river, passing the tree and little bush by the road. Everybody on the next side could see what they were doing over there. It was Mr. Coe. He have plenty daughters, and no one knew he was a duppy man. When it was twelve o'clock in the day they blow the conch shell, *Boooo*. If anybody is sick and they want help, they blow the horn and people come and give you a hand to carry the person. They put a blanket, you know, and they take an end with a bamboo. Everybody hold it there and bring him down. They take him down to Anse la Raye, but he dead on the way. His head turn a horse's head. That showed that he was a duppy man. Many men are dead duppy men. The kind of way he turn was the kind of way he spend his days. Anybody could see."

"Is that what you call a three-legged horse?"[32]

"Yes, that's a duppy woman or a duppy man. There was a three-legged horse in Marchand. It was a woman who had killed four husbands. You going up the road now and you hear, *Backala, backala, backala, backala*. That's a three-legged horse. You going to stand up. The horse stand up too. As you leave from there and go to the corner, you hear, *Backala, backala, backala*. It's a three-legged horse behind you. When you reach by the house, you have some nice stones there for to open [bleach] your clothes. You're going to hear a pig there, *Rrrrr, rrrrr*, in the stones. Tomorrow morning no stones are moved. The three-legged horse, that's the person humbugging you behind the house.

"Sometimes you will see a hundred mules in a pasture eating, and you is the one in charge of those mules. They come behind your house, eating the grass—*wum, wum, wum*. If you want to destroy them stay home next day. Make a hole for the gun mouth to pass and shoot through the hole. Never come outside because they will kill you. That mean to say, you in charge of the mule train, and they don't want you in that job. They come there to destroy you. When those mules start to kick, you don't know who's mules, but the last one behind—you shoot that one. That the one who is the ringleader. Don't mind the hundred you see, there's only one there. He make you see a hundred. He make you see a lot of things in your eye, but it's only one person. If a bunch of pigs are there, you shoot the last pig and it's only one man you shoot. If it's a woman, it's a woman you shoot. Sometimes a woman will tell you, 'Do you want a job?' She will tell you a certain place to come and meet her. When you come you see a dog. You pick up a stone and you strike that dog. It is the woman you strike. All these things got a method to destroy them. You just have to know what to do.

"Did you never pass Roseau in the night, child, going down to Anse la Raye? You're going to see duppy people there—you'll see the lights, like that—*feee, feee, feee.* One time I was sick with a cold in my belly in my canoe. I say, 'Well, I going to see about my boat.' I go down to Anse la Raye about eight o'clock in the night and I come back about twelve o'clock. When I reach at Roseau on top of the hill, I sit down, so, in a car. I went outside and I pass water. I think, 'Look at that son of a bitch. Instead of staying in their bed, look what they're doing. *Feee, feee, feee, feee.'* Tomorrow morning I was at Barnard. I just sweeping when I see a woman coming with an old basket. It haven't got no rim. She tell me, 'Charles.'

"I say, 'Yes, Madame.'

"'Where you from last night?'

"'Me?'

"'Yes.'

"'I been nowhere last night.'

"'Charles, you didn't been nowhere last night?'

"'I tell you, no.'

"'How about with the broomstick in your hand? Don't make

me give you two lashes. You lie. Tell me the truth. You been somewhere last night.' I stand up. 'Charles, I see you, you know. I the one that prevent them from breaking your neck. Charles, answer.'

"'I been to Anse la Raye last night.'

"'When you came out of the car, do you know what you say? "Look at that son of a bitch. Instead of staying in their bed, they're awake." What do you have to say to that? Suppose I wasn't there. Your neck would be broken inside the car, because the car would go right down over the hill.' She give me a bowl of farine in some milk and tell me to eat it. She take out a bottle and tell me drink it, and I drink. She tell me, 'You is a lucky boy that I love you.' Every Wednesday I give them twenty-five cents for the old people. That what saved my life. Don't tell me a duppy woman don't fly. A duppy woman go anywhere she want.

"A man called Anthony was carrying logwood in St. Pierre. A white lady like him. She have a nice hotel under the ground. They have plenty drink, and she give Mr. Anthony twenty pounds—that time it was pounds, not dollars—to buy some cloth in St. Lucia for her. Anthony take the money but he didn't bring the cloth. He spend the money and he not going to St. Pierre again. I stand a cruise with Captain Maismais to carry logwood. Now we don't know anything about that. We went ashore in the afternoon to go and get a drink, but we did not go to the place under the ground, because we knew it would cost something there. As we pass, the lady call us, 'Come here.' We came in. 'Sit down.' She say, 'Where is Anthony?'

"I say, 'In St. Lucia.'

"'He not sick?'

"'No.'

"'Well, tell Anthony to send the cloth with you when you all bring logwood.'

"We say, 'Yes, Madame. All right.'

"'When you're leaving here, come back and I will give you a letter to give to Mr. Anthony.'

"I take the letter to Mr. Anthony and hear what he say. 'Tell her it is good for her ass!'

"I go and give Madame the message. She laugh, she laugh, she laugh. 'When you go, tell Anthony, "Thank you very much." Tell him he going to see which one is good for his ass!' She suck Mr. Anthony's blood dry like that piece of wood. And he dead with not a bit of blood. Play with a duppy woman! Are you crazy? If you going to hurt a duppy woman, don't you believe, because you here and she there, that she can't be the place you is. A duppy woman flying. You cannot fool her. You fool your own self.

"You see that house up there by the red light? That's the Etienne house. She is a duppy woman. She has the biggest store in town. She have servants, she got cars, she got back store selling strong rum, and she was a poor girl. Her mother used to sell cocoa at Victoria Street. I could show you the house where they was living. Now the mother was a black woman, and the father was a red man. He bring the girl down, 'cause the man friend with the woman. Love is very funny—even you black, I could love you. You could be ugly, and who going to prevent me to love? All right. Mrs. Etienne at a party with her mother—in a crowd of people—and she don't find nothing else to do but insult her mother.[33] Right in front of everybody. She tell her, 'I don't know why my father took somebody black like you.' That word cause the lady to die. She took it to heart and she get up the next morning, pick up her trunk, take all her clothes, and she leave the house and go up in the country where her family is. The husband come to look for her, but she say, 'No. If you want me, get a next house to put me in and come live with the black.'

"And you know what Mrs. Etienne doing now? She married a nice big fat man, but she suck the man's blood and give him weak knees."

"She did that to her husband?"

"She got to do it for the journey. The Devil wants blood from her. You see, she could do anything when the man sleeping. After she give him the dope to sleep, she can take all what she wants. She weaken his two feet so he cannot have a good life while she have all the power and the property. That's what she asking the Devil for."

"Would this woman invoke the dead?"

"No. She was a duppy woman. Duppy women don't want nothing like that."

"Who invokes the dead, then?"

"If you have a business—a shop—you will invoke the dead to get more sale than the next person. On Saturday your shop will be full, block up with people, and the shop below there will have nobody."

"Well, do you do this yourself, or do you go to a duppy woman to learn how to do it?"

"Nah, Nah. You have a book—an obeah book, a Black Arts book—you never seen a Black Arts book yet?"

"No."

"You see, when it's a certain time in the night—about twelve o'clock—you got to stoop down and start to read this book in the cemetery. In Lagon that's why they put a big iron gate and a lock on it. For a long time it was free, but now, since people go there so often in the middle of the night making necromaney, making science, and raising the dead to get obeah, the government stop it. They put a gate there and they run wire all around. You got to go to a grave of a person who has died badly.[34] Then you'll see him coming up from six feet deep. A skeleton appear in front of you and you see the bones speaking."

"They speak!"

"Of course they speak, 'What do you want?' How he going to understand if he not speak to you? You have the power to bring him up, to talk, and when you finished let him go back down, and don't humbug him, eh? If he give you what you want this week, don't come back too fast, because he won't go right back. He'll go back, but not before he give you one slap in your face, and you won't live long. You're going to dead. He will tell you, let him rest in peace.

"I know a woman who went to the burying ground. She and three women go in the graveyard to get power from a wicked white man that dead. They waking the dead for power and luck. They raise him and ask what they want, but then they go back again the next night. They hear a big rush behind them and

'Leave me alone. I'm tired.' Two girls dead right there, the third have her mouth turned to one side, and the last one can't move from her bed.

"The dead will give you what you want, but what about the payment? Where you going to give him red blood? You could get a little child from somewhere far—that's the only way you could clear yourself good. And still people going to find out. The child going to come poor, poor, going lame, it wouldn't talk—like a dummy girl.

"There is a lady there by the market called Clarissa. On Saturdays her whole shop block up with people. Before you can go in the shop you have to wait for people to come out. When you wait and call what you want, they going to tell you, 'Wait, take your turn. I ain't no engine.' Clarissa went out and look for that, and she get it. Yeah she get everything, but it don't last. There is a time you will be broke. There's a time for everything. Now the shop is no use. The husband got to lock it up, because nobody can stay in the shop. The thing go *feeew,* and the shop empty now. That show you that nothing you get by force is good. Take little and live long. If you go in the Man's power you run along, but you will fail sometime and then you will out. He know all what you do. You have big business by force, compelling people to come in. You got everything, but what the use? When the time gone for you, you will go. Number one, he will start to seize all that you have. You might go loco, too—you and your husband. Both of you is going to sweat. And he is going to come and look for you."

"Is this the dead or the Devil you're dealing with?"

"When you're dealing with the dead, is it not the Devil you're dealing with? When you dealing with bad spirit, well, you're dealing with the Devil."

I knew that on other islands a grave digger was often sought after for assistance in certain supernatural dealings,[35] and so I asked Charles if such a person was important in St. Lucia.

"Here, too. It's the dirt you use. The dirt can kill. Take a little bit of dirt of a dead person's body, sprinkle it in somebody's food, and it is poisonous."

"Just regular grave dirt is poisonous?"

"Of course. Water comes down on a dead person's body, and all that dirt going to be poisonous. Eh, eh, you got to speak to the grave digger to give you that."

"Is the grave digger a kind of duppy man then?"

"No. He could do what he likes. He working at his job in the day. In the night he could do anything he likes. He's got better things to carry than a duppy man, because he's got the grave dirt. You grate it and it makes you disappear."

"It makes you disappear?" I had never heard that before.

"Yeah. You got to buy something to go with it from the doctor's shop. You put it in a glass, you see it boil, and then you swallow it. Your body change at the same time. You bound to. And after, you have something else to drink to make you come out."

"Well, the grave digger must be more powerful than a duppy person?"

"Of course he 's powerful. He can go anywhere he likes. He's flying."

"Does he fly?" Charles was becoming exasperated at my stupidity.

"Sure! Eh, eh," he clicked his tongue. "What you think he do if he not flying?"

"Well, he's not a duppy person though, is he?" I was still having some trouble with the duppy concept.

"He could do what he likes."

"But he's not dealing?" I had a dim idea that "dealers," as they were called, were a step above "duppy people" in that they had a clientele and didn't "deal" solely for their own benefit. I wanted to know how a grave digger fit into the company.

Charles explained simply, "He not bound to deal. But if he feel he could make it . . . just like you. If you feel to be a duppy woman, then you learn to turn a snake. All right. Suppose the grave digger bury a duppy man and he using the powder from that man's bones. He going to be wicked just like that man.[36] He bound to because that's what he have in the body."

"And then he becomes a duppy man?"

"That's right."

"Can the Devil take you then?"

"What do you mean? You're deep in that, because you have the dead person's spirit in you and you could do anything you like. You could kill, anything. Your face will be a man in the day, but when it is six o'clock in the night it will change. You disappear."

"Until the next morning?"

"Yes. Next morning when you come in, you drink your medicine and you come back. At night when your poor husband goes to sleep, you're gone through the window. He will sleep until you come back."

"And you don't leave your skin behind in the night when you're flying?" I was thinking of the sucoyan who flies off in the night to suck someone's blood. If a person finds her skin, he may destroy her by salting it. When the creature returns, she cannot put it back on and cries pitifully, "'Kin, 'kin, you no know me."

"The skin doesn't come out. You just have to drink your medicine and you're gone. This sight, it is terrifying, and when you got this kind of thing in your body, you cannot be in peace. You cannot rest one night at home, because when the time is up, you got to go to the Master. What the use that you got a whole fortune—that you got store, you got this, you got the other? What do you do now? The moment you blink the eyes, you lost it. How you lost it? Perhaps you went up to Roseau or you left for Vieux Fort. Tomorrow morning a woman dead with hole in her back. What happened? Nobody knows. Everybody asking, 'You know what happen? They stab Captain Beck's wife last night. She was a duppy woman.' Tomorrow morning Captain Beck's head is down because of his wife. Poor soul. He wouldn't live. He will take that to heart.

"When you going to deal with this grave dirt you could have it, but you cannot keep it in your house. You got to keep a big open vial—like a big jam vial with an open mouth. You put the dirt in there an you dig a hole by your house to put it in. Then you got the spirit in the vial. Anything you want to do you can do. You just take out a new spoon, shove it in, take a spoonful of it, and close it back. You see the person that humbugging you passing, and you sprinkle a little of that dirt in the back of his step—you don't do any harm, the person do you one thing. Then in a couple of days his two foot will swell and both foot are sore. No one can ever cure that. No!''

''What if I punged the little white pill you gave me and rubbed it on the foot?''

''Yes, that's what I told you the other day, but I didn't tell you the reason. But tonight you making me tell you everything. This tablet that I gave you—I told you good. When you get up in the morning, rub it under your feet so that during the day, while you walk barefoot, nobody can do you anything. If that kind of thing come under your feet, you can pass. You don't care, because you tend to your ownself. But if your feet is not dressed, after three days sores start to run water. They start to scratch you. Your water will run down and anywhere you got a drop it will be coming, so. In a couple of days now you can't walk. It coming to your legs now and going up. The doctor can't cure you. The only cure is to cut off your leg.'' I let out a gasp of alarm at such a prospect, and Charles gave a hoot of laughter. ''It's a damn good thing you meet me when you do.''

''Well, I guess so! I knew grave dirt was powerful but I didn't realize it was because it still contained the spirit of the dead person. I had heard that you could set a dead spirit on another person.''

''That's right. It's all according to the way you are dead. If somebody kill you before your time, well, it's easy. The family set the trap when they bury you. What they put in the coffin, that's what the dead will do. If they put a fork, or two forks—one in the coffin, one in your hand—you're going stabbing. It's your spirit that doing the stabbing.''

I was wondering what other things were put in the coffin besides forks, so I asked, ''What if you put a gun in the coffin?''

''No, no guns.'' And then he elaborated, ''They give you a whip[37] in your hand. A man could stand up there and *whack*, he's taking the whip in his back. He jump, he bawling, but it do no good. He getting whipped. What you do is what you get.

"There's a woman called Mrs. Branch, and she killed her husband for the next man. About five years after she killed her husband, they break the cave [vault] to put a next dead person there. They find Mr. Branch just like he put in yesterday. They throw him back [great laughter]. That's an example to show you. Now that woman dead. She bawl, she suffer, she do all kind of things. She suffer 'til she pass away, and her man, he have a next woman now, but his belly big, so. He will not live long. That's all right—you do yours—but what about the revenge the family going to take? Mr. Branch was a high society man, a Mason. Everybody knew how he dead. Well, they give she the revenge. The family gave Mr. Branch a whip in his hand, and with that whip he take his revenge. And Jesus Christ he whipping her backside—he don't stop. In two months she dead.

"Same thing with an animal. Do you remember the dog, Bruno, we have? Well, a lady they call 'Ma Mark,' she kill him— she kill two dogs, one for me and one for a next friend. I went up the hill by she house and I tell her, 'My dog is dead. He is an animal and he left seven young ones, and the whole seven young ones is dead. But I know the person that has killed my dog. She going to disfigure just how the dog done. The bone come out from the dog's skin. He's buried under the house, and you got to finish like the dog. All the flesh got to come out from your skin.' And Ma Mark come just like that. She's just skin and bone. I saw her just this morning and I couldn't believe it is Ma Mark."

"How did you fix her?"

"Well, it not me that fix her. She fix her ownself because she killed the dog. I give the dog what belongs to it."

I was trying to follow. "Oh, you buried the dog with something?"

"That's right. And she come like that—skin and bone. I pass her at the head of the hill. When I watch her, so, I see she have skin and bone."

I wanted to know what he had done, so I pressed, "What do you bury the dog with? A fork or a stick?" I wasn't sure he would tell me, but he answered in full.

"No, no. You rub it with dirt from in front of she door. I get that—I pay a dollar for it. I make a boy take it for me. The dog in the hole, and I sprinkle it in front of the dog and I cover it. I say, 'Bruno, Ma Mark kill you. She was jealous, but you got to make her turn the same way you turn.' And so say, so done. I sprinkle the medicine on top of the dog and cover it up."

I persisted, "You sprinkle medicine on top of the dog?"

"You got to do that. You got to put compelling powder on top of the dog. When I see her coming this morning with a little basket I say, 'You fucker. I will tell you something now. If you got heart to do harm to me, I telling you, I send it back. Me ain't responsible because you have heart to harm me. I don't leave that to God."

"Did you ever see a coffin in the road?" I asked. I had been told a number of stories from various people about coffins which appeared out of nowhere to block one's path in the night.

"That's a small matter," Charles answered me. "A coffin would be in the road and not let you pass. You will be courting with this man's daughter, and this man a duppy man. He will check up and see if you got heart or you is chickenhearted. You left his house at twelve o'clock in the night and you meet a coffin in the road. If you is a hero, just light your pipe and you sit down while you're smoking. After a while you hear, 'Get up boy. Leave me there. Get up.' He calling your name. 'Get up, Charles, I is your friend. Ain't nobody going to know. Get up.' If you is a damn fool you get up. He pull your neck and stab you. You got to stand up and stab the coffin. Don't stab the man, stab the coffin. 'All right,' I get up—but give a good stab, eh, because if you leave, he going to kill you. Never left without you stab it. If you want him to know you is a brave man, get up—say, 'I meet you last night.'"

"Oh," I said. That seemed simple enough. Questions piled into my mind, and I wanted to keep Charles in such a receptive mood to my queries. There were so many things I wanted answered in connection with obeah. So I began again with another question.

While working in Antigua I had been told about a jumby bead, something which was supposedly used in obeah.[38] I wondered if

Charles had ever seen such a thing, and I thought perhaps the time was ripe to ask him. "Have you ever heard of something called a jumby bead—a little berry—well, two-thirds of it is red and there's a black dot in the middle? It grows on a vine. Do you know what I mean?"

"Yeah." His answer was noncommittal.

"In Antigua they work obeah with this."

"In Antigua?"

"You know what I mean?"

"I know Antigua. I been Antigua." I groaned to myself. I didn't want to hear about Antigua at the moment, so I tried to cut that direction short.

"That's right, you had a girl in Antigua—children in Antigua."

"What are you doing with this?" Suddenly the tables were reversed and I began to wonder what I had gotten myself into. I backed off a bit.

"What am I doing with this? Nothing. Somebody just told me about it. I have never seen one. I just heard about it and thought you would know about it." There was a long silence and it began to make me uneasy, so I blundered on. "Have you seen one?"

Suddenly, indignantly, he snapped, "Who tell you about this thing?"

"Um, do you know a guy called . . ."

"Where that person belong to?" He was immediately distrusting.

"He belongs to Antigua. His father lived in St. John and he lives somewhere between St. John and the other end." I didn't know why, but I was deliberately vague.

"How he come to give you these words?" Suddenly I was getting the third degree. Knowing how Charles's mind might work, I shifted my emphasis a bit and said that actually the man had told my husband.

"What he said about the jumby?"

"The jumby bead, I think he called it."

"The jumby bead—yeah, that's what you call it. The flower is the jumby bead."

"It's a flower?" I was relieved to be back on the subject.

"Yeah, a flower."

"Well, he said that two-thirds of it was red and there was a black dot . . ."

"Set in the heart of it."

"And it grows on a vine, is that right?" There was another long silence while Charles just stared at me.

I said rather nervously, "What are you looking at me that way for?" Again there was silence. This time I kept it.

Finally he seemed to make up his mind to speak. "This flower," he started slowly and so quietly that I had to lean forward to hear him, "the tea of this flower will make the body change. You'd be human being in the day, but by the time it's the middle of the night, you're just like a duppy. Your face come a next kind of face. And you turn like the bees which sucking the flower."

"You turn like the bees and you fly in the night?"

"You is a midnight jumby."

"Oh." I thought to myself that I was reacting as if he had just told me bees produced honey.

"You take a bee that has just drunk from the flower and you put it in a vial, and it die and it turn a powder. The moment you put that powder in a glass and a drop of spirit of nitre, you shall be disappeared 'til daybreak."

"The sweet spirit of nitre—the same as you told me about before?" I asked with surprise.

"Yes. You disappear the moment you in the air. You going to do your job—you got to do it—and the only thing that could stop you would be if they beat you, and then you would be destroyed. Come." He led me up the steps to point at some ginger lilies which were blooming alongside the building. "You see this," he whispered. "You mind that. It have a flower, and the only way a bee can suck from the flower is the middle of the night. And the flower is so full of syrup when they taste it, they suck from it, of course. What about the bee sucking the flower?"

"Does the syrup kill the bee?" I guessed.

"No. It's a different bee come have a drop. If you catch that bee, grab the bee and put it in a vial. Do it the same way that I told you. That bee will turn a powder. When it about six o'clock the flower will open, and the bees will come and suck it, and you will have chance to kill that bee. Put it in a little vial and let him dry to a powder. Then put some in a glass with a little spirit of nitre. You see it making a froth. And you going to England in the night. You going to Martinique in the night. You going anywhere you like in the night and when day break you are to home."

"Gosh, and it's just that particular flower that the bees . . ."

"Exactly."

"What do you call the flower?"

"This flower is the lilies of the night. This flower we call lily of the valley because we don't want nobody to know its power.[39] This one is the master. This flower is the controller of big obeah. It's just like the Man's power. That's a job."

"Well, don't people try to come at night and get them?"

"What you think? You think my brain so small?"

"Well, you see I never knew that. No wonder you say it's such a dangerous job."

"What you think? You think I is a fool?"

"Oh, no."

"Let me tell you. Never make anybody know you are wise. Now, let us come to that business now. This flower—that's not for you."

"No, I was curious as to what it was, but I didn't want to use it."

"This flower and two seed at home by me are too much for you. You're too young and you're too beautiful and gay. Don't pay no mind, for you could be dead any moment you get this kind of way. There was a man from England, he was in the drugstore at eight o'clock in the night opening a tin of sweet biscuits. He give me a pack for twenty-five cents and open the next pack. He eat it. When it was twelve o'clock they bore a hole right here in his back, and he was quite to Pigeon Island. He was behind a white girl like you. That is the owner of this property here and the owner of the building there."

"They stuck him then?"

"Yeah. He have a beautiful wife. Nice wife, but he leaving his wife up the hill and making the black magic and take all white covers in the night. Every day the calabash go into the well, but one day it staying. He went to Pigeon Island behind a girl like you. Steel cannot cut steel. Two steel meet. The first time he sucks it and he back again. He gone."

"Well, when he's stuck is he killed?" I was still confused by the sticking.

"How you don't understand, Janie. You must understand. A man shove a dagger right in your back. He stab you, but you won't die on the spot."

"You'll die at home."

"Because the Devil bring you back."

"I see."

"When you drop him at home, by the door, they pick him up. They find he stabbed, and the lady report it. But catch the work. I will tell you something, Jane. You got to understand this thing. With these kind of people you will go to sleep dry—not taking with nobody—you sure you're not taking with nobody. You went and sleep with your panties on you. When you get up in the middle of the night, your panty on the ground and you're soaking wet. Tomorrow morning you're tired, you're sick, you don't know nothing because they done it in your sleep. That's why they kill them when they got a chance at them. God damn it, you can't get away.

"When they bore a hole in a man, they call Odisse Bataille from La Croix Maingot on top of the hill there, they take him to his mother's house, and he start to talk what he had done, that he was a black magic man. He repeat all kind of girl things—the kind of sheet, the kind of nightgown they have, how the body, how she so fat, how this and the other. He said he went in a room and he put two boys in a bag. He come outside, he laugh, and he go inside, and after he used the woman he put the man's head at the woman's foot. And he put the man's foot in the woman's face. That's the power he had. But how long the power last? The same power kill him. Every day he holding near, but not every day he going to get away. One day he catch. They bore a hole from his back to his guts. He was suffering, he start to talk all what he done, but he dead. Now you got to take sense from that. You got many sciences in the world, but know the kind of things that protect you. All the science, all these things got their master. Good. For black magic you're going to take a mortar and pestle and you put the medicine in the mortar. You pull the key and leave the keyhole empty—that is what he like, because he can come in free, and you buy a new pair of tailor's scissors because that scissors taking pin, taking needle,[40] and put them under your pillow. Now when he attempt to pass through the keyhole the thing hold him right there to his waist. The boy will be outside and this part will be the next side right to his fucking groin."

"Is that salt you put in the mortar?"

"It's a powder. You put it in the mortar, and his body got to come down the mortar pestle and heself outside."

"And he can't move."

"And he can't move," he repeated. "The only way he's going to move is if you let him go. When the red cock come to crow, and day break, he start to bawl and beg your pardon. This time you've got a wicked mind. You pass through the back door and go and call people—'There's him!' " Through his laughter Charles continued. "His private come long, so, on the ground, and everybody going to find him!" At this point he was laughing so hard he had to take a breath to control his voice. He began again, "He won't live though. No. At daybreak he will die. He going to be done dead. He will pass blood, and his body going to swell because the essence will be dry. He will stay until daybreak and he will bawl. People will have a chance to come and see."

"What kind of powder is that that you put in the mortar?" I persisted.

"That is l'essence okra."

"L'essence okra?"

"Okra in Patois meaning guabo—l'essence guabo—that's oil of okra he rubbing heself with to pass in the keyhole."

"Oh, he rubs that on himself?"

"Yes, but you going to put the powder of guabo in the mortar."

I wasn't sure what the okra was so I asked, "The guabo, is it a kind of okra?"

"No, it's a powder of guabo in the doctor's shop. That's to squeeze them."

"And in Patois it's poudre gombo?" I couldn't quite tell whether it was gombo or guabo.

"Yes, that's gombo powder. You telling the man you want a thing for magie nwe. That's black magic in Patois. But nothing can happen to you. This thing can't come across you. Nothing so. Uh unh. I will tell you—before you stand dummy—but not again. You could go anywhere in the forest—you could go anywhere—nothing can happen to you again. The will power will protect you.

"That happen to my wife already. She woke up, and all her legs get scratched, because they make you know they come, and it burning her like pepper. She call me when I come in the morning and say, 'Charlo, look at that. And when I get up in the morning I find myself wet.'

"I say, 'All right. He will come again.' I went and buy new sharp scissors, and Fati put them under her pillow. Next time he come he staying outside. He groan. The new scissors humbugging him. He cannot do the job. Once I stop it he never come back again. I just call him there. He tell me 'Good morning.'

"I tell him, 'Good morning,' and I say, 'Don't come back again. Alboney, let me tell you something. Don't come in my house again, because everybody going to know. I going to expose you and everybody will see.' He bark. He don't ask me what I talking about. He never tell me so, he just hear what I say and he turn he back. He don't come again."

"Does a duppy man practice black magic?" I queried.

"No. Black magic is black magic."

"Who practices black magic?"

Charles explained, "A duppy man doesn't do that. That's another job. But remember, a black-magic man is easy to kill."

"Does the black-magic man deal with the Devil?" For Charles my question was naive.

"That's the Devil's work," he barked at me. "What you want is what you ask him for. The job you want is the job you ask. None are good."

As long as we were having this kind of conversation, I decided to ask Charles about la jablesse. This is a creature who is well known throughout the islands, but I had never been too clear as to her origins. She was supposed to be a woman with one cow's foot (linking her with the Devil) who would carry off any luckless individual and lose him somewhere in the bush.

"Charles, who is a jablesse?"

"What they do is too much. God don't want them. Devil don't want them, so they go back in the earth and stop there. Make a spirit—just like a duppy woman who do too much. God don't want you, and Devil don't want you, and you stay in the bush and become jablesse."

"But she's dead?"

"But she's dead, yes. She going to hold you and carry you in the bush. How the jablesse take you? When your mother send you for wood in the bush. You go and cut wood and bring it home. She'll catch you there. Or if your mother send you in the garden without a dog, well, the jablesse will catch you. If you plant peas, she'll come in the garden to tief peas. And you can't cook them. She eats them raw. How you know? Where she going to get fire!" Charles guffawed at the thought and then went on. "She going to meet you in your garden. You know what she going to tell you? You going to see a woman there picking your peas. You going to say, 'Ah, you picking my peas?' She going to laugh at you. She going to take you and tie you upon the tree there. You stop by that tree there. If your husband or mother going to call you, you under the tree like that but you can't answer. They tie your hair behind your head upon the tree and leave you there in your own garden. And what they going to give you to eat—rotten wood but it will look like plantain, and a next kind of mess—they call it *poule bois*, a little worm [termite]. They will give you that as fish. You see it's fish. You cannot see it's poule bois. You cannot see it's rotten wood. You going to eat it for food, but when your family look and find you, you will be doped, you're like a dopey man. You have no sense. They have to carry you to the church for the priest to bring you back again.

"She live in the jungle and she singing like anything there. You don't know because she have a nice voice more than you. She go to dance too. You have a time just before Christmas you call 'contumba'—people dancing, you know—Congo dance, big drum, the tambou there. A man beating the tambou, and nice moonlight like tonight. Plenty people come. A jablesse dancing there and you don't even know. She got on a long dress. You cannot see the cow's foot because the dress is so long. When she there talking with you she just cover the foot, but now you're going to know what she is. As you pull your pipe, you light it. She going to tell you, 'It smell like shit' and she gone because the pipe humbugging her. She cannot stay. She cannot bear tobacco.

"There is a fellow called Davy—a short fellow by the wharf there. He was going up to Ti Rocher. He see a nice, good-looking girl going up. He meet the lady and he so inquisitive, he say, 'Good night.' The lady don't answer. He say, 'Good night' again. The lady say, *'Stttt.'* He say, 'Ay ay, I tell you good night.' He start to talk. The lady start to talk. He talk, he talk, he talk, he talk. He tell the lady a question. The lady say, 'All right, I agree with you. When we is more high up I will set.' Now we have a kind of tree that have a white leaf—we call it 'bois canon'—a big tree that have a lot of cashew, lot of prickles in it." Charles began to laugh. "When he reach there, the jablesse pick him up and put him up there. He don't even know. Ah, when he catch up heself, he see the prickle vine all around. He start to bawl. The jablesse tell him, 'You stay there. You too bloody vicious. When you see a woman you fresh too quick. Stay there. You won't do that again.' You see, when you see a woman going up, why should you interfere with the person. After he put he hand on the jablesse's wrist, he had no strength, nothing at all, and she put him in the top of the tree. When he start to bawl, people hear the bawling and they go and take a lamp up and find him in top of the bois canon. Everybody start asking what he doing. He say, 'It is a woman put me there.' They say, 'Well, only a jablesse would do this.' They cut the tree and it fall and he come out, the fucker.

"If you going somewhere and you meet a woman passing, say 'good night' and go on with your business now. That thing would never happen to you. I could meet a hundred women in the road. I pass straight. Me don't even tell her 'good night.' Me!"

"Have you ever seen a jablesse?"

"Sure. Roseau full of them. Eh, eh, it's there they got this kind of thing. They got hill for that, they got jungle for that."

I was very interested in the supernatural creatures that peopled Charles's world, so I took the occasion to ask him if he had ever come across a mermaid while he was out fishing.

"No, I never see one, but I hear about them. I will tell you where you going to meet mermaid. She have a kind of big stone and under it is empty. That's where mermaid sleep. That's she home. She sit down on top of it in the early morning. Sometime when you pass, you meet she combing her hair. If she see you she will say, '*Oooh!*' and *shooo* and she gone. When you see the sun is hot they glad to warm themselves. She's a white lady with plenty hair. It's just like your hair—sometimes black too. She's a human, only the tail is a fish."

Other West Indians had told me of trying to get the comb of a mermaid, so I asked Charles about that. "I heard if you could get her comb you could get great riches?"

"I wouldn't like to get her comb. No! If you get a mermaid's comb, the mermaid take you. She take you for a year or two. She ask you what kind of food you eat, but be careful. You got to tell her what's in the earth. Don't tell her what's in the sea. Tell her all what you eat is ground food. You will give yourself trouble, but the day you say you'll eat fish, you die, because you see, she is a fish."

"Will she take you under the sea then?"

"Sure. She will take you easy. And after you stop with her for about a year, you say you feel to go and see your family. She will bring you to your family and make you plenty money and gold and everything, but she will ask you, 'What day are you coming back? You going to come back in a month? In three months? Next year?' Now what you going to tell her? You say, 'Sometime I'll come back,' but that day have no date. If you say you'll come back next day at a certain time, don't talk about the sea, any river you go in—so long as you take the water she will take you because she smell you.''

''Are mermaids in the rivers as well as the sea?'' I asked.

''Mermaids are in the swamp. Eh, eh—mermaid is a fish, she living in swamp. I hear about the mermaid, but I could tell you better about the fairy maid.''[41]

My eyebrows must have shot up, for he nodded his head to my unspoken question. ''Uh huh. There's a fairy woman that was by the river, and a girl come to take water by the river. She was engaged to marry in one month. When she come she meet the fairy maid who had been doing her wash and had put out all her dress to take the sun. The girl say, 'Ah, good morning, mother.'

'' 'Good morning,' she say. 'Listen, my child, my head wants a comb. I got a lot of bush and things. Can you clean my head for me a little bit?'

''The girl say, 'Yes, I will clean your head for you. Only I wonder if you will lend me a dress, because you have a lot of nice dress by the river there.'

''The fairy maid say, 'You clean the head.'

''When the girl start to clean her head she find some prickles pricking her hand. 'Ah!' That humbug her. She say, 'My hand hurting me. I have to go.' She went at her home. Every day she find a pretty dress left for her. When she find that, she go back to find the woman and tell her that she want to try and see what she could do with her hair.

''The woman say, 'It is too late now. There's something behind that. Leave it alone.'

''The girl go, but she come back again. 'Maman?'

'' 'Yes.'

'' 'It was not my fault. My hand was prickled.'

''The woman say, 'The same prickle in my head still.'

''When it got the last week before she to get married, the girl come down by the river. She say, 'Maman, you still there?'

'' 'Yes, I still there.'

"'Well, can I clean your head today?'

"The woman say, 'I haven't got no comb.'

"'I'm going home to get a comb to comb your head.'

"'Well, go and get the comb.' She come back and she start to comb the fairy's head. When she combing, combing, combing, she in a hurry. The woman say, 'Listen, I don't want nobody to pull my hair so hard. If you cannot take your time to comb it, don't worry about it.'

"The girl say, 'Yes,' but she didn't do it. She combing the hair, but it's the dress she want. She say, 'Well, I done for now. Tomorrow I going to come back and finish it.' She will come back because she don't say what she got to say yet, and only one day remain before she get married. The next day she return. 'Ah, Maman, all what you want me to do for you today, I will do.' You see, she want to speak to her to get the nice-looking dress to get married.

"'Well, I still want you to comb my hair.' The girl start to comb.

"'Maman, I comb you nice today.'

"'Yes, I see that. What do you want now?'

"The girl say, 'The nice dress you have there, it's just like a rainbow. I would like to get a dress like a rainbow for to marry tomorrow.'

"'Really?'

"'Yes.'

"'It's the oldest thing. I will give it to you with the greatest pleasure, if you will send your sweetheart to pass a night with me. I will give it to you tomorrow morning.'

"'Oh, yes. I will do so.'

"The girl went up and she call the man. She says, 'Do you love me?'

"'Yes.'

"She say, 'Well, there's an old lady who says if you love me come and pass a night with her.'

"'An old lady?'

"'Yes.'

"He say, 'All right.' When he come he find a young girl sit down by the river washing.

"She say, 'Peter?'

"'Yes.'

"'Didn't I tell you when you go at your mother's, don't kiss the girl that was inside your house?'

"He say, 'Yes, you told me so, but I did forget.'

"'Well, I still waiting for you by the river.'

"He say, 'Come now.' But the girl never saw her sweetheart again. The fairy maid took all that belong to her and went with it. Jealousy cause that. The fairy girl take the man and go with him. What is yours is yours. The water cannot wash it out."

"The water can't wash it out?" I asked, rather blankly.

"No! That belongs to you. People could say what they like. If you is to be dead poor, you will be dead poor. You could work forever and you're dead poor. Many men tried to have plenty things, but they are dead before their time. Why? You didn't wait for your time. You want to do it before. That to show you. It's a click. The Lord tell you, 'Work, the sweat of your blood will have to support you,' but don't force it."

I realized he was through with the fairy maid, so I asked him if he knew of a baku, a small creature known on most of the islands south of St. Lucia. He was purported to bring you anything you asked, so long as you took care of him and fed him. This would sometimes become an impossible task, for his appetite and demands often grew to insatiable proportions.

Charles answered me with, "You got all different names. A baku mean a bolum."[42]

"I've heard the best place to get a baku is down in Guyana."

"Uh huh, uh huh."

"But I've also heard you could make them right here," I encouraged, hoping something more would be forthcoming. This time I was lucky.

"You know how you making a bolum? If you in the family way, and they know where you're passing, they'll fix up a big jar and they put the baby there. What you're carrying got to go in that bottle. You never know it's gone. Next morning you'll find blood. You think it's some fall you take.[43] The child will be in that jar, but you cannot trade that jar for anything. Anything you got in your mind, that guy knows. He'll give you money, but you got to feed him back. You cannot get clear of that guy. He'll bust you, for he have power more than you.[44]

"There was a man called Mr. Westall. He have a bolum. After he dead everyone find out, and that's no good. The only way he'll leave you is when you're dead. With a bolum you'll be a slave. You're helping yourself, yes. You have a lot of money, but you is a slave. You have the goddamn bolum inside your house in your chamber. You have a room by your ownself—suppose you have a big trunk. Then you're boring a lot of holes in it to get air. Sometime you got to let the trunk open, but nobody can go in that room besides you or your wife.

"I'll show you. You see that mark there—that exact mark, there." He held up the back of his hand and I could see a small scar. "When I was a little boy, every day I used to go at my godfather's. I go inside there and I'd play in the chamber. One day I saw the trunk like this," he demonstrated showing a half-open trunk, "and I see a little child there—he shoving the fingers and I playing with the fingers. My godmother tell me, come away from there. I see the boy go back in the trunk again. Now one day he shove his fingers, and I hold the fingers hard and I squeeze the fingers. He give me one kick. My godmother was ironing, and I throw my hand in the fire. I go like that and I get burnt, and I start to bawl and roll around on the ground, and I go tell my mama and show her how I get burnt. And my mother say, 'Come home.' She takes some coal and mash it up and put it upon my hand and my mother say, 'Too troublesome, too troublesome. Why should you go up there when I tell you no.' And when I come big I find out it is a bolum. After my godfather is dead, everybody come and know he had a bolum. That no good. It give you money. It make you rich. You have science, but after you're rich you got to get poor. You will be rich. You have horses, you have cars, got everything—big building, shop—but before you dead. . . . Mr. Westall have to sleep in a little coop before he dead. That no good. A bolum would choke you. Before you have your money you don't know what you're going to do. He choke you to death.

"There's a man up there. His name is Hubert. On Saturday you don't have a place to pass in the shop, it so crowd up with people. The next shop below him is empty. He got all the sale. You go looking for a shop selling fish. You cursing all those people clattering to buy fish. The fish is fifty cents but here it's sixty cents. Still the people rushing to buy from him. Now the time come when he can't even sell a piece of fish. Man better man. His shop remain. The message in the shop there—all that remain, but the next man got all the business. Hubert weep. No sale."

"And all that's the bolum's job?" I ventured.

"That the bolum job now. Without the bolum this man cannot sell anything. The bolum cause all that. You cannot kill a bolum. Never put that in your mind. When you have this thing, you say well, you could kill him, but he going to kill you before you kill him. The only chance you have is when you're sick—you're dying and somebody else going to pick him up in the night. Because he crying and calling your name. 'My father dead. My mother dead,' and you going to pick him up and carry him at your home in the night. You will hear him crying under the house. He call you and tell you he hungry. When you see him he a little, little boy. He have a new pants and a new shirt. But he's a man. He could slap you down and break your waist. You find that here. You find that in Dominica.

"You think Dominica good? Dominica got people turning snake, you know. There is a man—a policeman—he turn a snake and couldn't come back. He turned a big hell of a snake. He turned it good, but to come back a human, he cut the wrong card. Now there is a woman who come to look for him. When she pushed the door she find a snake inside the house. The woman bawl, and the snake watching her, like that. His friend come, and the next friend come and tell the girl, 'Why didn't you come and call us if you were going to call people?' They push the door and take the next vial. They just put it in a glass and lift up the snake and give it to the snake. And the snake back human. Son of a bitch. He didn't know what to do. He didn't know how to get out from the snake. He turn a snake. His father learn him that, his father was my father's brother, and he told me that was the biggest mistake he ever done. You know something—you know mostly everything. Good. Yes, you going to show either your son or your daughter some of it, but don't show him all you know—anyone—because that same learning you learn him, he going to turn back against you. When you think you do good, you do worse by yourself. Never show it all. My wife—I know what I show her. I show her something in case I sick or she sick or a child sick, but I wouldn't show her everything.

"My uncle learned me too, and after he learned me he tell me, 'I learning you this because you haven't got no mother or no father.' He know how to turn a bird.

"There is a little bird that stay right on top where you see the sea is by the bay. You hear him 'chick, chick, chick, chick, chick' and you call him 'zi rondelle.'⁴⁵ He on top there, making his nest on the wall. Any time you're sailing and you hugging the land, you're going to see this bird on top of the wall. And the eggs is hard to get. The only way you could get that is if you are a man fishing with a stick, and God give you a chance to meet a nest lower down. But you're happy to find that, because why? The eggs are all on top there, and these eggs are the best eggs in the world, because if you get them you can fly just like that bird, and the sight of you is just like that bird. You will have to get one or two of those eggs—those eggs going to turn a powder—and you will mix it with the flying powder I tell you about the other night, and you turn the bird. That's what you drink. You put it in the glass, and when you throw it and you mix it, the glass will be frozen. Then you swallow it and you is a bird. And you keeping it in a bottle by your bed. This thing got you going deep— going very, very, very deep. Hide it where nobody could get it. That's for you one alone. This thing you've got to hide where nobody can meet it, or they will destroy you. They find out what kind of thing you're doing. They put poison in the bloody article.

When you drink it, you think you know what you drink, but there's something wrong. They ain't killing you. They ain't eating you. But you kill your ownself. When you go and mix it, you didn't know somebody else find it out, and when you think you are right you are wrong. The moment it about eight o'clock, nine o'clock, you shut yourself in. You say you going to bed, but you don't sleep. You mix your powder, *Che, che, che, bam*—you're gone. Five o'clock in the morning, you're home already, combing yourself. And you done take your thing as you reach. You land, *brrrr*—as you reach. You just like the bird and you go in and take your message. Your two wings is the hands. As you reach you take it. You got the thing—number one outside. You just take the first one to drink—you have your two hands back. Take the next one, you solid human. You comb yourself, dress up and clean yourself. *Bam!* Back to your bed and sleeping."

Hoping to get him to elucidate a bit, I asked, "Is it something different you drink to turn yourself back?" But I didn't get much more information.

"Of course. One for you to go anywhere you like—you want to go to England, you go to England, you go to the Queen's Palace and you do what you want to do, you take what you want and you come back—nobody don't know—and one to come back human.

"And something else I'll tell you now. They got a kind of tree here—you cannot understand the name if I tell you. It's a kind of tree like a devil tree. At twelve o'clock in the night it groans like a human."

"And it cries when you cut it?" I had heard of this tree before, but never from Charles.

"How you know this?" he snapped at me.

"I'm just trying to remember the name."

"I don't want to hear that from you. How you know this kind of thing?"

I laughed. Once in a while surprises were good for Charles. I was trying to remember and then it came to me, "bois moudongue."

Charles looked at me in disbelief. "I want to know something from you. Where you know all this kind of talk from?"

"Mostly from you," I answered. "You've told me a lot of things. I try and remember."

"Wait. I'll tell you something more. Bois moudongue is a tree here. You will put a shilling there and you will dig for the root. You will say, 'Well, I want a piece from you and I paying you.'"

"And then it won't shriek?" I had heard something about that before, too.

Charles ignored me and continued, "And you dig there and you cut the piece. You hear, '*Hmmmm, ummmm.*' That's why you paying him. He groaning and he make you know that you pay him. You talk before you do your job. But if you don't speak, you going to hear, '*Oooh.*' You leave the wood, you leave the tree, and you gone because you never hear a tree do that. This tree, bois moudongue, will do for the balance of your life. Only a little piece of the wood you got to use. You put it in your mouth, and the moment you put it in your mouth you disappear, you know."

He had surprised me now. I had not heard that before and I said rather humbly, "I didn't know."

Charles continued, "You're five feet off the ground. You're walking, you're going to town, you could do anything. You just gone. You do it and come back and nobody see you. You could go to Vieux Fort. If you natural it going to take the whole night, but if you're not natural—*boing*—you're in Vieux Fort, and your friend helping you. You don't feel nothing."

"I never heard that," I reiterated.

"Young people who are working these kind of things—they don't know that. Who will tell you that? This boy who come in here and talk to me—my son's friend—my son put him on the track. Now he coaxing me to help him. I would never put him in front. I always put him in back. I wouldn't make him wise too young, because if I make him wise he will go too deep. He want too much thing—he want car, he want this, he want the other. Uh unh."

While in Dominica I had heard of a tree called bois diable, and

I wondered if that was the same thing as the bois moudongue, so I asked Charles. "No," he told me, "that's a next one. We call it 'fromager.'[46] There is a tree by my house. Moudongue is different. It carry a green leaf. When you come to get the root you put the money, so, and you dig it. When you come to dig it you going to see where other persons cut the root to take the piece."

"Does the moudongue look like the fromager?" I was trying to get the two separated in my mind.

"No, fromager is a big tree. Bois moudongue is a short tree. It have a green leaf. You think you can go in the daytime and get bois moudongue? You could never get it. You got to go in the night and do your business. If you want to make something serious, you have to go in the night unless you want a lot of people to see you. You don't know people going to watch you as you going up there to dig that. You don't know where the people going to watch you is, and your name will be called. It is easy to find out [recognize] the root. Any man could bring it to me now. He tell me, 'Here.' The moment I take it, I smell it, I tell you what kind of thing it is—moudongue.

"You can't use that in no way for sea. Sea! You can't use that atall, atall, atall. You will be a slave. Because you got to leave here to go windward of the land to go and fish. You got this bottle to go and fish. Yes, you never come out empty, but you is a slave. You cannot stay to finish your work how you want, because then twelve o'clock going to catch you, and the boss going to come."

"Just like when you use the oil of rose?"

"That's right. When you see the boss come the first time, he come different color. Then he go back and he come red. He bar up the whole place—that mean to say, he come this time for you—very serious. He will go about making the sea by your ownself and he, after sinking the boat. As you see that, he lift up the boat. He goes straight and passes under the boat. He giving you a sign, and the captain going to tell you go in the box there and take the thing and let it go. That what he want."

"And that's the bottle of moudongue?"

"They wash the boat with that in the morning inside and out. You got to pung maweepoui with that moudongue to wash the boat with and you put it in a bottle to soak."

"Is that the same maweepoui that you brought me?"

Charles nodded his head in approval. "Child, you is the first girl I know, when I talk, I don't talk twice and you never forget anything. I am going to bring you a little piece of the moudongue,[47] and you put a little piece of it in your mouth and you walking far. You walk so fast you're going to feel like you're flying. Sometime it is right for you to learn these things, because you don't know what's on your journey. But if you is a stupid girl, according to the Haitian, you is a human being without no soul, because you don't know what to do for yourself."

I knew that the bois moudongue was considered to be the Devil's tree, but I also wondered about the fromager. Was this the Devil's tree too? I asked Charles what the difference was. He clicked his tongue at me, "Eh, eh, you mustn't talk about that." But that night he seemed in a receptive mood so I pressed on. "Eh, eh," he clicked again. "This Devil thing. If the government know you're using it, they jail you for that. The cotton and the seed is especially dangerous."

"The seed of the fromager?"

"Yes. How could you get that seed? You cannot tell me though?"

"Is it like the bamboo seed?" I guessed.

"No."

"I don't know."

"You can get the seed when you hear the high wind. The cotton fly, and if God help you in this thing, the cotton fall by your door. You go and pick up the cotton. You will see the seed inside the cotton. But aside from that you cannot get the fromager seed. If the tree to windward of your place—just like at my house— well, the fromager tree on top and when the wind blows I could get the seed when I want."

"And what do you do with the seed?" I asked curiously.

"You collect your seed and put it in a vial, because you cannot get that seed as easy as you think. If you got that seed, you've got money too, because this do plenty work."

"Oh, what do you use it for?" I was pressing again. "All kinds of things?"

"All kinds of things—evil things. And if you want the seed to call the Master, you got the seed."

"Oh, you need the seed to call the Master?" My interest was quickening. Somehow power objects always seemed to play a part with the Devil.

"Yes, to call the Master," he repeated. "You could drink a tea with the seed, but you could not drink the tea of the seed only. You got to take faydo blanc with it. This faydo blanc is a delicate leaf, you know. Nobody doesn't plant that. A man which know medicine, he will find that like an iron under the dirt on a cliff— the cliff below and the dirt on top. Now that leaf going to grow behind your house. If you take one leaf to use it for yourself, you'll see it all behind your house in a couple of months—so long you go pick up a leaf anywhere and you carry it at home to use, you'll have it. That's a sign. She tell you, 'If you love me, I got to stay by you.' That's what that leaf will tell you, 'If you love me, I stay by you,' and it will come by you without your calling. When you see a couple of days you're going to see, one, two, three. When you have about a month, it's all behind your house and it doesn't choke out other bush. It send a nice flower. The flower got the seed in it, and when you see the seed dry, that's when you collect it for your tea. This all behind your house in your little garden, like the little garden I have behind my house. All what you find is different, different, different. You find charpentier, you find maweepoui. You get all that there. In case anything happen to you in the night, you just light the lamp and open the door."

"Do you drink the tea with the fromager and the faydo blanc?" I tried to nudge him gently back to that subject, but his mind was going in another direction now.

"Of course."

"And what does that do?" I was afraid there was to be no more talking of the Devil for the moment. He was on the subject of faydo blanc. I suspected he was purposely ignoring the fromager.

"What the reason you drink that? Well, the kind of way you feel—your bowels hurting you, and your stomach hurting you, and you was well and good, and you went out. Perhaps you might drink with somebody. You don't know what the person do, but in the middle of the night you feel sick. You just get up. You take that leaf, you boil it. You put in a grain of salt and you drink it. If it's anything bad, you going to start to feel you're getting your ease from your stomach. You want to puke—you cannot puke. When you drink that, you go by your basin or your bowl."

"You're sick immediately?"

He nodded. "And you're not sick again. You will puke it out in the basin." With that he gave me his rendition of being actively sick.

"Is that the tea of the fromager and the faydo blanc?" I asked, knowing perfectly well he had only been talking about the latter.

Apparently I hadn't pronounced it quite right, for he answered me with, "You forget it again? *Fay-do blanc*—you have it? *Fay-do blanc*. Watch it good. The two sides are quite different. As you take the parcel and open it, you're bound to see it there."

"Yes, I remember. It has a big leaf."

"It is a big, round leaf," he continued, "on one side it is green, and behind it is white. If you feel you need it next morning at daybreak, you take your maweepoui and charpentier with it. You could give that to everybody—to all the children—you don't have to make that by your ownself."

About this time a stranger made his way down the steps to the telephone which was on the wall above Charles's head. I did not pursue our conversation, as I figured the man had enough to do battling with the phone without the added confusion of a conversation buzzing around his ears. But once he had gone Charles rebuked me. "You got to hold there. That's why I told you—eh, eh. You cannot stop the conversation because, first thing they see you and me talking, and when they come, you stop it. Well. . . ."

I tried to explain that I had simply been trying to let the man talk on the phone, but Charles clicked his tongue at me again to assure me that such niceties were not necessities. I hoped maybe to get him back on the subject of the fromager, so I asked him about the fromager tree I'd seen outside Portsmouth. I started hesitantly. "In Portsmouth—there's a fromager tree."

"Yeah."

"And they told me that the sucoyan used to come there."

"Yeah."

"At night." I didn't think I was getting anywhere.

"Yes. You got to get the prickle [thorn] of the fromager."

"Oh?" I had never heard anything about a prickle before.

Three fromager prickles (about two inches in length)

"And that's what I'm going to give you—the three prickle. You take the cutlass and you shove it under, flat. Now the prickle is very dangerous. It is a poison. If that go through into your foot you can't get better. You could have shoes—you could have rubber shoes, you could have leather—it could go through the leather. It's a dangerous prickle. It's poison, and worser yet—if you take the prickle and put it in a teacup, and you throw the oil of coupier[48] on it—that person don't live because the coupier is poison, and the same poison meet poison again. If you cut off your leg you could not get rid of that poison. It going to still go back so again. Where are you going to tie that cut? When this foot get wounded the water of this one fall on the other."

"And so the other leg gets infected," I finished. Charles nodded, letting out a whoop of laughter at the thought. "Even if you burn up the foot, in the night you're sleeping, and it's dripping from that one, and both feet are going to catch. And the next thing again. The hand is dressing the feet. If a person don't know, he's going to pass it anywhere—in his eye, on his face, on the mouth—all that going.

"There's a man up there. I watched the man—he's a chauffeur. Both his hands are all cut up. I watch him and I say, 'You fucker you. You must have done something wrong. That's why you're like that.' The hand all cut up and still sowing [infected]. He can't cure."

"There's no cure at all?" I asked, wondering about the powers of the en tout cas.

"I tell you, no. He coming down the road. I watching him. He got house. He don't have no land, because why? The place he was living first, they put him out. They have to ask me. I didn't know at first, but after I know. He was making black magic and when they find out, they give him notice. Now he come and ask me where to go. I told him to go at Mrs. Spit. She give him a spot by the road. I only watch him pass down. I say, 'A nice man like you—your lips going, your hand going.' But he still have a wife. The wife have heart more than me because I wouldn't stay with him. That man—while doing wrong—the trap catch him. He can't get cure up to now. I tell you the hand so. Up to now, up to yesterday morning when I going down, I meet the man going down. I watch him head to foot. All that way. That to show you what he was doing there. They catch him. Fromager doing that thing for him.

"And the next fucking thing. When you got fromager at your house, you don't have to worry atall because the Man with you."

"Because what?" Was he talking about the Devil again?

"The Man with you," he repeated. "Where's your boss?"

"You mean you use the seed to call him?" Was he talking about the seed or the prickle? I wasn't sure, but he made it clear in the next instant.

"You have it there. And why do you have fromager at your house if it not a guardian?"

"It's a guardian?"

"Right. You have the prickle—you have three prickles—in a vial by your dresser. What do you care? You got the prickles there. The prickle have flesh in them. When one jams you it sure to bore a hole. It's not a little prickle, it's a heavy prickle, and when you go and stab your foot on it, it got thing to destroy you. The point is just like a needle point. My dear child, I passing by the thing. I told you, look my house there and the thing below me there."

I hadn't remembered seeing the tree and I told him so. It was so distinctive I was sure I'd recognize it. "It's a great big tree, isn't it?"

"Oh, Jesus Christ!"

"And a sort of flared bottom?"

"It a very big, big tree. All kind of side, and it go up in the air, and it making a place you can sit on. You could sit down on the ground like your home. That's where the duppy people sit down in the night and get their rest and chatter. Down in Conway they had one—right near where you see the bridge—where they put their shed for tourists to come. There they have a tree and there they find a woman right down in the ground saying, 'Let me go. Let me call.' That same Nancy[49] I tell you about, and Dr. Meyer come by she home. Her eyes were red and she naked as she born. And the doctor say, 'She's a duppy.'"

"Did they cut the tree down?" I asked in surprise. I had always heard there was great resistance to cutting down such a tree.

"Of course."

"Didn't they have any trouble?"

"The government cut it because they have to make the road." I had heard a story in Africa where the road had been moved to go around a silk cotton tree, and one from Grenada where the government wanted the tree cut down, but the people refused, so I asked again, "But wasn't there trouble?"[50]

"No, it was the government that build it, and they blast there. They have a big store there, but they bar it up. Well, it was there they had a big snake in the root of the fromager."

I had heard about the association of a snake with a silk cotton tree,[51] but I didn't know much more than that, so I tried to encourage Charles to enlighten me.

"Is there always a snake in the root of a fromager?" I asked.

"Yes, that's what they got dealing with bad people. That's people that put that there."

"People put it there?" I encouraged.

"Yeah. You could get snake just so long you ask for it. You pay for the snake and he bring it to you. If you have business at your home, you have a big business in a shop, or you have a rum shop, or a shop combined with a rum shop, then you have a snake in a barrel."

"What does the snake do for you? Bring you business like a bolum?"

Charles continued, "The snake is worse than a bolum, because it come out in the night and go back in the morning and you can't find it. You train your snake. The snake in a barrel and you have a bag of sugar at your home. And you put the bag under the counter and then you open it. What you think you do? You got a square hole in the center of the shop."[52]

"And that's where your snake is?" At this point I wasn't quite sure where the snake was. Maybe it was in the bag of sugar.

"Give me a chance. Give me a chance," he laughed at me. "You too fast—just like the dog trying to climb the tree. Don't rush me. In the center of the shop they have a big hole."

"Right," I said, rather contritely.

"Now, what I tell you? You're going to open the bag of sugar and pull up the door. You leave the snake there, and it can come out inside the store and go all around. Snake could climb tree, you know. You know that? Snake go and he lay down there. You cannot see him. He put his head outside there and he watching you like that. Now if he feel to come down, he coming down by your head there. You don't even feel it. In the night he go in the kitchen. He eat breadfruit and he go back in his place when day break. You got little child. It come and it nurse the baby and go back again. You would never know that. That snake will never harm you and it will never harm the child, but let somebody come and humbug you—let anything happen to you—he lay down there waiting for the person. When he hear the person, *nyah!* and he go back in the hole. You pass there every day and you never see it trouble you. You cooking in the kitchen and you leave the bottom of your foot there. He enjoys it. He eat all the grease."

"He's a guardian then?" I asked, somewhat hesitantly.

"Guardian of guardians," Charles emphasized. "You charming a snake very easy. You charming a snake like you're charming a human being." He looked at me. I was obviously puzzled. "You scratch your head. Ah, child, I'll tell you now. You will ask for a little snake. They'll [the Devil will] bring a little snake for you. You put the snake in a barrel. The snake enjoys it. That time he's there, he a little one. Now you give him a personal water food—because snake drinking water like human. So you put the water there in the barrel for it to drink. But this water is doped."

"You put a little something in it?"

"Yes. You put in a powder and you got to put something from your body in it."

"From your body?" I questioned. "Like a fingernail?"

"No, darling, not a fingernail. Nothing like that. You've got to put the water you clean yourself with in the barrel. The snake drink it. Then you got your guardian because he bound to drink the water."

"And what kind of powder?" I pressed.

"Compelling power powder."

"Compelling powder?"

"Dope, eh? A little sprinkle each time you give it its food. When you go to the drugstore you just ask for compelling powder. Compelling powder means what you say, goes. You could take compelling powder and put it in a glass and throw water on it and then you drink it. If you pass a bit of compelling powder under your arm and your face, and you go off to look for a job, when you talk the person got to listen. You putting the person to leeward, and you passing to windward."

"And they give you the job?" I asked incredulously.

"And they give you the job. When you stop by the store or anywhere you is, what you say goes. At that time, you know your business. You're serious and you make no truck with nobody. When you want to go out, you just go straight to your office and you go. When you come back, you come back. You don't even laugh. You're serious. It's not you, it's the medicine you're using controlling you now. Compelling powder—you got the oil and you got the powder."

"Do you use the oil for the same thing?"

"Sure. You got shore work and sea work. Right? You bring this for shore work. It's not different. They're dead the same, but one thing. No devil can come and meet you there because you not in the sea."

"Can you use the oil at sea?" I asked, remembering what he had told me about the oil of rose.

"Not too much. He cannot come. Because why won't he come? I not give you the next thing to put in it. There's a leaf. You call it 'gros deetin.'" He chuckled.

"Yeah, thick leaf."

"Oh, Jesus Christ. Who show you that?"

"You told me that—with maweepoui," I reminded him.

"Yes."

"The tea."

"You could drink that, but don't you take the compelling powder and mix it with gros deetin. The Boss come."

"The Boss comes?"

"Of course. It's too strong."

"You don't rub your boat with it then?" I questioned.

"If you're using one, don't use the other one," he explained. "If you're going to take gros deetin and maweepoui, don't use the oil. You know the gros deetin?"

"You've just told me about it. I've never seen it," I told him.

"You've not seen it? If you tell me you didn't know it, I would bring it to you. I don't want you to deal with me like that. Don't deal with me halfway. When you're going to deal, deal with me straight. If you tell me, 'Charles, I don't know that, I would like to see it,' I would bring the leaf to you."

"O.K. Well, next time you come?" I asked.

"Don't say next time! How I bring it without you telling me? Gros deetin is a thick leaf. You could drink it. You could put it in your food. When you put that in your food you eat it and you all right."

"Didn't you tell me it was bitter?"

"It's not so bitter. It not bitter atall." Then he reminded me, "The one that bitter is the one making the worm with two horns. That one bitter. Do you remember the name of it?"

"That's twef, isn't it?"

He nodded, satisfied, and added, "Racine twef—the root."

"What do you use the root for?"

"The root does the same thing as the leaf." He laughed, seeming to relish the thought. "The root is worse. You using the root in the rum too, you know, but you're not taking a heavy spoon. Take a baby spoonful and not often. You could do it this month and next month again make a sip. But you know any time your toe get rotten you have something to take. When you sit down, resting yourself, study the things in your head and you won't forget it. When I start to speak Spanish—the minute that I get up—I repeat the word that they tell me in my head. I'm doing it when I'm working on top of the horse riding. I'm studying at the same time, because I want to speak Spanish. Well, you do it that same way I tell you. If you study what Charles say tonight, tomorrow, or tomorrow afternoon, you will remember. Any time you sit down—you're sewing your clothes, yes, you're sewing your clothes—but your mind upon what I tell you. Study, 'cause I know what I say. I bound to tell nothing. Do like me. I just sleep and I is a goner, because I don't like no friend. I don't keep friend here. I don't keep people by me because I don't see no good.

"Now the next thing I got to show you is the place where the drugstore at. You don't know how long I going to live. You don't know if you're going to come back and meet me. Well, the place is owned by Mr. Barras, and you don't want to ask nobody about it, you hear. You take the track from the garden. You go up straight. When you reach the place to go up Monkey Hill to go at my house, you see the house there. You go in and you say, 'Is your name Mr. Barras?'

"'Yes.'

"'Good.' You open your book and tell him what you want. The man speaking nice and polite. When you finish, he going to call the things for you. You put them in your bag and close your book. But don't go and talk in the drugstore. Never do that. As you come, he will size you up good. He will give you the right thing, but when he see you he will price you over. How I go there? I come a poor man. He won't charge me because I a poor man, but if you go he will price you over. The same in the market. They will sell orange to me for four pence, but they will sell one to you for a shilling—and it will be the same one they sell to me. You'll go in a store. You will buy a shirt for me for six dollars and I going to go buy the same shirt for two. Good. I know, because you is a white person and you have the money. The poor man don't. What he lost upon the poor man, he'll take in from you. That's what they tell me already. I told Mr. Barnard that and he tell me, 'Yes.'

"I said, 'How that? Dr. Meyer make three visit for three sailors on board a ship, and you send two hundred sixty dollars for him.'

"He tell me, 'Yes, I supposed to send it, Charles, because I will tell you why. A white man got expenses to feed his wife and feed his ownself, but you going to take a penny macamboo, a penny fig, and a penny oil, and you're going to get a breakfast. But the white people don't do that. They got to eat something to keep him up and something good too. You will make it for a week on some sardine or salt fish, but not a white man. Them working for double money to support themselves.'

"I say, 'Oh.' Mr. Palmer getting more money than Mr. Cyril, but Mr. Palmer is a white man. Mr. Hamilton is getting more money because him is white people. And the black people—you're really working hard, more than those people—but they have different expenses. So you got to expect Mr. Barras to over-charge you. That's where I dealing. Today he was closed. He out round the coast. He got a doctor's shop down there and one here. That's where all the country people come to get what they want. Those country people doesn't speak English much—all Patois—and he's a Patois man too. That man have a big trade. His father dead, he left a lot of money. His mother dead, she left a lot of money. He's been quite to Panama to learn."

"He went to Panama to learn?" I was surprised, as I would have expected him to go to either Guyana or Haiti, known throughout the Lesser Antilles as the places where the best magic is wrought.

Charles nodded. "And all the article, he send for it every six months. He bring it in the shop. He not making all this kind of thing."

"Does he get it from Panama, then?"

"From Panama. I check on that. Now hear what he doing. He going to England to go and see his daughter, and when you think he in England, he in Panama. When I go there I sit down up-stairs. Then I tell him what I want. We two is good friends."

"I bet you know more than he does." I tried a challenge. I wanted to have some idea of the extent of Charles's knowledge.

"You're fucking well right, girl," he boasted. "When he tells me a thing, I laugh. He believe he learn me that. He tell me something, but he don't know that I know all of that."

"He doesn't know?" I should have known better than to ask that.

"Janie, what you think I is, a fool?"

"Oh no, I just thought he would know," I said weakly.

"Let me tell you now why I say that. If you go at a man's house, and he have to tell you his power, his instruction, and what he could do, then you stand out there like a little monkey. When you come there, why? You come there privately. You're calling the name to tell him what you want. You don't want others to know your business. When I was there, a woman come and ask, 'Give me something to tie a man to make him give me money.' She calling, 'Mr. Barras, what's so and so?' Mr. Barras sell it to her. A man come and ask all kind of different powder. Mr. Barras sell it. But I come, so. As he see me come, he just push the side door, and I go inside. I tell him what I want. I get all my message. I shove my paper in a paper bag, and nobody see what I come out with. Because I is a man. I don't have to expose my business."

I thought back to that night when Charles had brought me his first "messages" and remembered how quickly he had stuffed everything into a paper bag at the sound of a footstep.

Charles went over to the water spigot and had a drink. I stretched and looked at my watch and decided it was time to go. Even though Charles was a night watchman he liked to get in some sleep before daybreak. After all, if anything went wrong the dead watchman would waken him.

The next evening when Charles arrived, he beckoned me into the storeroom. "Here is your message." He thrust a worn, brown paper bag into my hand. I looked inside and found a little package wrapped in newspaper. Carefully I extricated three giant thorns about two inches in height with needle-like points on the end. "Are these the fromager prickles you were talking about?"

He nodded. "That's three men you got in the house now," and he explained how I should put one over each window and door in my house as a guardian against black magic. I asked him if the number three was important.

"That's right. Not only black doing this job. White doing it too. You will go and sleep with your panty on and when you get up in the morning, you find they have come off and somebody using you in your sleep. You will feel tired and sleepy. But so long as you got that you don't care, you could sleep without panties. . . ."

"And nobody could get in," I finished.

Charles laughed heartily at the thought. "What! You going to stamp your foot. He can't work. Eh, eh. That's why I give you that. All kind of way he come, he fucked. You don't know what you got there. It's hard for you to find out this kind of medicine. Me don't tell nobody that. Me don't give nobody that neither. Just for you ownself. But I know if I don't open the door it is me one that can open my door. My door is mine.

"You got many science in the world, but know the kind of things that protect you. All the science, all these things have their master. You mustn't stop like a bottle without a cork. Just like with a boat. You is the one to make the boat work. If you don't make medicine, it can't work. There's an old man who's got a boat by the wharf. They say, 'That boat have luck. Each time he come back he doesn't come back empty. He got luck.' Well, what they do now? They try and humbug him. The more they do it, the more he taking. Because why? You take the precautions first. What they put on the boat is no use. It only wash away. Now you could put a piece of the fromager in a canoe. Never, never, never, never put that in the head. Take a prickle like one of these and drive it in behind the rudder. No government can find that out.[53] Because why? You paint the boat and do everything. It right at the end of the tiller and that's the guardian for the boat. If you put the prickle there, the whole body bound to go in. Remember it is not a big shot of poison that kill you. A drop kill you quicker, because an overdose will make you suffer. Well, that's what you got there. A fool going to put a big drop, but it's all got the same blood. Those Carib people, they give it all kind of way for you to understand. They show you it is not a big piece doing the job. A little piece doing the same job a big piece does, because it's the same family there. But a man going to believe he going to take half a piece of that wood and put it in the bottom of the boat—he's mad. When they come to investigate you, they going to find that out and report you and jail you."

"Why will they jail you?" I asked naively.

"You know who you're dealing with?"

"The Devil?"

Charles nodded. "The Master. You go anywhere in the ocean—if you going to fish, you never out of fish. But some day your life is miserable, because he going to take you by your back—grab you behind your back—and take you down to the bottom. He give you a long time to make your bread, but some day he going to come for you. He not joking, this man. He not robbing you, but don't rob him. He not shaking you, don't shake him. A promise is a debt. Never say you will and you not do it. If you pay, you see job. If you not pay, you is a slave. That man will never settle. When it's his pleasure he will come. He won't knock.

"You can go from here to Jerusalem, but you don't bluff him. Better you pay all the money at one time. Just like a fellow there in Anse la Raye. He have a big net—seine net. His name is Micoud,[54] a big tall dark fellow. Mr. Micoud—he have a rum shop there, and he wife selling fish in the market. Micoud's a big man now, he's cleaned up full of gold. He was a poor man. He was in prison for gambling and everything and now he have a big house."

"And Micoud paid all at once?"

"Yes. He pay the job and he never loss. Fish is there, and when Micoud make a lash with the seine he get so many he got to send in the country all about."

"Will he ever have to pay again?" I queried.

Charles looked at me as if I had lost my mind. "You cannot pay if you not owe. You pay one time and you finish with Him. If you pay half, you pay half. You give the amount. A hundred is a hundred. 'Here's your hundred,' and you go with your bottle. That's all. You pay for your seine. You pay for your boat. After you see, you fumigate your boat and fumigate the seine. That's all. Your boat is clear. Your seine is clear. Nothing can happen.

"Now put that away." I had been absentmindedly twirling a prickle in my fingers as he talked, so I carefully wrapped it and returned it to the bag—out of sight from prying eyes. We walked out to where we usually sat at the foot of the steps. Charles pulled out his old canvas chair from the office, and I took my usual place on the bench. He began to speak about the pictures I had brought of himself and his family. "Fati, she shove that picture right in the grip. Nobody to see the picture. When she go to sleep she hide it so nobody would tief it. Zander, he carry one for his godmother and his godfather. Zander beat me, you know. Zander's picture is nicer." Suddenly he stopped and looked at me and said very quietly, "They could kill you with your own picture, you know."

"What?" For some reason I hadn't been expecting that right then, although I had wondered what Charles's attitude toward photographs was. He always had been delighted when I took his picture.

"They could kill you with your picture, you know," he repeated earnestly.

"I didn't know that," I said, hoping some more information would be forthcoming.

"Sure."

"How?"

"What!" Was he incredulous or was he avoiding the question?

"How?" I persisted.

"How!"

"Kill you with your picture?"

"Kill you with your picture. Yes, they shoot your picture. You could be from here to Vieux Fort, and they shoot you. All right. I will give it to you now. There's a man from Dominica who came here to go and dig some money[55] for a woman—Millie. When he dig the money, they pay him and then they shoot him in Martinique. He was my child's godfather. They find him here, dead with a khaki pants, a khaki suit, a black belt and a brown shoe, but the person that shoot him was in Martinique."

"You shoot the picture and then the person . . ."

"Dies," Charles finished.

"Do you have to say something special, though? You can't just shoot a picture and have the person die?" I asked skeptically.

Charles was shocked at my ignorance. "What are you talking about! You know what they call science?"

"Yeah."

"Well, a science man going to get you no matter where you are—so long as he have your picture. You quite upstairs sleeping. After he take the picture, put it in front of the science pot and he work it. He make you come out from upstairs fast asleep and go and break your neck."

"Well, don't let anybody get hold of your picture."

"No! You can't tell me nothing about that. I've been to a place where they have coolies—they using a kind of white hat that have a white ribbon behind it. They have a long pipe. Below, there's a hole, and they have fire there, and when they put the article there, they ask you what you want to do the person. So long as you got his picture, they do what they want to do. You could tief all what you want from him."

"Do they make little dolls to represent a person and stick it with pins, too?" I asked.

"No, Indians not making all that. They got the person in front of them and they making their work there. The man hold it, so, and bringing the smoke through the picture. He say, 'Look at him. What do you want to do him now? Kill him?'

"You say, 'Yes.' And he will kill him, but you got to pay plenty money to do that job. You cannot say no. If a person have the heart to hurt you, you must do him the same."

"Have you seen it done?"

"Sure, I've seen it done. If I see it done!" he spat between his remaining teeth. "There's an Indian man. You been Antigua?"

"Yes."

"You didn't meet an Indian man preaching in the street?"

"In St. Johns? No."

"There's a man with a long thing hanging behind his neck and he have a kind of turban. That man's an obeah man. He tie you up. Have I ever seen that! You think I not traveled yet?"

I held my breath and asked the question I'd been wanting to. "Can you do it?"

"My way is better than his. I doing quicker job than he."

"Really?"

"Sure. My way is better. When he doing it he have to make smoke and everything. I don't need to make smoke. I do mine with a candle."

"With a candle?" I was pressing again.

"Yes. Look here, Janie, I'm going to chase you to hell away just now because you make me go too deep. When you leave here that night, remember, water come out in my eye. I went behind there and I light a black candle for you. It light, it burn 'til it finish. It was a black candle."

"Why a black candle?"

"For your traveling."

"For traveling?"

"Light it. It will burn according to the way you're leaving. If you have a black road and if you're making a bad journey, it won't light bright. When I tell you black candle, black candle means serious trouble candle. All right. I light it inside there," he said motioning towards the storeroom, "and each time I went inside, I just understand what it say."

"And it makes you have a good journey?"

"The kind of way the candle read to me I see you make a good journey."

I remembered that trip well. It was the end of the summer and we had stopped in St. Lucia on our way home from Bequia, an island further south, to see Charles, and the following morning had flown standby to Barbados. I had been trying to make reservations for two weeks, only to be told there was no space on the plane. As it turned out it was a good-sized jet with only a handful of passengers. Once in Barbados we thought we had reservations for New York. That was the only part of the flight that had been confirmed. But this turned out to be a feeling of false security. We were told that we had no reservations and that there was a long waiting list without much hope held out to standbys. We drooped around the ticket desk with long faces, while others cracked their knuckles and shouted at the ticket man. Perhaps it was our silence, perhaps the man took pity on our young children, but whatever the reason, five minutes before the plane was to depart our family of four were the only passengers to be put on the plane, and, what's more, we were given first-class seats for our third-class rate. Maybe there was something to this black candle after all! I told Charles the whole story and he beamed at me.

"You was in a journey, going away, but you had somebody working for you. You didn't even know. That time you leave was a bad-weather time."

"That's right. It was hurricane season." And then changing the subject slightly, "Well, if you want to kill somebody, do you use a different kind of candle?"

"That's right. Did you ever see a candle dressed like a vessel? It have a rigging."

"Like a vessel?" I wasn't sure that I had heard right.

"It have a rigging, there. A red and black thread. It well dressed and it lighting. Oh, ho, ho, ho. Child, keep off. I will make you keep off from it, because you're rubbing pepper in my guts. I don't know if its God send you for me, but whoever it is, you got to have my blood, eh?" And he was off again, but there was no more talk of candles that night.

A week or so later I returned to our conversation. That night he was in a more receptive mood. "The other night you were telling me about how you could light a candle—you know, when we went on a trip."

"Ah, yes."

This time I was more direct. "Can you teach me about that?"

"Yes, I could teach you about that. It's very easy. It's very easy.

I will show you how to do it. You got to get a roll of black thread
and one of red thread and some pins. You see, just like the mast
of a ship." He demonstrated how to place the pins, putting two
rows down the candle so that their points would meet in the center of the candle. "You go down from head to the foot and then
you go down with the thread now, one by one. You take a turn
around the head of each pin. One side with the black and you
bring it down to the bottom and tie it there. The next side with
the red thread. This side is black and the next one is red. And be
careful, eh? You have the person's name under the candle and
you will call the person's name about three times and you going
to speak to the candle now, 'The same way you light, I light you
to do my offering and I want you to carry it' and you call the
person's name three times and let it burn."

"And let it burn?"

"Yes."

"And then what happens? It does your work?"

"Yes, of course it works."

I wanted to know more, and I figured that probably candles of
different colors were used for different things, so I asked about
the black candle he had lit for us.

He explained, "There is many work and many candle. You
could use a black candle for a different thing and you using a
white candle for a different job."

"Oh."

"Each job got a candle."

"What would you use a white candle for?" I persisted.

"A white candle according to the work you got to do. If somebody is aggravating you and you want to send him away, after
you dress it, you put the paper under it and you burn that
candle."

"Would you put the same pins in the white candle?"

"Yes, yes. You see, you put the paper in a jelly bottle."

"Uh huh." I nodded to let him know I was following him.
"And the candle on top of it."

"Yeah, but the candle will light in it, you know, because you put it down and you drop a bit of wax on top of the paper, and you put the candle there in the bottle and you cork it. You light it now."

"Yeah."

"Right. What you think you're going to do with that bottle?" I shook my head. "You don't know?"

"No."

"Well, you take that bottle, well corked. . . ."

"You cork it?"

"Of course you cork it."

"Won't the candle go out?" That was one of my earliest recollections of science class.

"No, they have a big vial," Charles explained. "Nothing will happen. The water can't get in, and then you take it and when you reach far in the ocean you throw it overboard."

"And that person goes away?"

"And that person is adrift. He will have no ticket. He pass on this side. He go on that side for the balance of his life. Your black candle is worse."

"It's worse? Well, that's the one you lit for us?"

"That's right. As you leave, I light my candle."

"With the pins too?"

"Yeah, pins and everything. What you think inside there now? That's your travel all about. That's what I do—the night you was going, the day you was going—everything."

"And how long do you let it burn for?"

"The whole night."

"Do you say special things?"

"Of course—special things. What you demand is what you get."

I was surprised that the same black candle was used both in killing someone and as the travel candle, so I questioned Charles a bit more on that. "Why do you use a black candle for a trip?"

"Because that's your travel candle—because you don't know what's going to happen. The kind of job you have, the kind of candle you use, you know. You use a red candle if you have a serious court case, or if you have danger. You using it that time when the person in court. Then you lighting the candle—a big candle. It will burn for three days, but this kind cost plenty money."

"Who taught you all that, Charles?" There was a long silence as Charles gave me one of his penetrating looks that always made me squirm a bit. "Did you learn it from Anton, from the Caribs, or did you just pick it up?" I finished lamely.

Still there was silence. Then suddenly he broke it. "How could I learn the job without somebody showing me? Yes, it was Anton. He is a Haitian, you know. But this thing come so funny. Just like me and you, Janie. When I reached a place they call Pintado, I meet the man—his head big like a lion and his face full of beard—and I pick him up—just like me and you come friends, Janie. He tell me he have no one to cut his hair. And so say, so done. He say he don't have no money to give me, but what he give me worth more than money. I tell you, if it not for this man you would not see me here today. I telling you, a person cannot be raised in this world without knowing something. That's not eticote [ethical?]. Yes, you find out. You going out of your way. You got to stick with somebody which know the wangawanga. God send you."

"The what?"

"The wangawanga."

"What's that?"

"Obeah."

"Oh! What language is wangawanga?"

He laughed at me and teased, "Oh, you want to know that kind of language? Well, you got to go in Haiti if you want to know that—that's wangawanga. When you go to a man's house, you see he carry you in a chamber. The chamber black, and bottles all around."

"Did Anton practice wangawanga, then?"

"Of course. Anton—eh, eh," he clicked.

"And he was very good at it?"

"Man, if the man good! Huh!" he exclaimed. "Anton was a digger. When you hear they pray for dead people, Anton going to get more than a hundred dollars expenses to make dinner for the dead people. He tell you, 'Come, go do something with me.' When you go, you find you're there cutting cane. You believe you alone cutting cane, but you hear cane cutting like there is four men cutting cane. And cane cutting. When you get up tomorrow morning—a heap of mountain of cane you have.[56] Sometime with Anton, rain falling. Everybody run and leave there. You cutting cane and no rain wet you."[57]

"Where did Anton learn all this?"

"Well, he is a king of this. He is an old man. What, you think he is a young man? And after I take Anton's rule, you don't ever see me with friends. Me don't keep friends at my house, and nobody can know my secrets. I don't want no man setting his backside upon my chair, because I don't know which one good, which one bad. After what I pass already you think I going to drown again? Oh God, not me. You stay by yourself because the person will come at your home. You believe he is your pal, and he call for your destruction. Huh!" He spat some tobacco juice for emphasis. "Ah hah!

"Anton learn me to talk to my mother when I like. You learn what you don't know, but when you know it's very easy, like a penny bread. There is only one trouble I got with you—the song of the Haitian song—and it's Haitian talk you got to talk. It's very easy. Here is the song."

With that Charles stretched out flat on the concrete, folded his hands over his chest, and began a low, moaning hum. After a few moments he stopped to instruct me. "You singing that song in the bottom of your heart, and the tear will come to your eye.

You lay down flat, so, and you singing that song how I show you. Then the first thing, you drop asleep. If your mother die, or your father—whoever it is—they come to you. Jane, you got to understand. You lay in a bed and you know the kind of work you have upon your account. It is not ha'penny you studying. You're studying your job.[58] And it's not to say God's sickness you have. Your own people put you there.[59] You have to defend yourself, child. You got to defend yourself. It is very easy with the song." He began to sing again.

"Every night I got to go at Anton's and clap myself there on the bench, and he sit down there and he make me singing that song—just as I have singing it to you." Once more he started humming.

"And the word coming out to me like a Yankee note," he continued. "That is the faith you have in your heart. That's why the tear come out in your eyes—'cause you're singing and crying. It pain for you. And now you calling the dead. That's the dead people you're calling there."

He lay back again, chanting his song. It had a mesmerizing effect. "Suppose I carry on now. I would fall asleep. I can't show you more than that now. Try and see if you can carry the song by your ownself. If you practice it about three nights here, on the fourth night you bound to take the tune up."

Once more he began to sing in an effort to teach me. As I watched, the water started to well up in his eyes, and I sensed he would go into a trance. "I got to stop that. It start to come on me. They [the dead] are around there. If I carry on singing the song, I drop asleep, and the first person I meet as I drop asleep would be my mother."

"Is it the dead person who matters the most to you who comes?" I asked.

"That's the right person to call. If your father is dead and your mother alive, then your father come. It is after your mother dead that there's nobody there. Don't tell me you're going to trust anybody besides your mother or your father, because they wouldn't have no heart for you."

"What about your grandparents?" Both my parents were alive.

"Oh, that is worse again. That worse. So long you know that grandfather before he dead. Did you know him before he dead?" I nodded. "Well, you have the key in your hands. You have the key. It's worse. That's your own blood—your main blood—and he know what to do for you. Some night you going to sleep. You take a cup of water, you send it, so, out the door, and you're going to hear a person tell you, 'Janie, you wet me.' You didn't know he was there, but he get vexed. In the next day or so your foot begin to swell. You got to know what to do for it. The old people will know. Your grandfather will help you.

"If a person have a heart to hurt you, why can't I hurt him back? Eh, eh. If somebody do me something, I send it back for them. Don't do me first because I ain't doing nobody no harm. I watching the man there with my watch. I laughing, you know. I show you something. I never vexed with him. No. I never vexed with him. I passing nicely, say 'hello' to him. He believe I love him, but he don't know. If I vexed with him I couldn't catch him. I go in the shop. He lets me there. I could put something in that same shop. But if I vexed with him, I can't go in the shop. You think I do a fool thing like that? Obeah man never vexed with nobody. No, you do me harm, I know what to do. He talking, he left me there, he go in the back. I say, 'Well, I watching him good.' I will make his two foot swell up as big as a whole night, and he can't get better."

Charles had pawned the watch I had given him for five dollars just before Christmas. When he went to retrieve it, the man told him that he had lost it. Apparently it had been reported in the neighborhood that the pawn dealer's son was wearing a new watch. Charles was muttering to me about taking him to court.

"Can't you put something on him? I'd think he'd be afraid of that."

"Uh huh. Yes, Ma'am. If he say no, he will be miserable inside that house, because he not living far from the road. You could stay in the road yourself and send it inside the house."

"Really?" I was all ears.

"He have a shop downstairs and he living upstairs. You don't have to worry about that. You could send it in the eggs."

"How would you do that?" I asked.

"I could do that. Do you know how to suck an egg? You draw all the egg out with your mouth, and the whole egg empty. Well, you put those eggs somewhere else to spoil. You put something in it to spoil, and that egg will spoil so much—when you fire the eggs upstairs, when they burst—the whole lot of them sick inside the house, one on top of the other."

"What do you do to make it spoil so?"

"Poison powder—just like a tin. You fix up this medicine and you poisoning the tin. You cover it for fifteen days and let it spoil. The eggs turn a poison, and you just have them in a paper bag, like so. When you reach, you fire it upstairs and let it go. The smell of the egg is poison. Who's watching? You don't know anything."

"And the smell makes you pass out?" I queried.

"The smell of the disease exploded inside. Every man inside that house sick. It's just like you blow a gas. 'You stole my watch. This has nothing to do with me. Fuck you. You have a heart to do me a job. I don't have heart to do you?'"

"What kind of poison is that?" I pursued. I was at the point where it was comfortable to ask him any question. He might refuse to answer, but he didn't seem to mind. I thought this might be one of those times.

"Ah, Janie. You like a devil. I caught with you. You going so deep with me. It's not for you. Why should I tell you what it is? You want to know what it is? Number one, to make it spoil, you have some acid and you mix two powder together. If you want, you put cat poison in the cup and poude brisée—the row powder."

In this case, however, Charles never resorted to such ends. Nor to my knowledge did he ever retrieve his watch. At a later date I asked him why he hadn't used the eggs, and he responded, "Don't be too much in a hurry for that." As an alternative he asked me to write a letter to Mr. Mosette, threatening him with a court action if he did not return the watch. "He will know I not write that. He will be frightened and make the boy give me my watch back." We sent the letter but from all I could gather, its effect was nil. The eggs would have been more impressive!

As long as we were talking so freely, I thought it might be a good time to ask Charles about divining. He had mentioned how the Caribs could see things in a bowl, so I asked him if he could do it as well.

"Sure—like the Caribs?"

"Yeah."

"I told you, the girl told me what she done."

"Yeah, but can you do it, too?" I persisted. He seemed to misunderstand me, but what followed was every bit as interesting to me.

"Janie, it is very easy. It is not to say 'can you do it?' It is if you have the heart. If you be a coward you wouldn't be able to do that. You got to have the heart to stand it. Not to say 'could you do it?' It is very easy to do." He laughed and repeated, "It is the heart to stand it. Janie, you'll go in your room by your ownself and you could sit down upon a chair by your ownself. You sing a song by your ownself and you lock the door. You calling him in private. You inside there. You want nobody to turn up watching you. To sing the song is nothing, but standing this is something. If you know you could not stand it, don't worry yourself, because you're not singing it in your mouth. He's there. He stand there and he sit down there. And you ask what concerns you—what you want. He watching you like that. If you're in trouble and in distress, you're sick and you need him, you will call him. But you won't call him for a joke. Call for what you need and speak for what you want. It's very easy when you understand it. If you fooling, you might get your neck turned to one side. You have to stand to speak. You speak with the power. You've got to get the message for the power."

"Is that the fromager and the faydo blanc mixed together?"

"How you know that?" He threw me one of his looks. "You catch things good, girl. You call this the power. You have it inside of you, because the moment you drink that thing, you man to beast. You've got to take some in a glass to give you the power to sing the song. You just like a desperaro, just a man out for business. You need and you want to get what you want. You drink that stuff to deal with him."

"And you drink it all at once?"

"One dose, and you get a next thing there for when you finish. You drink the last one after you're done. After he finish with you, then you are free. He drink half and you drink half—two glasses. Then when you come out from there, no door doesn't open. The same way he come, the same way he go. It's no use to believe you going to hide, or that you going to give him a bluff and tell him this and the other, or say you will shut yourself in a room and say he cannot get in there. You is a fool."

"But why does he drink half?"

"What!" Charles was shocked at my lack of understanding. "To give you the power."

"By drinking with you he gives you the power?"

"Yes, you drinking half the power. Both of you drink half. It is he who give it to you, not you give it to him. After that you belong to him because you promise him something to pay him. But you have enough time to pay for that, and the pay is very simple. What he ask you, you give him."

"And you give it all at once?"

"You will give all of it because you're going to have it. You'll get it. What he ask for, you must give him. That's the payment."

"What kind of a thing would he ask you for—a life?" I questioned.

"No, a white cock, and he will tell you where to put it—where to leave it—under a bamboo tree. Just tie the white cock there. About eleven o'clock in the night you go with your white cock. You just put a weight on the cock to prevent the cock from dragging it. And tomorrow morning when you come back you find the cock on the ground, his neck broken. He don't want the flesh. He want the blood."

"The blood of a white cock," I repeated.

"What kind of a white cock do you think? A pure white cock. When you see a man got a white cock at his home, you think it is for boiling, eh? There's a lady got a white cock in Conway, and she feeding them to eat, yes. Sometime you see about three or four cocks there."

"Do a lot of people know that song?" I was hoping maybe he would break down and teach it to me, but he quickly dashed any hopes I had.

"This song not for you. No, it not everybody that know this song. It's those who dealing with the Devil. There are many men and many ways."

"I see," I said meekly. "Did you learn this from Anton, or did you learn it from the Caribs?"

"From the Caribs. Anton learn me a lot too, but the Caribs—I didn't make one trip with them. Remember, I stopped in Dominica for seven years. It was the Caribs who put me on my feet." And Charles launched into his tale of how the Caribs had brought him back "natural" after his sister had sprinkled something in his food. I knew that all talk of calling the Devil was over for the night. I decided to try another tack and changed the subject altogether.

"Charles, I have a friend who's having a lot of bad luck—a lot of sickness in her family. Can I do anything for her?"

"Of course," came his quick response. "If that person is a good friend of yours, I will send medicine. Look here, I send medicine quite to Anguilla for a Captain Mister who have a boat called *Sunbeam*. The fellow told me about the man—that he have a bad leg and he cannot walk. I send the medicine for him in Anguilla and, do you know, the gentleman got better. He came to St. Lucia to find out who is the man that make the medicine for him."

"What kind of medicine would I get my friend?"

And just as any doctor might inquire for the symptoms, Charles asked me, "What kind of sickness does she have?"

"Well, more than anything it seems like a run of bad luck. Her children get sick, her mother-in-law had a heart attack, she gets the flu."

Charles nodded knowingly, "She got too much for she one."

"Yes."

"Janie, Janie, you see the same thing that person get—you get away quick. You get away from that."

That wasn't quite the response I had expected to my somewhat hypothetical problem. "Get away from that?"

"Yeah, for you don't know what may happen to you. She's doing something wrong. Do you feel to help her?"

"Yes." There was a long silence, then a sigh. This was turning into something more than I had bargained for. "I'll give you a bottle of medicine for her and I will give you something to send her to bathe and to clean up herself, and tell her to do what you say."

"What kind of medicine is it?" I asked.

"For her to drink a little tiny glass twice a day."

"What's it called?" When Charles didn't want to give out information, questioning him was like battling with the tar baby.

"The medicine? You don't need that. What you want it for?" Then he weakened and started to laugh at me.

"Well, I wondered what I was giving her," I said weakly in my defense.

"Well, you giving her sweet spirit of nitre and a next medicine to go with that."

"And what's that?"

Again he gave a great laugh. I was glad he wasn't angry. "You want to be a doctor, do you?"

"Well, I want to learn from you."

That seemed to satisfy him. "Ah, good. Child, you killing me, you killing me."

"I'm not killing you," I laughed at him.

"Well, what's the use, what's the use—I talk to you tonight, and you don't have a pencil to write it down."

"Yes, I do." I produced pencil and paper, and Charles gave in.

"Now you got to get these things. Mark down the sweet spirit of nitre. And you got to get a next bottle too. You know porter?"

"Porter?" My mind was a blank. All I could think of was somebody who carried bags.

"Porter, a kind of stout, or if not that, a bottle of wine."

"Right. I know what you mean." I was with it again.

"You got to get two bottles of porter, one which you mix with the sweet spirit of nitre. That one going to be white. And she to drink that after she drink the porter. That to clean her up nice. Now you got to get linsen seed."

"Like linseed? Is it oily?" I asked.

"It's a small, small seed. It's called 'grain de lain' in Patois. You boil it by your ownself, strain it, and throw it in the porter." Charles waited as I wrote that all down. Then he added, "Isinglass."

"Isinglass?" I couldn't believe my ears.

"Yes. You see that is a kind of thing, thin like a little thread. It's tiny tiny. When you put it in the bottle, you have to hold it, so, and shove it in the porter. And there's a next thing, too. I got to get something else for you. I'm studying. The name I forget. It is a powder. When you drink it, it make you sweat and get out the core of the sickness. It just coming to me. I will get it. No, I well sure I don't remember it now. But I will ask Mr. Barras. It's something like potasse. It's a kind of powder—a kind of lotion. When you put it in the basin you shake it, and it come like blood.

"After she drink that, she going to drink a dose of senna pods. That's to clean her out, and then she must go and bathe and rub sheself with the tobacco and seasonings. I will get all that in the drugstore for you tomorrow. She will be all right."

The following evening turned out to be the last time I would ever see Alexander Charles. As I was leaving St. Lucia the next day, he had brought me a number of "messages" to replenish my supply and ensure my safety until we would meet again. He also brought the ingredients to cure my friend, along with a scrunched-up piece of paper with "potassium iodide" written on it. "That's what I couldn't remember. Mr. Barras didn't have none, but when you reach, the first doctor's shop you meet, go inside and you will ask nothing. Tell them to give you what you need, eh. Now when you get it, just take a little grain of that and put it in the porter. Tell her to drink that at night. Now you got all your things."

I thanked him and said I had something for him as well. His

eyes sparkled. I handed him a pipe and some tobacco. Eagerly he filled it and leaned back contentedly in his chair. "Every time I smoke this I will think of you," he told me.

"I've got something else for you too, but this is for the roof of your house, not for rum."

"For my roof? How much is that?" he asked, looking at the bill in his hand.

"Ten, American," I said.

"Are you sure I can have that? Did you tell anybody?" For a moment I felt like a conspirator. It was as if I were a child and had purloined some change I had found lying around the house.

"No, I didn't tell anybody," I assured him. He whistled and looked at me. "Janie, Janie, what! You got to come home and see it next time you come."

We chatted on through the showers that night to the first crowing of the cock. Just quiet conversation. There were no questions, no proddings by me to elicit information. It was the quiet talk of two friends, and inevitably we drifted onto the subject which was common to both of us: the sea and its vagaries. When I finally took my leave, it was a sad moment. He encouraged me with, "You are not like you was before. Before you was a cow that just went to slaughter in the slaughterhouse, because you didn't know nothing and you didn't have nothing, but now you are a vessel with a mast in and all the rigging. If you are wise you will catch what I mean."

As I turned to wave for the last time I saw him leaning back smoking his pipe. His face was a mask, and he seemed to be following his own advice, "Never make anyone know you're wise. Just all what they ask you, say, 'I don't know.' Never make them wise. I here like a dummy."

Conclusion

Charles died in February of 1974, but it wasn't until a year later that I first heard of it. I sent him a Christmas card, and sometime in February, 1975, back came the card with "Deceased" scrawled across it. I looked at it, stunned. He had seemed so vital when I last saw him. My first reaction was that there must be some mistake. I knew that new management had taken over the company where he worked, and I had heard rumors that Charles had been in the hospital and that he had been fired for sleeping on the job, but I couldn't get any solid information, only hearsay.

In April, 1975, I decided to go and see what I could find out for myself. My husband had been doing research on an island farther south, so I went home via St. Lucia. I arrived on a Sunday afternoon and went straight over to where Charles had worked. The place seemed dead as I wandered around. The old bench and the chair were gone, and a gate had been erected where Charles and I had spent so many evenings. Even the store where the rats had scurried in and out was defunct. I looked around for the new owner, and when I finally found him he dashed any glimmer of hope I might have had by telling me that Charles *had* died. He had been sick for a couple of weeks in December and said he was going to have to leave. His new employer suggested that, rather than quitting, Charles should be fired—that way he would get compensation. Charles agreed. Shortly after that he went into the hospital and he did not linger long. His employer suspected that he had had lung cancer.

While I was in St. Lucia I telephoned Mr. Barnard's daughter, a person Charles had constantly mentioned throughout our conversations. I had hoped that perhaps I could talk with her about her memories of some of the same incidents. She was very pleasant on the phone, but told me she honestly did not remember an Alexander Charles. I kicked myself for not appearing on her doorstep with photograph in hand. I tried to jog her memory, but to no avail. She sounded amused as I recounted some of the incidents and told her of the fondness Charles had for her. I suspect she probably had never known his name, and I felt a sadness for the man who had spoken of her so reverently. To her he hadn't existed; to him she was an important figure in his life. It seemed a sad commentary.

The following year I stopped in St. Lucia again—once more with the hope of answering some of the questions that bothered me. This time I was more fortunate. I met Ti Son, quite by chance. He was home for a day while the Geest boat took on cargo, but it was to sail that night. We had gone into Castries to get supplies, and the man who had taken us happened to be a friend of Ti Son's. Thomas pointed him out to me and called him over. I had a picture of Charles with me, in case I had the opportunity of finding Ti Son, and I handed it to him. He stared in disbelief, and as he gazed at me I saw that same inquiring look which I had seen so often on the face of his father. "Charlo," he murmured. "Where did you get this? How did you find me? You must come home and have a drink." Words spilled out in rapid succession. He called a friend over, "Look at Charlo!"

Ti Son was obviously pleased that we had found him. He looked just as Charles had described him—robust, bearded, and jovial. Nothing would do but to go home with him and have a drink. He bought Cokes for the children and a bottle of Scotch to celebrate our meeting. As Charles was a man of an older traditional generation, Ti Son appeared to be very much of the now generation. While Charles lived in a two-room wooden shack, Ti Son had a modern house complete with indoor plumbing, telephone, television, stereo tape deck, and record player, along with various pieces of art picked up during his travels to different continents. No wonder Charles was so proud of him. He had all the accouterments of a big man in the West Indies and was truly successful in modern terms.

Ti Son spoke warmly about his father's last days. He had just returned from Japan for two weeks' leave from the Geest Line when the phone rang and he received a message that his father was very ill in Marchand and wanted to see him. "I tended to him every day until he died," he told me. It was Ti Son who had closed his eyes and put his death on the radio. "We had a big party—a good party. A lot of people—my friends and everybody—came." Charles would have liked that. For this man who had prepared for death so long, it came peacefully and quietly—a good death indeed. In the end he preferred to stay at Marchand, and when he was laid out in his black suit for all to see, everybody would remember, "He looked great upon the bed."

Although Charles can never be anything but unique to me, his lifestyle is representative of that of many lower-class West Indians. Perhaps his family experience is somewhat unusual, in that he apparently was rejected by them—yet even so, the kinship network was there and intact. His aunt in Dominica appeared to recognize the necessity of caring for him, although she did no more than the minimum. In St. Lucia his mother's sister, who turned him away while she was cooking breadfruit and tripe, was not only considered reprehensible by Charles, but would for this act also be censured by West Indian society in general. As Herskovits writes concerning Trinidad, lower-class kinship ties in St. Lucia seem to be

> activated for emergency help such as food and shelter—in short, for survival rather than for success or security. This is especially the case where the kinsmen are homogeneously of lower-class background, and where little or no help for achievement can be expected from a kinsman.[1]

It is also interesting to note that although Charles's St. Lucian aunt refused him food and shelter he still believed it his responsibility to bury her.

Charles's relationships led him to be a man of two islands, which is a frequent occurrence in the Lesser Antilles, particularly in the case of St. Lucia and Dominica, which are known as sister islands and whose people are closely connected by language (the local Patois) and kinship.

In typical West Indian fashion, Charles's career was varied. Throughout his life he applied himself to a number of different jobs, returning always to the sea and fishing as a constant. The sea is every West Indian's basic provider, as well as his testing ground. And so it proved for Charles with his fishing, traveling, and smuggling escapades. Living by one's wits and paying little heed to the law often leads to the development of a trickster prototype character, and Charles performed successfully as such, confounding the police by dispatching the evidence into the river or courting Enid under the nose of her fatuous mate. As Anansi, the well-known trickster-hero of African and West Indian folktale, Charles reveled in the plumage of finery and ostentatious display. Again and again he described a well-dressed individual, and he was rendered speechless—no mean thing for Charles—by Captain Pantobe in full military dress.

There was also something very West Indian about Charles's humor. Often he would tell me, "I nearly kill myself laughing." His humor seemed stirred by violence and "one-upmanship," and at times he would laugh so hard at something he conjured up from the past he was helpless to continue. Seldom if ever was his humor directed at himself, but rather at others' misfortunes. It was humor of situation. For example, the man who had all his money stolen by the woman he had picked up for the night got little sympathy from Charles—only loud hoots of laughter. The tale of the man whose finger became entangled in the wire of the winch and was dashed to his death on the concrete below evoked such a ludicrous image that Charles laughed uncontrollably. In the same manner the onlookers shook with laughter when one

man feigned being hit in a pistol duel in order to shoot his oppo-
nent. When he succeeded, nobody gave a thought to the victim.
The situation was much too funny. The trick had succeeded, and
all were delighted.

In our society we don't usually laugh at such things. We are
taught to evince shock and emit a gasp of horror. Often American
tourists shudder when they witness West Indian children amus-
ing themselves by pulling off bird's legs or provoking dog fights.
The West Indian response to violence and cruelty may well be a
reaction brought on by a harsh and elemental life.

Mark Twain once said that all humor was based on human
misery. If this premise is accepted it is only natural that the West
Indian find humor in acts that would shock those from a more
opulent and softer society. Violence is then, perhaps, a relative
quality: what is considered violent in one society may be commonplace in another. For the West Indian, laughter and rage are
two sides of a revolving coin, and the rapidity with which one
follows the other is an indication of the quixotic and volatile West
Indian nature.

There is another important consideration in West Indian
humor. This is the capacity for one-upmanship. By way of humor
one gains power over his fellow man. It is through laughter that
one individual loses face and the other gains stature. Once more
we see the constant interplay that occurs at all levels of West Indian life, where one individual attempts to gain power over
another—be it accomplished by a volley of words, laughter,
physical action, or supernatural dealings.

As pointed out earlier, courage in the face of superior force or
power is a virtue highly prized among West Indians. Charles took
pains to affirm his own. He fished to windward of the land and
suggested he could stand firm before the Devil. He believed that
the dead watchman would call him at work if there was any
trouble in the night, but at the same time he wanted to make sure
that he always had at least one cutlass within easy reach. One
night when he came to work his cutlass had disappeared. He was
furious. He went straight to Mrs. Ganter, telling her, if she

wouldn't supply him with a gun, he must at least have a cutlass. The night before, the night watchman at Peter and Company had had his arm badly cut by thieves, and Charles was adamant and vocal as to his needs. Eventually we solved the situation by giving him our cutlass, and once more he settled into his chair in relative calm. Sometimes I sensed the difference between talk and action; this is always something to keep in mind when dealing with autobiography.

The first part of this book is Alexander Charles's presentation of himself and how he would like to be remembered. It is therefore understandable that he liked to play the hero and perhaps made more of his courage than was sometimes warranted. "If I wasn't a hero, I don't believe you would see me today." Only a hero can deal with the supernatural successfully. To an extent, then, Charles was playing a role in presenting himself as heroic—heroic in terms of his own society. His seventeen children and his travels attested to his virility. He had scattered his seed "all about." He was generous, he was kind, but when necessary he could be counted. And most important of all, he was wise, and his wisdom and courage gave him power.

In the role of hero Charles underscored the "ideal" in terms of his life-style. This does not mean that his story was not true, but that he molded his experiences to present his own ideal. The fact that Charles told the same stories consistently indicates to me that his view was well formed and that he believed them to be totally truthful. He not only believed in his system but was representative of it.

It was a long time before I actually came to the realization that Charles was not simply relating but teaching me a well-integrated system of knowledge as well. Listening attentively night after night, probing for new incidents in his life story, and carefully noting each new cure or potion, I found myself concentrating on specifics. It was not until after Charles's death, when I began to sift through and organize some of the material into themes and patterns, that I began to shift my focus and view it in a larger matrix.

Slowly I came to realize that Charles's life story as well as his teachings covered the whole spectrum of his system—from his basic view of man to his belief in the supernatural world. It was a working, functioning system with a number of conflict points. Because Charles was attempting to teach me how his system functioned at its best, he glossed over or to some extent ignored these points of conflict. The result was somewhat confusing to me at first, for often his material seemed full of inconsistencies. Was Charles really telling me to stay by myself and have nothing to do with anybody but my husband and children? Did he really distrust everyone? At other times he would frequently preface his remarks with, "What you plant is what you reap" or explain, "Kindness done that." Apparently generous, he gave to the poor, shared his food with those who were hungry, and helped his friends (who weren't supposed to exist) with no thought of remuneration. Despite his admonishments to me, Charles had the reputation of being very sociable. I was told on several occasions that he was "a gay man who liked to go to dances and was loved by everybody." At one moment I was warned to distrust everyone, but in the next I was told that it was important to "live nice together." What did he really mean?

As I puzzled over this I came to realize that there was an essential difference in Charles's view of man and his society's traditional social code: man was not totally evil, because nothing in the West Indies is strictly good or bad. Just as God makes evil, the Devil can do good. Thus man is a mixture of good and evil. The problem is knowing. "You believe a man is your pal, and he call for your destruction." This basic distrust of man is not typical of Charles alone, but seems to be the basic view a West Indian holds concerning his fellow man. Despite this deep-seeded distrust, the traditional social code requires a behavior that apparently presupposes a high degree of trust—that every man is your brother. One is supposed to "live nice" with his neighbors, to be generous, cooperative, and friendly. The man who "loves party," buys drinks for everyone, and is always laughing and joking is a popular ideal. But beneath this jovial and friendly mask that his friends know lies suspicion, jealousy, and a temper quick to take offense. Flashes of his inner being run the gamut from volatile arguments that spring from a single word that shatters the surroundings with threatening violence and then disappear once more into joking or laughing, to covert acts of obeah, heavy with malicious intent but concealed in pleasantries. "Obeah man never vexed with nobody." And so when Charles saw his watch on Mr. Mosette's son's wrist he never released his internal fury. "I passing nicely, say hello to him. He believe I love him, but he don't know. If I vexed with him I couldn't catch him."

With the view that man can be harmful—capable of treachery, jealousy, and trickery—and the code that man must live nice together, suppressing all hostilities, there is obviously great ambiguity built into the system which leads to a stress situation and to apparent fickle changes in attitude towards people and situations.

Herskovits witnessed the same type of behavior in Haiti, terming it "socialized ambivalence" and describing it as a

> tendency to manifest those rapid shifts in attitude toward people and situations that characterize the responses of the Haitian peasant to such a marked degree that the same man will hold in high regard a person, an institution, an experience, or even an object that has personal significance to him and simultaneously manifest great disdain and even hatred for it. As outwardly observable, this takes the form of recurring and often rapid changes in behavior toward the object of attention. In attitude, there is vacillation from one emotional tone to another.[2]

This vacillation would be caused by the deep-seeded difference which is built into West Indian culture—the gulf between feeling and acting.

George Foster generalizes well beyond the West Indies and suggests that these attitudes and social behavior are characteristic of folk society or what he terms "a peasant village." As he wrote,

> An objective appraisal of a peasant village . . . will in all likelihood reveal basic strains and tensions in interpersonal relations that make it difficult to understand how the community continues to function.[3]

Hazel Weidman takes Foster one step further and explains

> When ambiguity is characteristic of many interpersonal relationships, people relate to each other on two levels at once. They attempt to protect themselves from the uncertainties of situations by phrasing their conversations so that no one really knows for sure what is intended.[4]

Such a description is certainly characteristic of Charles's dealings with people. Often he would tell me something, sit back a minute, and say, "Did you catch what I say?" I learned to look for the second meaning rather than the apparent one.

Charles schooled me well, inculcating within me the values of his system. He was teaching me to perform in a hostile environment and therefore never to trust anyone—not even my own sister. Constantly he reemphasized the idea that I must learn to protect myself, to doctor myself without having to ask anybody. No one must know what I am thinking, what I am doing. I am to be an island unto myself—in one sense a totally antisocial being. No one is to know my business. As I learned this first lesson I was considered ready for more and more teachings, and these teachings were to make me a grown woman in West Indian society. As the Haitian said so significantly, "If you don't know how to keep yourself in a house, you're not a woman yet."

Charles was schooling me in ambivalence. Through him I would be equipped to exist antisocially within a social complex. It has long been thought that such ambivalence fosters the belief in and use of witchcraft,[5] and this was certainly demonstrated through Charles's system. Obeah proved to be at the very heart of it. Obeah was Charles's system of knowledge, his road to power and to that elusive status of a big man. But there was an ambivalence to obeah as well. Within the social situation one was only supposed to use obeah defensively. "If a person have the heart to hurt you, you must do him the same." One was not supposed to manipulate the environment—social or otherwise—for his own individual profit. This was the aggressive aspect of obeah—although lucrative for the individual, harmful to society. It was also fraught with dangers, and could prove to be too powerful and therefore the downfall of the individual. As Charles warned me, "The Lord tell you, work, the sweat of your blood will have to support you, but don't force it" or "Nothing you get by force is good." When I pressed to learn the blacker arts he would sidestep my questions, "Child, keep off," or "That too powerful for you." He did not wish to make a potential duppy woman of me. When one learns too much, too young, it is far more of a temptation to put it to a personal use than one should be expected to resist. It was the young person who would have used the poisoned eggs on Mr. Mosette; Charles preferred to try other methods first. The young man is "too much in hurry to climb tree. He want too many things." Thus obeah in the fullest sense was generally the province of the old heads.

Charles genuinely believed in his system, but while instructing me he was also teaching me the "ideal" situation. There was always a direct cause-effect-and-cure relationship. Only once did he deviate from that pattern, and for a long time I found these stories particularly confusing. They all centered around the duppy woman, Mrs. Alcindor, and her attempts to drive Charles's keeper, Ann Marie, mad.

At first I thought she alone was responsible in Charles's eyes for his keeper's trips to the lunatic asylum, but as I went over his different accounts I realized that he was not always referring to Mrs. Alcindor—there was at least one other person involved. Mrs. Alcindor died in the early '70s, but as of 1973 one woman whom he held responsible for Ann Marie's earliest fits and to whom he had sent the sickness back was still alive. He described her as "sometime she well, sometime she bad," and he had seen her "just the other morning."

I suspect the confusion here is due to the way Charles's system of magic actually worked. When a problem arose, a number of solutions were tried in a kind of trial-and-error technique until eventually the cure was effected. When one was finally successful it was the terminal solution that would be most clearly remembered.

According to Charles, Ann Marie was driven mad a number of

times. These periods of madness seem to coincide with the birth of each of her three children. Thus Charles must have found a number of culprits along the way. One of these was the woman who was jealous of Ann Marie and who put her astray by making off with her "panties." But when Ann Marie had another child she apparently was subjected to more fits, and another explanation I was given was that Mrs. Alcindor had caused Ann Marie's madness. Again jealousy was the reason. When Charles discovered that Mrs. Alcindor, a duppy woman, was the culprit, he claims he brought her a poisoned fish, and "the day she dead everything work out."[6]

In actuality it is doubtful that Charles did kill Mrs. Alcindor. In another story he attributed her death to someone "sticking her too hard." How or what Mrs. Alcindor died of we will probably never know, but the important fact in Charles's mind was that she was a duppy woman, and her death was typical of such people. He was very consistent when it came to the details of her death—that her head became "small, small, small," her mouth was "red like fire," and the priest would not accept her body in the Church. On five different occasions, almost word for word he described her appearance at death to be the visible indication of a duppy woman.

Although we can never be sure, I think there is a plausible explanation for these inconsistencies. Angela, Charles's last child was born in September, 1970, shortly before Mrs. Alcindor's death. Ann Marie, again subject to her "fits" after the baby was born, was once more taken to the asylum. About the time she returned home, supposedly cured, Mrs. Alcindor died. Further, Ann Marie, not having had any more children since that time, appeared to be permanently cured. The relationship between the two facts was clear in Charles's mind. Apparently during the years he had lived next to Mrs. Alcindor he had seen this woman as a real threat, whether as a duppy woman, landlady, or simply as a powerful woman. Perhaps in the end he really believed he *had* killed her—at least he had triumphed over her. The discrepancy, I suggest, is a refinement of Charles's life story and the confounding of the real and the ideal. By killing Mrs. Alcindor, Charles played the hero by remedying an intolerable situation and therefore demonstrated that his knowledge was superior to hers.

Charles's road to knowledge was followed in traditional manner. He learned from the "old heads" and from all who would teach him. What he held up for me to see was a well-developed psychomedical complex which was both a functional and well-integrated part of his cultural system. Not only does it provide a basic view of human nature and man's relationship with the natural and supernatural environment but also a kind of folk theory of medicine which administers to both the mental and physical health of the individual as he functions within a social situation.

As it has already been pointed out, Charles was a general practitioner. He coped with the usual, run-of-the-mill complaints and administered to these minor ills apparently successfully with bush teas, poultices, or medicines.[7] Illnesses that were thought to be due to unnatural causes often manifested apparent psychological as well as physical symptoms. And these were usually treated by both bush and magical medicine. Charles frequently employed some kind of ritual cleansing, most often in the form of a bath. The sense of smell was also apparently very important in his cures and potions. "Will power" has an overwhelming sweet smell, and often when he was teaching me to recognize different ingredients he would emphasize that this one smelled sweet, that one fetid. Those items with sweet smells were generally employed for protection, while those of an unpleasant nature usually caused some kind of harm.

Charles apparently could distinguish between a natural and unnatural illness. His diagnosis seemed to be intuitive. When he saw the chauffeur with his hands "all cut up and still sowing" his immediate reaction was "You fucker, you must have done something wrong," and sure enough, others whispered it about that he had been practicing black magic in the night. When I asked about my friend, Charles affirmed significantly, "You mean she got too much for she one." In the West Indies, the unusual always seems to be grounds for suspicion.

One piece of knowledge raised Charles above the ranks of the general practitioner. This was his ability to talk to his mother when he liked. He indicated to me that he had never taught the Haitian song to anyone else and he apparently only used it under the most stressful situations and only for himself. There is no question in my mind that this song or rather monotonous chant induced a trance. As I. M. Lewis points out,

> . . . trance states can be readily induced in most normal people by a wide range of stimuli, applied either separately or in a combination. Time-honoured techniques include the use of alcoholic spirits, hypnotic suggestion, rapid over-breathing, the inhalation of smoke and vapours, music and dancing; and the ingestion of such drugs . . . [8]

Always Charles would lie down, flat on his back, legs outstretched and hands crossed on his chest. As he began to hum, tears flowed from his closed eyes, and he would apparently be on the verge of sleep. Because he was trying to teach me the song he resisted falling into the trance, but he had to break off his singing. Even when he took another position to sing, he said he felt "sleep" coming on him and had to desist.

Although Charles's trance was intentionally induced, in his view the dream which resulted had a life of its own. It did not originate with him, but instead with his dead mother. This was the magic or power of the song. Thus his mother appeared and explained his sickness to him, revealing who was responsible and what to do about it. She brought a special mixture for him to drink, bathing him in the remnants, and she told him he must brew a tea with three stones collected in a special manner from the cemetery. He drank in the dream state but went to the cemetery after he awoke. There was no doubt in Charles's mind that he had actually spoken with his mother and that she alone was responsible for his cure.

This is typically the case with self-induced trances. Erika Bourguignon notes that despite the fact that the trance may be intentionally induced the events which follow "are not experienced as deriving from the self but are reified through cultural concepts and cultural patterning."[9] In this case it is the strongly held West Indian belief that the dead return in dreams to bring important messages.

Through supernatural aid Charles cured himself of a sickness that was of unnatural origin—one that had been sent to him through jealousy with malign intent. Whatever Charles's illness, it was obviously both psychological and physical and probably indicates a crisis in his own life and a breakdown of his ability to function within a social context.

It has been pointed out in the introduction that illness in St. Lucia is not just a biological phenomenon but a social condition as well, where both social and psychological forces affect the health of the individual. Thus "illness is a consequence of breakdowns or changes in patterns of interpersonal relations."[10] This has been termed the "interpersonal theory of disease." Richard Robbins refines this theory and postulates that when illness results from such social and psychological pressures operating on the individual "a person's health will be a function of the degree of consonance between his self, social, and public identity."[11] In order to reduce the disruption in a person's social field Robbins suggests three tactics: to reorder the patient's social field, to change a person's social field, or to remove the patient from his social field "possibly attempting during the isolation to refashion his identity."[12]

For Charles the interpersonal pressures appear to have focused on his job and his keeper. His rival, Yankee Charles, appeared to want both. As Charles told us, for three months as he lay on his bed, his rival worked toward his goal. But then he called his dead mother to him, and there was a reversal of the situation. By means of his trance Charles was apparently able to reconstruct or reassert his own identity. He came out on top of his rival, whom he then punished through magical means according to his mother's directions.

I might also suggest that Charles's mysterious sickness in

Dominica—supposedly something done to him by his sister—might also be considered in terms of the interpersonal disease theory. In this case the Caribs removed him from "his social field." During the time spent in Carib country, Charles's identity was again reformed, and with his return to his aunt's he had become "natural" and "understood what he had to do." In both sicknesses, after the cure Charles committed some kind of positive action, such as going to St. Lucia to sell his property, to reaffirm his cure. Such action is probably as important to his recovery as the "cure" itself.

Thus bush and magical medicine cope with both the natural and supernatural elements of the universe and the physical and psychological well-being of the individual. It made no difference whether Charles's self-invoked trance was termed a magical song or a method of self-hypnosis. It apparently worked for him.

Charles's method of calling his mother also suggests an insight into his song used for summoning the Devil. Although he would never teach it to me, I suspect that the technique was very similar to that which I had already observed when he was calling his mother. In other words, this song also induced a trance, and what followed would again be explainable within cultural terms. The Devil would appear and act just as he was believed to act when an individual had the courage to tryst him.

I would further suggest that the ingestion of liquids—both to seal an agreement with the Devil and to enable one to fly at night—also caused a kind of trance or series of hallucinations. Unfortunately I never obtained any of these flying powders, but I do know that sweet spirit of nitre, which Charles said he mixed with the dried powder of a particular bee, can be hallucinatory. What properties the root of the moudongue possesses I cannot say for sure, but again it would seem reasonable that it might contain hallucinogenic properties.

These were the basic tools with which Charles worked, and there is no question that his techniques had therapeutic value for him and his patients. He could cope with drunkenness, colds in the bowels, cutting in the stomach, strain, some varieties of worm, and he could administer to those illnesses which seemed to result from the basic drives of sex and jealousy. Love magic was just as big a part of his craft as were the guards or potions which protected against revenge or insured greater luck than one's neighbor. It is significant to note that these two motivating forces are personified in the extreme by the duppy man or woman who ministers to the requirements of jealousy and the black magic man who indulges in wanton sex.

Charles's system was one of checks and balances. "Everything has its master." The problem was to know the master. "There are many men and many ways," and one man could not possibly know all. Thus Charles strove "to make himself wise" in as many ways as possible. As a general practitioner he was willing to administer to sicknesses of natural or unnatural origin, but he was not willing to aggressively pursue the blacker arts such as dealing with the Devil or the invocation of the dead. Constantly he warned me that such power was too strong. Before you used such power you should have the proper check for it—often simply the stipulated payment—otherwise it would destroy you. Charles rubbed his boat, but he was careful not to overdo it or to dirty the sea too much.

The same kind of caution was expressed as a kind of social conscience within Charles. Despite his distrustful view of man, he seemed to possess certain rigid attitudes as to just how far one should go against his neighbor. If his neighbor tried to kill him, there would be no holds barred, but if the offense was less, like should be repaid with like. Thus he was not ready to poison Mr. Mosette for the theft of his watch. Likewise he was highly disapproving of the man who poisoned all of Mr. Sam Boyce's cattle because of the latter's stinginess. "That man didn't have no conscience. He could have killed two, but don't kill all."

Although folk seldom present a completely coherent philosophical system, through his life and his teaching Charles exhibited a functioning magico-medicinal system which permeated his whole life-style. This system dictates how the individual acts within society, what it is necessary to do when things don't go as they should, and, at the aggressive end of the scale, what to do to make things happen, how to cope with power, and how to control it. There is a balance of weakness and fear, power and courage—a social code to maintain this balance and individualism to upset it. Such individualism is personified in terms of the duppy woman or the black magic man and socialized by the way of the obeah man or gadeur.

This is the system in the terms of which Charles operated. It remains to be asked, how did he make out? I think the answer must be: not badly—although there is perhaps a discrepancy between the answer he gave in his autobiography and what he revealed in the second part through his conversations. As has already been suggested he was presenting himself much as a trickster-hero who had gained his knowledge (translated power) throughout his life chiefly from the old heads and frequently in return for kindnesses he performed. As the master of this knowledge, Charles commanded respect. The visible evidence was that he could sleep on the job and not be robbed; it did not appear as riches or material wealth.

But between the lines of our conversations I read another message. Sometimes his courage quaked. Sometimes his methods did not succeed. Perhaps he wasn't the invincible hero he attempted to portray, but rather a man who believed in his way of life and glossed over its shortcomings. He had learned how to cope—in fact he had done more than cope. He owned his own house and he had his own fishing canoe. For the last twenty years of his life he had held a steady job. He was a man of the world and knew how to keep his own counsel in hostile surroundings. He was small but always quick. He was the underdog but ever clever. And at once he was both violent and kind. What's more, he dared to go to windward of the land.

Appendix

"This woman, Madame Alcindor, was like a crooked woman. Every day the woman sit down by the door and I passing and begging me—give her a pound of sugar, bring her a pound of fish. She watch my woman and say, "Ah, you won't enjoy that house you buy." You know she send my wife five times in the madhouse. She make my wife come crazy—running all about, doing like a cat and like a dog—*how, how, how, how, yeow, yeow, yeow, yeow*. I take her in the station and she start to bawl the same way—like a pig.

"People say, 'Mr. Charles, Madame Alcindor is duppy woman.'

"I say, 'Are you sure?'

"'Yes.'

"She come to me and say, 'Mr. Charles, if you going to town bring up some more fish for me.'

"I say, 'Yes.' I bring the pound of fish and I open the fish and I throw the powder on it and the time for me to come up from town, that powder melt and that fish is poison. Now she clean the fish and eat it. A couple of days she start to kick inside the house. She start to bawl. She head come small, small, small, and the mouth come red like fire. They went and call the priest. The priest give all what she want inside the house and say, 'Don't take her to the church. Go and carry her to bury.' If I didn't poison that fish, I would have lost my wife. Madame Alcindor was doing that. The day she dead everything work out."

BIBLIOGRAPHY

Abrahams, Roger. *Deep the Water, Shallow the Shore.* Publication of the American Folklore Society Memoir Series, vol. 60, 1974.

——. "Patterns of Performance in the British West Indies." In *Afro-American Anthropology,* edited by John F. Szwed and Norman E. Whitten, Jr. New York: The Free Press, 1970.

——. "A Performance Centered Approach to Gossip." *Man* 5(n.s., 1970):290–301.

——. "The Shaping of Folklore Traditions in the British West Indies." *Journal of Inter-American Studies* 9(1967):456–80.

Adams, C. D. *Flowering Plants of Jamaica.* Mona, Jamaica: University of The West Indies, 1972.

Adams, John E. "Shore Whaling in St. Vincent, West Indies." *Caribbean Quarterly* 19(1973):42–50.

Allayne, Mervin C. "Language and Society in St. Lucia." *Caribbean Studies* 1(1961):1–10.

Aronoff, Joel Craig. "The Inter-Relationship of Psychological and Cultural Systems: A Case Study of a Rural West Indian Village." Ph.D. thesis, Brandeis University, 1965.

Aspinall, Algernon. *A Pocket Guide to the West Indies.* London: Methuen & Co. (Originally published 1907), 1954.

——. *A Wayfarer in the West Indies.* London: Methuen and Co., Ltd., 1928.

Asprey, G. F., and Thornton, Phyllis. "Medicinal Plants of Jamaica." *West Indian Medical Journal.* Part I, 2(1953):233–52; Part II, 3(1954):17–41; Part III, 4(1955):69–82; Part IV, 4(1955):145–168.

Atwood, Thomas. *The History of the Island of Dominica.* London: Frank Cass and Co., Ltd., 1971.

Banbury, Thomas. *Jamaica Superstitions, or the Obeah Book.* Jamaica, 1894.

Banton, Michael, ed. *Anthropological Approaches to the Study of Religion.* London: Tavistock Publications, Ltd., 1966.

Barham, Henry. *Hortus Americanus: Containing an account of the trees, shrubs, and other vegetable productions of South America and the West India Islands, and particularly of the Island of Jamaica. . . .* Kingston, Jamaica: A. Aikman, printer, 1794.

Barrett, Leonard. "Portrait of a Jamaican Healer: African Medical Lore in the Caribbean." *Caribbean Quarterly* 19(1973):6–19.

Bascom, William. "Yoruba Concepts of Soul." In *Selected Papers of the Fifth International Congress and Anthropological and Ethnological Sciences,* edited by Anthony Wallace. Philadelphia: University of Pennsylvania Press, 1960.

Bastide, Roger. *African Civilizations in the New World.* Translated by Peter Green. New York, Evanston, San Francisco, London: Harper & Row, 1971.

Bayley, Iris. "The Bush-Teas of Barbados." *The Journal of the Barbados Museum and Historical Society* 16(1949):103–109.

Beck, Jane C. "Dream Messages from the Dead." *Journal of the Folklore Institute* 10(1973):173–86.

———. "The Implied Obeah Man." *Western Folklore* 35(1976):23–33.

———. "West Indian Sea Magic." *Folklore* 88(1977):194–202.

———. "The West Indian Supernatural World." *Journal of American Folklore* 88(1975):235–44.

Beckwith, Martha. *Black Roadways.* 1929. Reprint. New York: Negro University Press, 1969.

———. "Ethnobotany of the Jamaica Negro." *Vassar College Folklore Publication* 8:47.

———. "Plant Medicines." *Jamaica Folklore.* Publication of the American Folklore Society Memoir Series, vol. 21, 1928.

Bell, Sir Hesketh J. *Obeah: Witchcraft in the West Indies.* London: Sampson Low, Marston, Searle and Rivington, 1889.

Blume, Helmut. *The Caribbean Islands.* Translated by Johannes Maczewski and Ann Norton. London: Longman Group, Ltd., 1974.

Bourguignon, Erika. "Dreams and Altered States of Consciousness in Anthropological Research." In *Psychological Anthropology,* edited by L. K. Hsu. Cambridge, Mass.: Schenkman Publishing Co., Inc., 1972.

———. "Dreams and Dream Interpretation in Haiti." *American Anthropologist* 56(1954):262–68.

———. "The Persistence of Folk Belief: Notes on Cannibalism and Zombies in Haiti." *Journal of American Folklore* 72(1959):36–46.

Breen, Henry H. *St. Lucia.* London: Frank Cass and Co., Ltd., 1970.

Carmichael, Mrs. A. C. *Domestic Manners and Social Activities of the White, Coloured and Negro Population of the West Indies.* 2 vols. New York: Negro University Press, 1969.

Cassidy, Frederic G. *Jamaica Talk.* London: MacMillan and Co., Ltd., 1961.

Cassidy, Frederic G., and LePage, R. B. *Dictionary of Jamaican English.* Cambridge: Cambridge University Press, 1967.

Clarke, Edith. *My Mother Who Fathered Me.* London: George Allen and Unwin, Ltd., 1957.

Comitas, Lambros. *Caribbeana 1900–1965*. Seattle and London: University of Washington Press, 1968.

Courlander, Harold. *The Drum and the Hoe*. Berkeley and Los Angeles: University of California Press, 1960.

Cracknell, Basil E. *Dominica*. Harrisburg: Stackpole Books, 1973.

Criminal Code of St. Lucia (1957). Castries: Voice Publishing Co., 1959.

Crowley, Daniel J. "Conservatism and Change in St. Lucia." In *33rd International Congress of Americanists,* vol. II(1958):704–15.

———. "Cultural Assimilation in a Multiracial Society." In *Social and Cultural Pluralism in the Caribbean,* edited by Vera Rubin. Annals of the New York Academy of Sciences 83(1960):850–54.

———. "Naming Customs in St. Lucia." *Social and Economic Studies* 5(1956):87–92.

———. "Supernatural Beings in St. Lucia." *The Caribbean* 8(1955):241–44, 264–65.

———. "The View from Tobago: National Character in Folklore." In *Folklore International,* edited by D. K. Wilgus. Hatboro: Folklore Associates, 1967.

Cumper, George E. "Household and Occupation in Barbados." *Social and Economic Studies* 10(1961):386–419.

D'Andrade, Roy G. "Anthropological Studies of Dreams." In *Psychological Anthropology,* edited by Francis L. K. Hsu. Homewood, Ill.: The Dorsey Press, Inc., 1961.

Davenport, William. "The Family System of Jamaica." *Social and Economic Studies* 10(1961):420–54.

———. "Jamaican Fishing: A Game Theory Analysis." *Yale University Publications in Anthropology,* No. 59(1970). New Haven.

Devaux, Robert. *St. Lucia Historic Sites,* No. 1. St. Lucia National Trust. Castries: St. Lucia National Trust, 1975.

Dix, Jabez. "Adolphe—one of the most terrible of Obeah-Men." *Canada-West Indies Magazine* 22(1933):53–55.

Durham, Harriet F., and Lewisohn, Florence. *St. Lucia: Tours and Tales.* New York: Robertson Printing Co., 1971.

Edwards, Bryan. *The History, Civil and Commercial of the British Colonies in the West Indies.* 4th edition. 4 vols. Philadelphia: J. Humphreys, 1805.

Emerick, Abraham J. "Jamaica Duppies." In *Woodstock Letters.* Woodstock: Privately published, 1916.

———. "Jamaica Mialism." Ibid.

———. "Obeah and Duppyism in Jamaica." Ibid., 1915.

Fenger, Frederic A. *Alone in the Caribbean.* London: Hodder and Stoughton, 1919.

Fermor, Patrick Leigh. *The Traveller's Tree.* New York: Harper and Bros., 1950.

Fitzgerald, Thomas K., ed. *Social and Cultural Identity.* Southern Anthropological Society Proceedings, No. 8(1974), Athens, Georgia.

Flowers, Helen L. "A Classification of the Folktale of the West Indies by Types and Motifs." Ph.D. thesis, Indiana University, 1952.

Foster, George M. "Interpersonal Relations in Peasant Society." *Human Organization* 19(1960):174–84.

Franck, Harry. *Roaming Through the West Indies.* New York: The Century Company, 1920.

Fraser, Thomas M. "Class and the Changing Bases of Elite Support in St. Vincent, West Indies." *Ethnology* 15(1976):197–209.

Glick, Leonard. "Magic, Science and Religion in a St. Lucian Pharmacy." Paper read at meeting of American Anthropological Association, December 1967, Washington.

———. "Notes on St. Lucia: A Report to the Rockefeller Foundation." Unpublished ms., 1969.

Goode, William J. "Illegitimacy in the Caribbean." *American Sociological Review* 26(1961):910–25.

Gooding, E. G. B. "Facts and Beliefs about Barbadian Plants." *The Journal of the Barbados Museum and Historical Society* 7(1940):170–83; 8(1940):32–35; 8(1941):70–73, 103–106, 194–97; 9(1941):17–19; 9(1942):84–88, 126–29, 192–94; 10(1942):3–6.

Goodman, Felicitas D.; Henney, Jeannett H.; and Pressel, Esther. *Trance, Healing, and Hallucination: Three Field Studies in Religious Experience.* New York, London, Sydney, Toronto: John Wiley and Sons, 1974.

Greenfield, Sidney M. *English Rustics in Black Skin.* New Haven, Conn.: College and University Press, 1966.

Groome, J. R. *A Natural History of the Island of Grenada, W.I.* Trinidad: Caribbean Printers, Ltd., 1970.

Hadley, C. V. D. "Personality Patterns, Social Class, and Aggression in the British West Indies." *Human Relations* 2(1949):349–62.

Hall, Douglas. "Slaves and Slavery in the British West Indies." *Social and Economic Studies* 11(1962):305–18.

Hall, Robert A. *Haitian Creole.* Publication of the American Folklore Society Memoir Series, vol. 43, 1953.

Hambley, Wilfrid D. *Serpent Worship in Africa.* Chicago: Field Museum of Natural History Publication 289, Anthropological Series vol. xxi, No. 1, 1931.

Henney, Jeannett H., "Spirit Possession Belief and Trance Behavior in a Religious Group in St. Vincent, British West Indies." Ph.D. thesis, Ohio State University, 1968.

————. "Spirit-Possession Belief and Trance Behavior in Two Fundamentalist Groups in St. Vincent." In *Trance, Healing and Hallucination,* edited by Goodman, Henney, and Pressel. New York: John Wiley and Sons, 1974.

Herskovits, Melville J. *Dahomey.* 2 vols. New York: Northwestern University Press, 1938.

————. *Life in a Haitian Valley.* Garden City: Doubleday and Co., 1971.

————. *The Myth of the Negro Past.* Boston: Beacon Press, 1958.

————. "Trinidad Proverbs ('Old Time Saying So')." *Journal of American Folklore* 58(1945):195–207.

Herskovits, Melville J., and Herskovits, Frances S. *Trinidad Village.* New York: Octagon Books, 1976.

————. *Suriname Folk-lore.* New York: Columbia University Press, 1936.

Hill, Carole E., ed. *Symbols and Society: Essays on Belief Systems in Action.* Southern Anthropological Society Proceedings, No. 9(1975), Athens, Georgia.

Hill, Donald R. *The Impact of Migration on the Metropolitan and Folk Society of Carriacou, Grenada.* Anthropological Papers of the American Museum of Natural History, vol. 54(1977), Part 2. New York.

Hodge, W. H., and Taylor, Douglas. "The Ethnobotany of the Island Caribs of Dominica." *Webbia* 12(1957):513–645.

Honychurch, Lennox. *The Dominica Story: A History of the Island.* Privately printed, 1975.

Horowitz, Michael M. "A Decision Model of Conjugal Patterns in Martinique." *Man* 2(n.s.,1967):445–53.

————. *Morne-Paysan, Peasant Village in Martinique.* New York: Holt, Rinehart and Winston. 1967.

————, ed. *Peoples and Cultures of the Caribbean.* Garden City: The Natural History Press, 1971.

Huxley, Francis. *The Invisibles: Voodoo Gods in Haiti.* New York: McGraw Hill, 1966.

Jesse, Rev. C. "Early Days: 1493–1763." In *St. Lucia Miscellany,* vol. II. St. Lucia Archeological and Historical Society, Castries, 1969.

————. "Kembois or Chembois." *The Bajan,* January 1960:27–30.

————. *Outlines of St. Lucia History.* St. Lucia Archeological and Historical Society, Castries, 1964.

————. "St. Lucia: The Romance of its Place Names." In *St. Lucia Miscellany,* vol. I. St. Lucia Archeological and Historical Society, Castries, 1966.

Johnson, J. H. "Folklore from Antigua, British West Indies." *Journal of American Folklore* 34(1921):40–88.

Kerr, Madeline. *Personality and Conflict in Jamaica.* Liverpool: Collins, 1952.

Kiev, Ari. *Curanderismo: Mexican-American Folk Psychiatry*. New York: The Free Press, 1968.

———. "Folk Psychiatry in Haiti." *Journal of Nervous and Mental Disorders* 132(1961):260–65.

Kluckhohn, Clyde. *Navaho Witchcraft*. Boston: Beacon Press, 1944.

Knight, Melvin M. *The Americans in Santo Domingo*. New York: Vanguard Press, 1928.

Labat, Père. *The Memoirs of Père Labat* (1695–1705). Translated and abridged by J. Eaden. London: Frank Cass and Co., Ltd., 1970.

Laguerre, Michael. "The Place of Voodoo in the Social Structure of Haiti." *Caribbean Quarterly* 19(1973):36–50.

Larose, Serge, "The Meaning of Africa in Haitian Vodu." In *Symbols and Sentiments*, edited by I. M. Lewis (London, New York, San Francisco: Academic Press, 1977).

Leach, MacEdward. "Jamaican Duppy Lore." *Journal of American Folklore* 74(1961:207–15.

Lewis, I. M. *Ecstatic Religion: an Anthropological Study of Spirit Possession and Shamanism*. Middlesex, England: Penguin Books, 1975.

———, ed. *Symbols and Sentiments: Cross-Cultural Studies in Symbolism*. London, New York, San Francisco: Academic Press, 1977.

Lewis, M. C. *Journal of a West India Proprietor*. Boston and New York: Houghton Mifflin Co., 1929.

Lieberman, Dana. "Bilingual Behavior in a St. Lucian Community." Ph.D. thesis, University of Wisconsin, 1974.

Lowenthal, David. "The Range and Variation of Caribbean Societies." In *Social and Cultural Pluralism in the Caribbean*, edited by Vera Rubin. Annals of the New York Academy of Sciences 83(1960):786–95.

Maclean, Una. *Magical Medicine: A Nigerian Case Study*. London: Allen Lane, 1971.

Matthews, Don Basil. *The Crisis in the West Indian Family*. Port of Spain, Trinidad: Extra Mural Dept., 1953.

Meikle, H. B. "Mermaids and Fairymaids or Water Gods and Goddesses of Tobago." *Caribbean Quarterly* 5(1958):103–108.

Metraux, Alfred. *Haiti: Black Peasants and their Religion*. London, Toronto, Wellington, Sydney: George G. Harrap and Co., Ltd., 1960.

———. *Voodoo in Haiti*. Translated by Hugo Charteris. New York: Oxford University Press, 1959.

Mintz, Sidney W. "The Folk-urban Continuum and the Rural Proletarian Community." *American Journal of Sociology* 59(1953):194–204.

———. "The Question of Caribbean Peasantries." *Caribbean Studies* 1(1961):31–34.

———. *Worker in the Cane: a Puerto Rican Life History*. New York: W. W. Norton and Co., Inc., 1974.

Mintz, Sidney W., and Davenport, William, eds. "Working Papers in Caribbean Social Organization." In *Social and Economic Studies,* vol. X, No. 4, 1961.

Mintz, Sidney W., and Hall, Douglas. "The Origins of the Jamaican Internal Marketing System." In *Yale University Publications in Anthropology* No. 57(1970), New Haven.

Mischel, Frances. "Faith healing and Medical Practice in the southern Caribbean." *Southwestern Journal of Anthropology* 15(1959):407–17.

Moore, Joseph G., and Simpson, George E. "A Comparative Study of Acculturation in Morant Bay and West Kingston, Jamaica." *Zaire* 11(1957):989–1019.

Oakley, Amy. *Behold the West Indies.* New York: D. Appleton-Century Co., 1941.

O'Neale, H. W. "The Economy of St. Lucia." *Social and Economic Studies* 13(1964):440–70.

Otterbein, Keith W. "Caribbean Family Organization: A Comparative Analysis." *American Anthropologist* 67(1965):66–79.

Parsons, Elsie Clews. *Folk-lore of the Antilles, French and English.* Publication of the American Folklore Society Memoir Series, No. 26, 3 vols., 1933–1942.

———. *Folk-Tales of Andros Island, Bahamas.* Ibid., No. 13, 1918.

———. "Spirit Cult in Hayti." *Journal de la Société des Americanistes de Paris* 20(1928):157–79.

Patterson, Orlando. *The Sociology of Slavery.* London: MacGibbon and Kee, 1967.

Pearse, Andrew C. "The Big Drum Dance of Carriacou." In *Ethnic Folkways Library* Album No. P1011, 1956.

Price, Richard. "Caribbean Fishing and Fishermen." *American Anthropologist* 68(1966):1363–83.

———. "Fishing Rites and Recipes in a Martiniquan Village." *Caribbean Studies* 6(1966):3–24.

Renzo, Sereno. "Obeah." *Psychiatry* 11(1948):15–31.

Robbins, Richard Howard. "Identity and the Interpersonal Theory of Disease." In *Social and Cultural Identity,* edited by Thomas K. Fitzgerald. Southern Anthropological Society Proceedings, No. 8(1974), Athens, Georgia.

Rodman, Hyman. *Lower-class Families: The Culture of Poverty in Negro Trinidad.* New York, London, Toronto: Oxford University Press, 1971.

Romalis, Coleman. "Barbados and St. Lucia: a comparative Analysis of Social and Economic Development in the British West Indian Islands." Ph.D. thesis, Washington University, 1969.

Romalis, Rochelle E. "The Rural Community and the Total Society During Economic Change in St. Lucia: A Case Study." Ph.D. thesis, McGill University, 1968.

Roscoe, John. *The Baganda, an Account of their Native Customs and Beliefs.* London: Macmillan and Co. Ltd., 1911.

Rubel, Arthur J. "The Epidemiology of a Folk Illness: Susto in Hispanic America." *Ethnology* 3(1964):268–83.

Rubin, Vera, ed. *Caribbean Studies: a Symposium.* Monograph 34. Ethnological Society. Seattle and London: University of Washington Press, 1971.

Sanford, Margaret. "A Socialization in Ambiguity: Child-Lending in a British West Indian Society." *Ethnology* 14(1975):393–400.

Shurcliff, Alice, and Wellemeyer, J. F. *Economic Development in the Eastern Caribbean Islands: St. Lucia.* Series 4. Manpower Surveys. Barbados: Institute of Social and Economic Research, 1967.

Simpson, George Eaton. "Afro-American Religions and Religious Behavior." *Caribbean Studies* 12(1972):5–30.

———. "Folk Medicine in Trinidad." *Folklore* 75(1962):330.

———. "Haitian Magic." *Social Forces* 19(1940):95–100.

———. "The Kele (Chango) Cult in St. Lucia." *Caribbean Studies* 13(1973):110–16.

———. "Magical Practices in Northern Haiti." *Journal of American Folklore* 67(1954):395–403.

———. "The Ninth-Night Ceremony in Jamaica." *Journal of American Folklore* 70(1957):329–35.

———. "The Peoples and Cultures of the Caribbean Area." *Phylon* 23(1962):240–57.

———. *Religious Cults of the Caribbean: Trinidad, Jamaica, and Haiti.* Caribbean Monograph Series No. 7(1970), Institute of Caribbean Studies.

———. "Social Stratification in the Caribbean." *Phylon* 23(1962):29–46.

Smith, Michael G. *Dark Puritan.* Kingston, Jamaica: Dept. of Extra-Mural Studies, University of the West Indies, 1973.

———. *Kinship and Community in Carriacou.* New Haven: Yale University Press, 1962.

———. *The Plural Society in the British West Indies.* Berkeley and Los Angeles: University of California Press, 1965.

———. *West Indian Family Structure.* Seattle: University of Seattle Press, 1962.

Smith, Raymond T. "Culture and Social Structure in the Caribbean." *Comparative Studies in Society and History* 6(1963):24–46.

———. *The Negro Family in British Guiana.* New York: Routledge and Kegan Paul, Ltd., 1956.

Starkey, O. P. "Commercial Geography of St. Lucia." In *Technical Report* No. 8, Department of Geography, Indiana University, Bloomington, Indiana, 1961.

Steggerda, M. "Plants of Jamaica Used by Natives for Medical Purposes." *American Anthropologist* 31(n.s.,1929):431–34.

Stewart, William A. "Creole Languages in the Caribbean." In *Study of the Role of Second Languages in Asia, Africa, and Latin America,* edited by Frank A. Rice. Washington: Washington Center for Applied Linguistics, 1962.

Szwed, John F., and Whitten, Norman E., Jr., eds. *Afro-American Anthropology: Contemporary Perspectives.* New York: The Free Press, 1970.

Taylor, Douglas. "Carib Folk-Beliefs." *Southwestern Journal of Anthropology* 1(1945):507–30.

———. "The Caribs of Dominica." In *Anthropological Papers,* Bulletin No. 119. Washington, D.C.: Bureau of American Ethnology, Smithsonian Institution, 1938.

Tench, M. F. A. "West Indian Folklore, the Zombi." *Folklore* 25(1914):370–71.

Udal, J. S. "Obeah in the West Indies." *Folklore* 26(1915):255–95.

Underwood, Frances W. "The Marketing System in Peasant Haiti." *Yale University Publications in Anthropology,* No. 60(1970). New Haven.

Underwood, Frances W., and Honigmann, Irma. "A Comparison of Socialization and Personality in Two Simple Societies." *American Anthropologist* 49(1947):565–77.

van Beek, W. E. A. "The Religion of Everyday Life: an Ethnoscience Investigation into the Concepts of Religion and Magic." In *Explorations in the Anthropology of Religion* No. 74. The Hague: Martinus Nijhoff, 1975.

Walker, Sheila S. *Ceremonial Spirit Possession in Africa and Afro-America.* Leiden: E. J. Brill, 1972.

Weidman, Hazel H. "Anthropological Theory and the Psychological Function of Belief in Witchcraft." In *Essays in Medical Anthropology.* Southern Anthropological Society Proceedings, No. 1(1968), Athens, Georgia.

Weisbrod, Burton A.; Andreano, Ralph L.; Baldwin, Robert E.; Epstein, Erwin H.; and Kelley, Allen C. *Disease and Economic Development.* Madison, Wisconsin: University of Wisconsin Press, 1973.

Williams, Joseph John. *Psychic Phenomena in Jamaica.* New York: The Dial Press, 1934.

———. *Voodoos and Obeahs.* New York: The Dial Press, 1933.

Wilson, Peter J. *Crab Antics: The Social Anthropology of English-Speaking Negro Societies of the Caribbean.* New Haven and London: Yale University Press, 1973.

———. "Household and Family of Providencia." *Social and Economic Studies* 10(1961):511–27.

———. *Oscar: an Inquiry into the Nature of Sanity.* New York: Random House, 1974.

————. "Reputation and Respectability: A Suggestion for Caribbean Ethnology." *Man* 4(n.s.,1969):70–84.

Wooding, Charles J. "The Winti-Cult in the Para-district." *Caribbean Studies* 12(1972):51–78.

Young, Sir William. *An Account of the Black Charaibs in the Island of St. Vincent's.* London: Frank Cass and Co., Ltd., 1971.

NOTES

Foreword

1. Peter J. Wilson, *Oscar: An Inquiry into the Nature of Sanity* (New York, 1974) and M. G. Smith, *Dark Puritan* (Kingston: Department of Extramural Studies, University of the West Indies, 1963).

Introduction

1. Queen Victoria was buried February 4, 1901.

2. George Foster defines the folk community as "the peasant society," a community which represents "the rural expression of large, class-structured, economically complex, pre-industrial civilizations in which trade and commerce and craft specialization are well developed, in which money is commonly used, and in which market disposition is the goal for a part of the producer's efforts." In Foster's definition a fisherman is as much a peasant as a farmer. George M. Foster, "Interpersonal Relations in Peasant Society," *Human Organization* 19(1960):175.

3. St. Lucia is the second largest of the Windward Islands in the Lesser Antilles and contains some 238 square miles. Its topography is varied. Generally mountainous, it also has fertile alluvial valleys and low-lying pasture and swamp areas.

4. Whites of European ancestry comprise less than half of one percent of the total population, while blacks of African origin comprise about seventy percent. The remainder includes a small number of East Indians who were first brought in after the abolition of slave labor as indentured servants and the much larger group of "coloureds"—a racial mixture somewhere between black and white. Burton A. Weisbrod, Ralph L. Andreano, Robert E. Baldwin, Erwin H. Epstein, and Allen C. Kelley, *Disease and Economic Development* (Madison: University of Wisconsin Press, 1973), p. 31.

5. Coleman Romalis, *Barbados and St. Lucia: A Comparative Analysis of*

Social and Economic Development in the British West Indian Islands (Ph.D. thesis, Washington University, 1969), p. 114.

6. Leonard B. Glick, "Notes on St. Lucia: A Report to the Rockefeller Foundation," (unpublished, 1969), Social Conditions, p. 16.

7. F. G. Cassidy and R. B. LePage, *Dictionary of Jamaican English* (Cambridge: Cambridge University Press, 1967), p. 326. Also Orlando Patterson, *The Sociology of Slavery* (London: MacGibbon and Kee, 1967), p. 185.

8. Indeed it has been pointed out by Shurcliff and Wellemeyer that St. Lucians have long been the most mobile people in the Windward Islands, migrating to England, the United States, Canada, other West Indian islands, and the Caribbean Mainland as well. Alice Shurcliff and J. F. Wellemeyer, *Economic Development in the Eastern Caribbean Islands: St. Lucia,* Series 4, Manpower Surveys (Barbados: Institute of Social and Economic Research, 1967), p. 27.

9. Charles uses the term "duppy" man or woman to describe a person who deals with the Devil for his or her own personal gain. A more common term found in St. Lucia is pronounced "gahjay" from the French "engagé."

10. See Jane C. Beck, "The Implied Obeah Man," *Western Folklore* 35(1976):23–33.

11. The use of roots and leaves for medicinal or magico-medicinal purposes.

12. Weisbrod et al., *Disease and Economic Development,* p. 3.

13. Ibid.

14. Glick, "Notes on St. Lucia."

15. Ari Kiev, *Curanderismo: Mexican-American Folk Psychiatry* (New York: The Free Press, 1968), p. 177. See also Richard Robbins, "Identity and the Interpersonal Theory of Disease" in *Social and Cultural Identity,* Southern Anthropological Society Proceedings, No. 8(1974), Athens, Georgia, pp. 5–14.

16. Another legacy from the period of French occupancy. While the language of the Government has been English, that of the Church has been French, and the priests have easily picked up the local Patois. As a result the Church has had a greater influence over the people than the Government and has tended to preserve the status quo.

17. The manta ray is also known as the Sea Devil and, as such, probably feeds the tradition. See J. C. Beck, "A Study of the West Indian Devil," Manuscript, p.12.

18. Francis Huxley, *The Invisibles: Voodoo Gods in Haiti* (New York: McGraw Hill, 1966), p. 50. See also Melville J. and Frances S. Herskovits, *Suriname Folk-lore* (New York: Columbia University Press, 1936), p. 111.

19. See page 224.

20. Wilfrid D. Hambley, *Serpent Worship in Africa* (Chicago: Field Museum of Natural History Publication 289, Anthropological Series vol. xxi, No. 1, 1931), p. 18.

21. John Roscoe, *The Baganda, An Account of Their Native Customs and Beliefs* (London: Macmillan and Co. Ltd. 1911), p. 44. For Charles's discussion see pp. 237–39.

22. Melville J. and Frances S. Herskovits, *Trinidad Village* (New York: Octagon Books, 1976), p. 225.

23. Martha Beckwith, *Black Roadways* (New York: Negro University Press, 1969), p. 122.

24. These Black Arts books often turn out to be editions of the seventeenth and eighteenth century French magic books such as *Le Petit Albert* or *La Poule Noire*. More recent acquisitions prove to be catalogues put out by the DeLaurence Company of Chicago, whose address is a jealously guarded secret.

25. George E. Simpson, "Afro-American Religions and Religious Behavior," *Caribbean Studies* 12(1972):9.

26. See M. J. Herskovits, *Dahomey*, volume II (New York: Northwestern University Press, 1938), p. 238, and William Bascom, "Yoruba Concepts of Soul," in *Selected Papers of the Fifth International Congress of Anthropological and Ethnological Sciences,* edited by Anthony F. C. Wallace (Philadelphia: University of Pennsylvania Press, 1960), p. 401.

27. Cassidy and LePage, *Dictionary of Jamaican English*, p. 164.

28. M. J. Herskovits, *The Myth of the Negro Past* (Boston: Beacon Press, 1958), pp.252–53.

29. A demon, especially one assuming female form to have sexual intercourse with men in their sleep.

30. In Grenada black magic men are known as "door-openers."

31. See J. C. Beck, "Dream Messages from the Dead," *Journal of the Folklore Institute* 10(1973):173–86.

32. Some exceptions are Sidney W. Mintz, *Worker in the Cane: a Puerto Rican Life History* (New York: W. W. Norton and Co., Inc., 1974); M. G. Smith, *Dark Puritan* (Kingston, Jamaica: Dept. of Extra-Mural Studies, University of the West Indies, 1973); Peter J. Wilson, *Oscar: an Inquiry into the Nature of Sanity* (New York: Random House, 1974).

33. Patois is a spoken rather than a written language and, although scholars are working on it, there is no standard means of rendering it in written form as yet. The reader must keep this in mind in terms of the Patois used in this text. I am particularly indebted to Mrs. Iohn Ford, who is herself engaged in writing a Patois dictionary, for her help with the Patois language.

34. Charles refers to the Spanish Creole of the Santo Domingans as "Haitian."

35. In the islands tremendous respect and deference are paid to the "old heads" who are looked upon as bearers of great wisdom because of their age.

36. Obeah. "Wanga" or "ouanga" usually refers to a charm intended to harm someone. See George E. Simpson, "Haitian Magic," *Social Forces* 19(1940):98.

37. See W.H. Hodge and Douglas Taylor, "The Ethnobotany of the Island Caribs of Dominica," *Webbia* 12(1957):513–645.

38. Ibid., p. 523.

39. M. G. Smith, *The Plural Society in the British West Indies* (Berkeley: University of California Press, 1965).

40. See J. C. Beck, "The West Indian Supernatural World," *JAF* 88(1975):235–44.

41. This is a common attitude in the West Indies. See Serge Larose, "The Meaning of Africa in Haitian Vodu," In *Symbols and Sentiments,* edited by I. M. Lewis (London, New York, San Francisco: Academic Press, 1977), p. 87.

42. A variant of the proverb, "The same stick that beat the black dog is beating the white dog."

The Early Years

1. Bourgeois is not a family name but rather a denotation of wealth. Those Dominicans who are known as bourgeois might be likened to the mercantile class.

2. A cobble is a small, cargo-carrying sloop distinguished by a tombstone stern and a deep forefront.

3. "Table au Diable" on the chart—a shoal off the northeastern point, Presqu'ile de la Caravelle, of Martinique.

4. Here he is referring to a half-sister who attempted to "fix" Charles by putting something in his food and whom he didn't care to think about.

5. This is a commonly held belief in St. Lucia. If one's body is over-heated from any kind of activity and is then subjected to cold (the half-roasted banana), the person will take a chill. The Patois term for such an illness is "fewdi" and covers a wide range of minor illnesses. Leonard Glick reports that an individual "would not go swimming immediately after lying in the hot sun, nor should one eat ice cream or drink cold liquids when hot and thirsty. The young woman who worked as our house servant was very reluctant even to open the refrigerator after walking in the sun or after ironing clothes." Leonard Glick, "Medical Beliefs and Practices," in "Notes on St. Lucia: A Report to the Rockefeller Foundation," (unpublished, 1969), p. 2.

6. Choco was in fact Charles's father's aunt and therefore his great aunt.

7. A man want to "get me."

8. See page 71.

9. When I asked what would happen to a child in St. Lucia whose mother and father had died, I was told that "everyone has family" and that a child would be taken in by various relations, usually by the child's grandmother or an aunt, most often the mother's sister. Frequently, because of the rather fluid mating system, a child of a former lover will be farmed out to a close relative when the woman is living with another man.

10. April, 1907. "The trouble began with a strike of coal-carriers in Castries on the 19th day of April; they went to see the Governor at Government House. Three days later the strikers rushed the wharf and prevented a ship from being coaled by those carriers who were willing to work. Several persons were injured. The situation grew worse when ten policemen were pressed into a dangerous position, and fired volleys upon the rioters; four of these were wounded. That evening some provision shops were destroyed. The next day the rioters looted the Castries Market. The labourers at Cul-de-Sac went on strike, and a crowd from there went down into Castries. Representatives of these strikers went to state their grievances before the Governor and the manager of the Cul-de-Sac Factory." Reverend C. Jesse, *Outlines of St. Lucia History*, St. Lucia Archeological and Historical Society, Castries, 1964, p. 39.

11. Here Charles means the same "class" of people. Governor Moore was not the governor of St. Lucia but was apparently an Englishman who may have held that title elsewhere.

12. He was probably about twelve years old and no longer considered himself a boy. In St. Lucia, where every economic contribution to the household is utilized, a boy's desire to become a man is fostered from an early age.

13. By the 1880s Castries, because of its excellent harbor, had become the principal coaling station in the West Indies. Helmut Blume reports that "more than a thousand steamships called on St. Lucia annually to bunker the coal imported from Great Britain and the U.S.A." Helmut Blume, *The Caribbean Islands*, trans. Johannes Maczewski and Ann Norton (London: Longman Group, Ltd., 1974), p. 346.

14. After the outbreak of World War I guns were brought from Martinique and a company of soldiers was imported from Canada to fortify the Vigie from 1915 to 1918.

Prison and Santo Domingo

1. It is doubtful that Charles was ever married. This was said early in our relationship—I suspect for my benefit. In later conversations Charles referred to his wife as "my keeper."

2. This occurred while Charles was under sentence for hard labor. He was evidently with a work-gang from the prison.

3. Charles never expanded on what he had done, but from further conversation he must have been involved in some kind of fight.

4. Working in the bakery and kitchen was much preferable to hard labor.

5. St. Lucia has changed over to Eastern Caribbean currency, but Charles often referred to the old British pound and pence. In a number of instances he seemed to have little comprehension of actual value. His mind was more oriented toward a barter economy than toward a monetary one.

6. Gobi made a supernatural charm to cause harm to Braffett.

7. Gobi "set" the charm on Braffett.

8. All natives of other West Indian islands had to register within four months of arrival and be prepared to leave if their presence was deemed undesirable. Those who came in had to have fifty dollars in their possession. Harry Franck, *Roaming Through the West Indies* (New York: The Century Company, 1920), p. 209. At this time Haitian and British West Indian laborers were brought into the Dominican Republic to work on the sugar estates.

9. I have been unable to determine what these "prickles" actually were. Perhaps they were some kind of rash or skin infection.

10. Anton was Charles's greatest instructor in supernatural lore. See pages 252–254 and 259.

11. This belief in cannibalism in Haiti was widespread. Elsie Clews Parsons writes, "Some St. Lucia boys shipwrecked in San Domingo told me there that they had become afraid of going on to Hayti, as they once thought of doing, since they had heard how they killed and ate people in Hayti." Elsie Clews Parsons, "The Spirit Cult in Hayti," *Journal de la Société des Americanistes de Paris* 20(1928):157. See also Erika Bourguignon, "The Persistence of Folk Belief: Notes on Cannibalism and Zombies in Haiti," *Journal of American Folklore* 72(1959):36–46.

12. A long thin knife. See page 27 for further description.

13. Metraux comments on the frequency of such situations, pointing out that, although custom permits it, when polygamy occurs with women jealousy often takes a physical turn. "When a wife or mistress

meets the woman who is sharing the favors of her 'husband,' . . . then a swearing match, peppered with insults and threats, breaks out. It is on such occasions that there are the 'scandals' which call for the intervention of the rural constable and end up before the justice of the peace." Alfred Metraux, *Haiti: Black Peasants and Their Religion* (London, Toronto, Wellington, Sydney: George G. Harrap and Co., Ltd., 1960), p. 48.

14. I work building or maintaining the roads.

15. The headquarters of the sugar estate.

16. A small wagon brought into the cane fields on rails to carry out the cane.

17. A premium is put on burial rites in the West Indies. Often West Indians join societies and pay a nominal sum per week to insure a proper burial. The Herskovitses record a similar reaction to the burial of a man in Trinidad. "Why, you wouldn't bury a pet dog like that! It's just like getting rid of a carcass of a pig—a hole in the ground, in he goes and stamp down the earth. I hope nothing like that ever happen to me." Melville J. and Frances S. Herskovits, *Trinidad Village* (New York: Octagon Books, 1976), p. 146.

18. This was the disastrous fire of Castries of May 14 and 15, 1927.

Employment with Mr. Barnard

1. Logwood was sold abroad for dye.

2. "Nasty hand people" is an expression for workers of obeah.

3. The Family (*terre famille*) system of land tenure in St. Lucia leads to many disputes over inherited property. All descendants, both legitimate and illegitimate, of the deceased owner, the living spouse, and sometimes a host of collateral relatives are considered to have equal rights to the land.

4. Black pudding is a sausage made from the blood of cows or pigs and seasoned with herbs and hot pepper. Souse is pickled pig trotters and parts of the head served with cucumbers.

5. Much of the fishing and trading in the West Indies is done on a system of shares in which the men and the boat each get a varying percentage. See page 107 for a discussion of "shares" in terms of black fishing.

6. Mr. Barnard owned Barnard & Company, which was one of the three agents in Castries controlling the commerce of the port. His competitors were Peter & Company and Chastanet (later Minvielle & Chastanet, Ltd.).

7. This was the strike of May, 1941, which continued until June 10. According to Romalis, ". . . the strikers held out for a short while before

capitulating with no gain." Coleman Romalis, "Barbados and St. Lucia: a comparative Analysis of Social and Economic Development in the British West Indian Islands" (Ph.D. thesis, Washington University, 1969), p. 132.

8. A long drum made from a hollow length of tree trunk.

9. Coal was unloaded by hand into baskets. A man and a woman would work as a team, the man loading the basket while the woman carried it to its destination. Pay was a penny a basket, each basket holding one hundred nine pounds of coal. Singing and carrying coal was not a novel idea of Charles's, for Aspinall reports the singing of shanties in his *Pocket Guide to the West Indies* in 1907. The coal would then be loaded onto other ships when they called into Castries for fueling. Algernon Aspinall, *A Pocket Guide to the West Indies* (London: Methuen & Co., 1907), p. 172.

10. By "turning the medicine" Charles's enemy would render it ineffective.

11. A roadside shrine with the stations of the cross.

12. I cut down all the baskets.

13. He's probably referring to the terrible landslides of November, 1938.

14. March 9, 1942. A German submarine actually entered Castries Harbor and torpedoed the C.N.S. *Lady Nelson* and the *Umtata*. The Reverend Jesse reports that "several lives were lost" and comments that "A regrettable sequel to the incident was an outbreak of pilfering and stealing of cargo from one of the damaged vessels, which actually brought about the death of an innocent man." Reverend C. Jesse, *Outlines of St. Lucia History*, St. Lucia Archeological and Historical Society, Castries, 1964, p. 48.

15. Coolie means East Indian. There were Lascars on the *Umtata*.

16. The implication is that he was "done something" by somebody who was jealous of his position as a "big man."

The Dominica Years and Smuggling

1. Dominica became the last stronghold of the Carib Indians, the native inhabitants found by Columbus when he discovered the islands. The Carib reserve was established in 1903 on the middle of the windward (eastern) side of the island. Today there are few full-blooded Caribs left; there has been a great deal of intermingling with the blacks, and hence the name "Black Caribs." Writing in 1945, Douglas Taylor estimated that the inhabitants of the reserve "number about 450, one hundred of whom may be considered reasonably as 'fullblooded' In-

dians." Douglas Taylor, "Carib Folk-Beliefs," *Southwestern Journal of Anthropology* 1(1945):507–30.

2. For a long time this incident was confusing to me. Originally, I had thought it took place shortly after his mother and father had been drowned. In actuality it occurred many years after and must have coincided with some property dispute in St. Lucia.

3. "Tawa" is the Carib word for chalk or pipe clay (personal communication from Douglas Taylor).

4. Also known as balizier leaf. These would be dried and bound together horizontally with Bromelia twine. See Douglas Taylor, "The Caribs of Dominica," in Anthropological Papers, Bulletin no. 119 (Washington, D.C.: Bureau of American Ethnology, Smithsonian Institution, 1938), p. 132.

5. Gouge or squash. Apparently the squash was scooped out and the covering was used as a drinking vessel.

6. Charles is referring to his aunt's knowledge of bush medicine.

7. Here he is referring to his sister and her family.

8. George William, the natural son of Governor George William Dervais, was a member of the local aristocracy, known as a good businessman, who ran a successful store.

9. In actuality, the relationship was not that simple. Choco was O'Farrell Hughes's half-brother's aunt, but no blood relation to O'Farrell himself.

10. Couscous is a kind of gruel probably made from farine (cassava flour).

11. Probably Charles means a couple of weeks.

12. The island of St. Martins is divided between the French and the Dutch.

13. O'Farrell Hughes told us that in fact Chesterfield was dead.

14. Charles means days. O'Farrell Hughes confirmed that they had stayed three days.

15. This fire occurred on June 19–20, 1948, and destroyed about four-fifths of Castries.

16. In actuality no lives were lost.

17. In a later conversation Charles indicated that this was part of a Kele ceremony for the dead. This was a line of questioning that I had hoped to pursue at a later date but unfortunately did not return to it soon enough. The Kele cult in St. Lucia is seen as deriving from Africa and is involved in ancestor worship. See George Eaton Simpson, "The Kele (Chango) Cult in St. Lucia," *Caribbean Studies* 13(1973):110–16.

18. Charles has switched from speaking about his aunt's death to telling me how things should be. This is the way I should act if my hus-

band were to die. In actual life this "ideal" kind of behavior is seldom followed.

19. My thanks go to Dr. Yvonne Lange for her help with the Patois and translation of this song.

20. Charles uses eight-day and nine-day wake interchangeably. Sometimes it is known as the Ninth Night. See George E. Simpson, "The Ninth-Night Ceremony in Jamaica," *Journal of American Folklore* 70(1957):329–35.

21. Also known as crapaud, *Leptodactylus pentadaetylus.*

22. These huge frogs are hunted at night with a flambeau (homemade torch). A wick is placed in a bottle full of gasoline. A lime plugs the neck of the bottle and prevents it from becoming too hot.

23. D'eau benite—holy water.

24. Probably Coulibistri.

Fishing

1. A circular net attached to a bamboo rim, carried by all St. Lucian fishermen.

2. True fog is almost unknown in the Caribbean. Charles refers to limited visibility.

3. Charles is referring to the reflection of himself in the lamp.

4. Chichima is used much as curry and is generally an ingredient of curry powders; it is also thought to be good for stiffness.

5. A small boat that made commerical trips from Soufriere to Castries.

6. A flat, round cake made of flour, sugar, salt, and baking powder.

7. Green turtle, *Chelone mydas.*

8. Hawksbill turtle, *Eretmochelys imbricata.*

9. Loggerhead turtle or "Cowette," *Caretta caretta.* Actually used in making a kind of bracelet, rather than a wristwatch.

10. The sampson post or logger head. For a comparative study of blackfishing on St. Vincent see Roger Abrahams, *Deep the Water, Shallow the Shore,* publication of the American Folklore Society Memoir Series, vol. 60, 1974, pp. 67–70. See also John E. Adams, "Shore Whaling in St. Vincent, West Indies," *Caribbean Quarterly* 19(1973):42–50.

11. He could work obeah on you.

12. Anyone can work obeah to hinder you.

13. See W. H. Hodge and Douglas Taylor, "The Ethnobotany of the Island Caribs of Dominica," *Webbia* 12(1957):584. Chardon beni has a peculiar fetid odor.

14. The "something" is oil of rose which has a pungent, sweet smell.

15. Charles is referring to an "East" Indian man. Obeah is not practiced by blacks alone.

16. I was told that another local name for maweepoui was "girly root." It is known by the old people as a protection against obeah and was often used for scrubbing as well as for tea.

17. Durocher was plugging the drain hole.

18. This is a kind of fish stew.

19. The Shouters is a religious cult in St. Vincent, also known as the Shakers or Spiritual Baptists. See Jeannett Hillman Henney, "Spirit Possession Belief and Trance Behavior in a Religious Group in St. Vincent, British West Indies" (Ph.D. thesis, Ohio State University, 1968). See also Henney, "Spirit-Possession Belief and Trance Behavior in Two Fundamentalist Groups in St. Vincent," in *Trance, Healing and Hallucination,* ed. Goodman, Henney, and Pressel (New York: John Wiley and Sons, 1974).

20. See pages 155–159 and 192 for further discussion of will power.

21. Often a fisherman will "rub" his boat with a special concoction which supposedly enables him to catch fish. This is done in the early morning before he puts to sea.

22. See pages 155–157, 230, and 239–40.

23. Charles is referring to the ballast stones in the boat.

"Watchie"

1. See W. H. Hodge and Douglas Taylor, "The Ethnobotany of the Island Caribs of Dominica," *Webbia* 12(1957):596.

2. Actually it is the apple-like fruit of the babara which is used, by being crushed and enclosed in the basket. Douglas Taylor makes the point that the basket is only immersed for a short time, "as it would poison the water for almost a week were it left there." Douglas Taylor, "The Caribs of Dominica," in *Anthropological Papers,* Bulletin no. 119 (Washington, D.C.: Bureau of American Ethnology, Smithsonian Institution, 1938), p. 145.

3. Intimate garments are known to be extremely valuable in working any kind of evil magic on a person. Herskovits mentions this in relation to Trinidad, reporting that "Care is taken not to leave [menstrual] clothes about, for they are potent in concocting evil magic. To insure against this, the first cloth used by a girl during her first period is burned and the ashes are poured into the water and given the girl to drink. This, it is believed, will forever prevent her being harmed by anyone who might utilize her menstrual fluid to make magic with which to control, or otherwise overpower her." Melville J. and Frances S. Herskovits, *Trinidad Village* (New York: Octagon Books, 1976), pp. 127–28.

4. Probably a poison egg which is believed to have powers to harm.

5. The attitude here is that it is easier to work "something" on a person and thereby gain revenge if the individual suspects nothing.

6. Another version of Ann Marie's madness and cure can be found in the Appendix. For the sake of continuity only one version has been presented in the text. The discrepancy between the two is, perhaps, a refinement of Charles's life story and a confounding of the real and the ideal. See pages 272–74 for a discussion of this.

7. Here Charles is referring to "en tout cas," his personal antidote to poison. This mixture was taught to him by Anton, the Haitian. In Haiti such a mixture is known as a "drogue," and its sole function is to protect the individual against poisoning. "After taking a drogue a glass with poison in it will break in your hands, or you will immediately vomit the contents of the glass." George Eaton Simpson, "Haitian Magic," *Social Forces* 19(1940):98. See also pages 146–47, 154–55, 190, and 240 of that text.

8. Mrs. Ganter told me a slightly different version of this story. Apparently Peter & Company had been losing quite a number of parts—wheels and carburetors—and Mr. Moyle, the man in charge, made the statement that the next night watchman to have anything stolen during his tenure would be fired. Charles was the unlucky individual. Later, when Mrs. Ganter needed a night watchman she called Mr. Moyle for a recommendation. He immediately suggested Charles, explaining that he hadn't wanted to fire him—that "he was as good as you can get" and "as honest as the day was long"—but he couldn't go back on his word. The result was that Mrs. Ganter hired Charles, and he worked there until he died.

9. It did not seem to matter that Mrs. Ganter was younger than he.

10. It is customary for every Catholic St. Lucian child to have three given names as well as a last name or surname. In Angela's case, she was Angela Matilda Dorothy Morris—Morris being her mother's surname. See Daniel J. Crowley, "Naming Customs in St. Lucia," *Social and Economic Studies* 5(1956):87–92.

11. See J. R. Groome, *A Natural History of the Island of Grenada, W.I.* (Trinidad: Caribbean Printers, Ltd., 1970), pp. 90, 91. It is also referred to as "fonsa."

12. This is the traditional attitude—that the family of the young man must be investigated by the girl's family. See Herskovits, *Trinidad Village,* p. 294.

13. Session means the Assizes of High Court in Criminal Jurisdiction.

Conversations

1. See pages 159–160 and 162.

2. Ingredients needed for magical as well as medicinal purposes are obtained at the doctor's shop or local pharmacist. Leonard Glick in his unpublished paper, "Magic, Science, and Religion in a St. Lucian Pharmacy," divides the clientele of the local pharmacy into four categories: "First are those who come for purposes that might be characterized as 'religious' or 'magical' but not medical. Second are those seeking Mr. Beaubrun's [pharmacist] advice and treatment for illness. Third are those with prescriptions written by physicians. Finally, a small but significant minority bring prescriptions from local curers—diviners called gadé," (p. 2).

3. "Spoil" means to harm an individual, usually by working obeah on him.

4. George Simpson mentions this in his article "Folk Medicine in Trinidad," *Folklore* 75(1962):330.

5. Mulberry worm.

6. "Sheenie" is Patois for caterpillar.

7. Euphemism for Sea Devil.

8. Someone is one step ahead and has already "set" something on you.

9. Charles is probably referring to some form of gonorrhea.

10. Possibly hookworm.

11. Unidentified. Another local name is Christmas worm.

12. Charles is referring to British West Indian currency, now Eastern Caribbean currency. At that time it was roughly $2 BWI for $1 American.

13. This is very similar to the well-known folk illness, "susto," in Hispanic America. Rubel characterizes its symptoms generally as "(1) while asleep a patient evidences restlessness, and (2) during waking hours he manifests listlessness, loss of appetite, disinterest in costume or personal hygiene, loss of strength and weight, depression, and introversion." Arthur J. Rubel, "The Epidemiology of a Folk Illness: Susto in Hispanic America," *Ethnology* 3(1964):268–83.

14. Again this is very similar to the Hispanic American "susto" sickness. Instead of "soul loss," which is usually thought to be the cause of this illness, a woman had "put something" on this man so that she can do what she wants with him.

15. Ti Son is Charles's second son by Enid.

16. A part of Castries Harbor known as Prince Alfred's Basin.

17. The boat is probably closer to forty miles from Guadeloupe.

18. "Galé" is Patois for facial sores.

19. Peter & Company store.

20. Sweet spirit of nitre is an organic compound—about 3 to 4½ percent ethyl nitrate, the spirit being an alcoholic solution of around 190 proof.

21. This is a common belief in the West Indies. Herskovits mentions it in regard to Trinidad, reporting that such a guard must be removed during intercourse and that many carry additional taboos "such as prohibitions on given foods while wearing them, or taboos against touching the ground." Melville J. and Frances S. Herskovits, *Trinidad village* (New York: Octagon Books, 1976), p. 244.

22. When a duppy woman is about to die she is often believed to confess her dastardly deeds. In Patois the woman is said to "dépalé," something that is considered very undesirable, for a person will confess all that he has done in life—naming those she has killed or harmed as well as those for whom she has worked obeah. In order to stop the tongue from "calling the list," special teas are brewed and given the person. See page 200.

23. The bamboo seed is very rare, for the bamboo tree seldom flowers; once it actually flowers and produces seed it dies.

24. The crossroads is significant for it is a place where "bad and good must cross," where human and spiritual being can meet. See Melville J. and Frances S. Herskovits, *Suriname Folk-lore* (New York: Columbia University Press, 1936), p. 67.

25. Fire is connected with many supernatural creatures. A sucoyan or ligaroo is characterized by balls of fire under its arms; a bolum or baku often burns houses.

26. Zander, Charles's second son with Ann Marie.

27. See pages 272–73 for a discussion of Mrs. Alcindor.

28. A thin blade with a sharp point hidden in a walking stick called a "flerrie" or "flayree."

29. In other words, it was the Devil who took her.

30. Better known as Horse-eye bean, the seed of the Mucuna. It has a rough pod on which the Cow Itch grows.

31. Another tea which is supposed to serve the same purpose is made from a bush known as "twenty-one shillings." See Daniel J. Crowley, "Supernatural Beings in St. Lucia," *The Caribbean* 8(1955):242.

32. I have not found the three-legged horse to be a well-known creature throughout the Lesser Antilles, but it is more common in Jamaica, where it is thought to be a "demon in the form of a horse with one foreleg and two hind legs." See Frederic G. Cassidy and R. B. LePage, *Dictionary of Jamaican English* (Cambridge: Cambridge University Press, 1967), p. 442.

33. The worst insult to a West Indian is to have his mother insulted.

One day a young boy shouted abuse at a man because he felt he hadn't been given adequate remuneration for climbing a tree and shaking down some mangoes. The man ignored the words until the boy cursed the man's mother. With that, the man shot out of his car, grabbed the boy, gave him a good shaking and a verbal lambasting. Climbing back into the car, he explained to us that it was very bad luck to curse one's mother; if you heard someone cursing your mother you must stop him or things would go badly in the future.

34. It is also believed that one must invoke a dead person who has been buried for over forty days.

35. See Michael G. Smith, *Kinship and Community in Carriacou* (New Haven: Yale University Press, 1962), pp. 145–46.

36. Here we note the concept that the dead man's soul is contained in the powder made from his bones.

37. There is no question that the whip remains an important symbol of power in the West Indies. Roger Abrahams makes an accurate observation when he writes:

> The amount of beating, whipping, and flogging in the life of the West Indian is really startling to the outsider. Children are trained by stick beating and lashings, often only vaguely connected with an offense. Teachers treat children in the same way should lesson recitations be faulty or behavior unruly. Marriages or other sexual unions are similarly controlled by the rod and the hand, leading to the widely found proverb, 'they don't love you 'less they beat you . . . ' With a background of this sort, coupled with the remembrance of the slave-masters' nine-tail cat, it is not surprising that the whip and the stick have become symbols of masculine power, and are so used in a number of traditions.

Roger Abrahams, "The Shaping of Folklore Traditions in the British West Indies," *Journal of Inter-American Studies* 9(1967):475.

38. Jumby beads grow wild in St. Lucia and are poisonous. The bead is a black and red seed that falls from the dried pod.

39. Actually Ginger Lilies and Lilies of the Valley are two different plants. I assume he was referring to the former as this was the flower he pointed out to me.

40. Here Charles is referring to the scissors' magnetic ability.

41. H. B. Meikle makes a distinction between mermaids and fairymaids in Tobago. He writes, "Mermaids according to local tradition are male in sex, Fairymaids female. The former 'live in the sea,' the latter 'in the rivers.'" H. B. Meikle, "Mermaids and Fairymaids or Water Gods and Goddesses of Tobago," *Caribbean Quarterly* 5(1958):103. However, I

have not heard such a distinction made. In Charles's story the fairymaid is simply a fairy woman, not a mermaid. As a fairy woman, however, she has been "West Indianized."

42. In Suriname a sorcerer makes the baku—creatures which are half flesh and half wood and "have the appearance of very black two-year-olds, except that their heads are large. . . . They have human voices and human speech and are given to teasing, which they do to trick and disarm people. Those who own them keep them under the bed, or locked in an empty room and there they feed and care for them." Herskovits, *Suriname Folk-lore*, p. 105.

At the other end of the culture area, in Haiti, the baku are described as "small and evil creatures, human in form, with red eyes, and legs or arms covered with skin but no flesh." Harold Courlander, *The Drum and the Hoe* (Berkeley and Los Angeles: University of California Press, 1960), p. 95.

There are several types of these creatures, all of whom perform malevolent acts. Among them are those who, like the bolum, "stay in the house of their master, go forth only to procure him riches." These baku are described as "jealous spirits" who "ultimately destroy the members of their master's family, particularly his children, or, should a man repent of his bargain and dismiss them they will return to kill him." Melville J. Herskovits, *Life in a Haitian Valley* (Garden City: Doubleday and Co., 1971), p. 245. The name "bolum" or "ti bolum" is probably a Patois corruption of "le petit bel homme" and is used in both St. Lucia and Dominica.

43. In the light of this method of obtaining a bolum it is interesting to note that one of the most common means of destroying unwanted children among the Paramaribo Negroes of Suriname was "to get a *baku* from a sorcerer, for since the *baku* are especially jealous of children, the child is killed in the womb without any overt act on the part of the mother." Herskovits, *Suriname Folk-lore*, p. 50.

The direct ancestor of these creatures is probably the "spirits of abiku" known among the Dahomeans and Yoruba as "children who are born to die." These spirits are thought to be "waiting to enter her womb and usurp the place of her [a woman's] own precious child." Una Maclean, *Magical Medicine: A Nigerian Case Study* (London: Allen Lane, 1971), pp. 50–51.

44. Another belief concerning the way to obtain a bolum is to take a hen's first egg on Good Friday. A person takes this egg, places it under his arm, and goes to bed for a year. From the egg, cared for in such a manner, will come a bolum.

45. Swallow, (French) *hirondelle*.

46. In Dominica the bois diable and the fromager are known as different trees. Charles's confusion is probably in the fromager's connection with the Devil. I suspect also that he might have misunderstood me. The silk cotton tree is sacred throughout West Africa and the West Indies as well. Stories of obeah being worked at its roots and jumbies living in its branches abound.

47. Charles never did bring me a piece of the moudongue. He explained that many of the moudongue treas had been cut down to make room for banana trees when bananas became an important industry for St. Lucia. Now, he explained, you had to go far into the jungle. Next trip he would bring it for me. But he died before that ever came to be.

48. Unidentified.

49. See page 195.

50. The Herskovitses report in *Suriname Folk-lore* that the silk cotton tree is the habitat of Gro Mama, the Earth Goddess, and when angry "she manifests herself as a snake." To appease her a generous offering of eggs and a prayer for forgiveness must be forthcoming (p. 63). *Dagowe* is used as the generic term for all snake spirits believed to live in the silk cotton tree, and "when food is placed as an offering at the foot of one of these trees, it is not for any spirit in the tree itself, but for the spirit of the *Dagowe*." Herskovits, *Suriname Folk-lore*, p. 67.

51. See also Herskovits, *Trinidad Village*, p. 66, and Sir Hesketh J. Bell, *Obeah: Witchcraft in the West Indies* (London: Sampson Low, Marston, Searle and Rivington, 1889), p. 125.

52. This same belief is reported by the Herskovitses from Suriname people who are believed to purchase a snake from a *wisiman* (obeah man) "to keep in the house for 'luck.'" The snake feeds on eggs and sometimes consumes as many as fifty a day. In return the owner gains wealth. Apparently, the owner must speak to the snake in endearing terms at night; it is believed that when children are born the snake will become jealous and kill them. This is quite different from the protective attitude of the guardian snake in St. Lucia. Herskovits, *Suriname Folklore*, p. 104.

53. The government in most West Indian islands has laws on the books making the practice of obeah illegal. Sections 276–284 of the Criminal Code of St. Lucia reads as follows:

276—"A person practising obeah" means any person who, to effect any fraudulent or unlawful purpose, or for gain, or for the purpose of frightening any person, uses or pretends to use any occult means, mesmeric or otherwise, or pretends to possess any supernatural power or knowledge . . .

281—In any prosecution for any offence under this section, it is not necessary that any witness should despose directly to any precise consideration or to the fact of the offence having been committed with his participation or his own personal or certain knowledge . . . But so soon as it appears to the Court that the circumstances in evidence sufficiently establish the offence complained of, the Court shall put the defendant on his defence and in default of such evidence being rebutted shall convict the defendant accordingly.

Criminal Code of St. Lucia, 1957 (Castries: Voice Publishing Company, 1959), pp. 532–34. Courtesy of Leonard B. Glick.

54. Micoud is well known as a big man in Anse la Raye. He wears studs made from raw nuggets of gold and claims to have three chains and a belt of solid gold as well. He is of striking stature and apparently has a way with the women, as he has sired thirty-six children—stretching in age from forty-four to one month old. None were with his wife.

When we first met him he was in his early sixties and told us that he had come from Micoud (hence his nickname), which is on the windward side of St. Lucia, to Anse la Raye over forty years ago. At that time all he brought with him was a seine net valued at four hundred dollars. He was successful in fishing and traded this net in for one worth a thousand dollars, but other men were jealous of his success and poured acid on the net and cut his boat loose, causing the boat and its contents to be lost on the rocks. Angry but not laid low, Micoud went out and bought a two-thousand-dollar net that was later lost in Hurricane Janet in the fifties, when again two of his boats were cut loose.

At this point in his story Micoud added that he was usually successful in getting even with those who did him wrong. However, he was also quick to say that he would help any man who was sick and would charge him only the price of the medicine—if anyone should trouble us, we were to come to him and he'd take care of it.

According to Micoud, his money was made not only in fishing but also through the buying and selling of houses and gold. Rather than trusting his money to a bank, he would put it in land, houses, gold, boats, and nets. Of course, this would make his wealth that much more visible to all around him; it is no wonder that he became the target of both stories and jealousy.

55. It is generally believed that one is "given" money in a dream. He must dig for it exactly as he is told, bringing only those persons indicated in the dream. If he follows everything to the letter it is believed

that he will successfully recover the treasure. See J. C. Beck, "Dream Messages from the Dead," *Journal of the Folklore Institute* 10(1973):182–86.

56. The magical cutting of cane is associated with Haiti in many of the other islands. As far south as Bequia I was told, "They say in Haiti they had this cane field and some men who do devil dealing, who don't want the workers to work, they just tell the Devil to cut down all the cane, and you just see cutlass flying through the cane. If you don't move out of the way you get chopped up too."

57. Herskovits speaks of this last phenomenon in Haiti in terms of "good magic." "It is said to be secret knowledge, transmitted in certain families from generation to generation, of how to control the rains. Those who have control of magic of this sort are to be recognized when they are seen to be completely dry while walking in a downpour. Generally such powers are used to insure a rainless day for a *combite* or *service*, or to cause rain to fall the day after a *combite* has made the field ready for hoeing, or when the proper time for planting is at hand. Eventually, it is said, in response to a temptation too great to be resisted, the possessor of such magic will put it to other, evil ends." Herskovits, *Life in a Haitian Valley*, p. 229.

58. Charles is once again referring to his sickness suffered while working for Mr. Barnard.

59. When Herskovits asked in Trinidad whether it was friends or enemies that would tie an individual, he was told, "Friends, friends. Enemies, you don't have business with. No trouble. It's your friends do it. They call you and tie." Herskovits, *Trinidad Village*, p. 239. The same could be said in St. Lucia.

Conclusion

1. Melville J. and Frances S. Herskovits, *Trinidad Village* (New York: Octagon Books, 1976), p. 106.

2. Melville J. and Frances S. Herskovits, *Life in a Haitian Valley* (Garden City: Doubleday and Co., 1971), p. 299.

3. George M. Foster, "Interpersonal Relations in Peasant Society," *Human Organization* 19(1960):176.

4. Hazel H. Weidman, "Anthropological Theory and the Psychological Function of Belief in Witchcraft," in *Essays in Medical Anthropology*. Southern Anthropological Society Proceedings, No. 1(1968), Athens, Georgia, p. 29.

5. Clyde Kluckhohn, *Navaho Witchcraft* (Boston: Beacon Press, 1944), p. 127.

6. See the appendix, page 280.

7. There is a distinction made by the West Indian between bush tea and bush medicine: a tea may be good for you, but a medicine has the ability to cure.

8. I. M. Lewis, *Ecstatic Religion: an Anthropological Study of Spirit Possession and Shamanism* (Middlesex, England: Penguin Books, 1975), p. 38.

9. Erika Bourguignon, "Dreams and Altered States of Consciousness in Anthropological Research," in *Psychological Anthropology*, ed. L. K. Hsu (Cambridge, Mass.: Schenkman Publishing Co., Inc., 1972), p. 426.

10. Richard H. Robbins, "Identity and the Interpersonal Theory of Disease," *Social and Cultural Identity*, ed. Thomas K. Fitzgerald. Southern Anthropological Society Proceedings, No. 8(1974), Athens, Georgia, p. 7.

11. Ibid., p. 10.

12. Robbins defines self-identity as the individual's "view of himself" and "what he perceives his position to be in regard to others," social identity as the individual's "appraisal of what others believe his social position to be," and public identity as "the view that others hold of the person's social position." Robbins, "Identity and the Interpersonal Theory of Disease," p. 6.

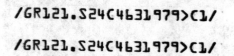